KS3 Maths Progress

Confidence • Fluency • Problem-solving • Progression

δ TWO

δ

Series editors:

Dr Naomi Norman • Katherine Pate

ALWAYS LEARNING

PEARSON

Published by Pearson Education Limited, Edinburgh Gate, Harlow, Essex, CM20 2JE.

www.pearsonschoolsandfecolleges.co.uk

Text © Pearson Education Limited 2014
Typeset by Tech-Set Ltd, Gateshead
Original illustrations © Pearson Education Limited 2014
Cover illustration by Robert Samuel Hanson
Index by Wendy Simpson

The rights of Nick Asker, Jack Barraclough, Sharon Bolger, Lynn Byrd, Andrew Edmondson
and Catherine Murphy, to be identified as authors of this work have been asserted by them in
accordance with the Copyright, Designs and Patents Act 1988.

First published 2014

17 16 15 14
10 9 8 7 6 5 4 3 2 1

British Library Cataloguing in Publication Data
A catalogue record for this book is available from the British Library

ISBN 978 1 447 96235 9

Printed in Italy by Lego S.p.A

Acknowledgements
The publisher would like to thank the following for their kind permission to reproduce their
photographs:

Alamy Images: age fotostock Spain, S.L. 101; **Fotolia.com:** Ashwin 225, Christian Schwier 87,
cottonfioc 201, igor 235, Kadmy 210, Maksym Dykha 205, Max Topchii 78, Mopic 84, Petair 30,
roger ashford 203, Tan Kian Khoon 48, yang yu 58; **Getty Images:** Fanatic Studio 111, Lonely
Planet Images 202, 206, 216, 219, 223, The Image Bank / Jeffrey Coolidge 129; **Pearson
Education Ltd:** Gareth Boden 154; **Rex Features:** Geoffrey Robinson 8; **Science Photo Library
Ltd:** Gary Hincks 60; **Shutterstock.com:** ArchMan 114, blvdone 237, Boris Rabtsevich 23, Brian
Goodman 179, Claudio Divizia 75, FERNANDO BLANCO CALZADA 157, Fotosenmeer 176,
IM_photo 27, kazoka 55, Nataliya Hora 207, qingqing 104, Rehan Qureshi 149, Shots Studio
45, stefano spezi 109, zentilia 173; **Veer / Corbis:** 18percentgrey 107, alexraths 4, 50, Alliance
131, Andrey Armyagov 184, Monkey Business Images 186, Brebca 135, Brian Jackson 81, Illia
Uriadnikov 182, Inga Nielsen 6, javarman 116, Kitch 152, Ohmega1982 233, Olechowski 25,
Olivier Le Moal 133, Paul Fleet 159, rudi1976 52, timurpix 227

All other images © Pearson Education

We are grateful to the following for permission to reproduce copyright material:
UK populations (p19), statswales.wales.gov.uk, Welsh Government; Cost of 1GB of data storage
(p88) from 'A history of storage data', www.mkomo.com; UK population data (p96) from '2011
Census', Office for National Statistics licensed under the Open Government License v.2.0;
Number of websites (p97), from 'Internet Live Stats', internetlivestats.com; House price data
(p80, p93) from 'House Price Index', Land Registry (Crown Copyright), licensed under the Open
Government License v.2.0; Data on oil use in the UK (p145) from 'Energy Consumption in the UK',
Department of Energy and Climate Change licensed under the Open Government License v.2.0.

Every effort has been made to contact copyright holders of material reproduced in this book.
Any omissions will be rectified in subsequent printings if notice is given to the publishers.

CONTENTS

Unit 4 Real life graphs

Unit 5 Transformations

Unit 6 Fractions, decimals and percentages

Unit 7 Constructions and loci

Unit 8 Probability

Unit 9 Scale drawings and measures

Unit 10 Graphs

KS3 Maths Progress

Confidence • Fluency • Problem-solving • Progression

Pedagogy at the heart – This new course is built around a unique pedagogy that's been created by leading mathematics educational researchers and Key Stage 3 teachers. The result is an innovative learning structure based around 10 key principles designed to nurture confidence and raise achievement.

Pedagogy – our 10 key principles

- Fluency
- Mathematical Reasoning
- Multiplicative Reasoning
- Problem Solving
- Progression
- Concrete-Pictorial - Abstract (CPA)
- Relevance
- Modelling
- Reflection (metacognition)
- Linking

Progression to Key Stage 4 – In line with the 2014 National Curriculum, there is a strong focus on fluency, problem-solving and progression to help prepare your students' progress through their studies.

Stretch, challenge and support – Catering for students of all abilities, these Student Books are structured to deliver engaging and accessible content across three differentiated tiers, each offering a wealth of worked examples and questions, supported by key points, literacy and strategy hints, and clearly defined objectives.

Within each unit:

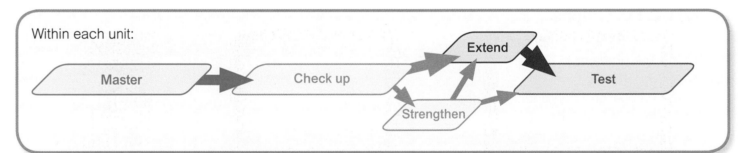

Differentiated for students of all abilities:

Alpha	Pi	Theta	Delta
Tier Access	Tier 1	Tier 2	Tier 3

Progress with confidence!

This innovative Key Stage 3 Maths course embeds a modern pedagogical approach around our trusted suite of digital and print resources, to create confident and numerate students ready to progress further.

Help at the front-of-class – **ActiveTeach Presentation** is our tried and tested service that makes all of the Student Books available for display on a whiteboard. The books are supplemented with a range of videos and animations that present mathematical concepts along a concrete - pictorial - abstract pathway, allowing your class to progress their conceptual understanding at the right speed.

Learning beyond the classroom – Focussing on online homework, **ActiveCourse** offers students unprecedented extra practice (with automarking) and a chance to reflect on their learning with the confidence-checker. Powerful reporting tools can be used to track student progression and confidence levels.

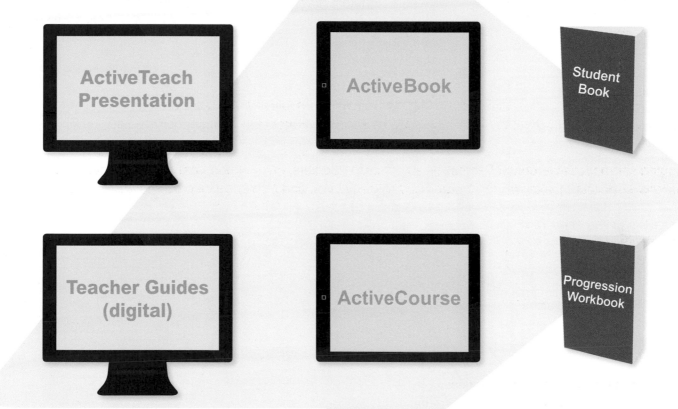

ActiveTeach Presentation

ActiveBook

Student Book

Teacher Guides (digital)

ActiveCourse

Progression Workbook

Easy to plan, teach and assess – Downloadable **Teacher Guides** provide assistance with planning through the Schemes of Work. Lesson plans link both front-of-class **ActiveTeach Presentation** and **ActiveCourse** and provide help with reporting, functionality and progression. Both **Teacher Guides** and **ActiveTeach Presentation** contain the **answers** to the Student Book exercises.

Teacher Guides include **Class Progression Charts** and **Student Progression Charts** to support formative and summative assessment through the course.

Practice to progress – KS3 Maths Progress has an extensive range of practice across a range of topics and abilities. From the **Student Books** to write-in **Progression Workbooks** through to **ActiveCourse**, there is plenty of practice available in a variety of formats whether for in the classroom or for learning at home independently.

> For more information, visit
> **www.pearsonschools.co.uk/ks3mathsprogress**

Welcome to KS3 Maths Progress student books!

Confidence · **Fluency** · **Problem-solving** · **Progression**

Starting a new course is exciting! We believe you will have fun with maths, at the same time nurturing your confidence and raising your achievement.

Here's how:

At the end of the *Master* lessons, take a *Check up* test to help you decide to *Strengthen*, or *Extend* your learning. You may be able to mark this test yourself.

Choose only the topics in *Strengthen* that you need a bit more practice with. You'll find more hints here to lead you through specific questions. Then move on to *Extend*.

Extend helps you to apply the maths you know to some different situations. *Strengthen* and *Extend* both include *Enrichment* or *Investigations*.

When you have finished the whole unit, a *Unit test* helps you see how much progress you are making.

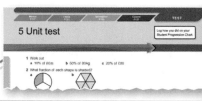

Clear *Objectives,* showing what you will cover in each lesson, are followed by a *Confidence* panel to boost your understanding and engage your interest.

Have a look at *Why Learn This?* This shows you how maths is useful in everyday life.

Improve your *Fluency* – practise answering questions using maths you already know.

The first questions are *Warm up*. Here you can show what you already know about this topic or related ones…

…before moving on to further questions, with *Worked examples* and *Hints* for help when you need it.

Your teacher has access to Answers in either ActiveTeach Presentation or the Teacher Guides.

Topic links show you how the maths in a lesson is connected to other mathematical topics. Use the *Subject links* to find out where you might use the maths you have learned here in your other lessons, such as science, geography and computing .

Explore a real-life problem by discussing and having a go. By the end of the lesson you'll have gained the skills you need to start finding a solution to the question using maths.

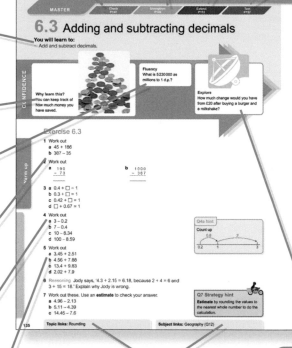

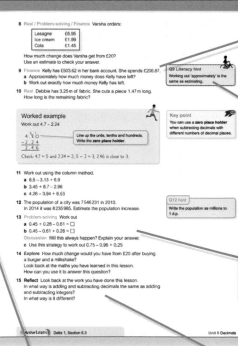

STEM and Finance lessons

Context lessons expand on *Real, STEM* and *Finance* maths. Finance questions are related to money. STEM stands for Science, Technology, Engineering and Maths. You can find out how charities use maths in their fundraising, how engineers monitor water flow in rivers, and why diamonds sparkle (among other things!)

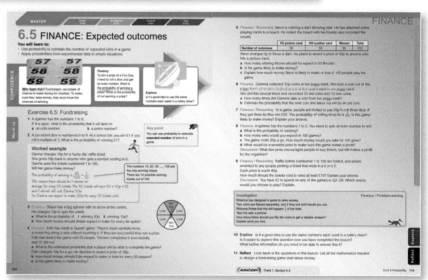

Some questions are tagged as *Finance* or *STEM*. These questions show how the real world relies on maths. Follow these up with whole lessons that focus on how maths is used in the fields of finance, science and technology.

As well as hints that help you with specific questions, you'll find *Literacy hints* (to explain some unfamiliar terms) and *Strategy hints* (to help with working out).

You can improve your ability to use maths in everyday situations by tackling *Modelling, Reasoning, Problem-solving* and *Real* questions. *Discussions* prompt you to explain your reasoning or explore new ideas with a partner.

At the end of each lesson, you get a chance to *Reflect* on how confident you feel about the topic.

Your teacher may give you a Student Progression Chart to help you see your progression through the units.

Further support

You can easily access extra resources that tie in to each lesson – look for the ActiveLearn icon on the lesson pages for ActiveCourse online homework links. These are clearly mapped to lessons and provide fun, interactive exercises linked to helpful worked examples and videos.

The Progression Workbooks, full of extra practice for key questions will help you reinforce your learning and track your own progress.

Enjoy!

1.1 Prime factor decomposition

You will learn to:
- Write the prime factor decomposition of a number
- Use prime factor decomposition to find the HCF or LCM of two numbers.

CONFIDENCE

$48 \overline{)336}$

HCF of 99 and 165?

Why learn this?
Writing a number as a product of its prime factors can help you work out divisions, HCFs and LCMs.

Fluency
Which of these numbers are prime?
- 12, 7, 9, 2, 5, 4, 1

Write using powers
- 3 × 3 × 3 × 3
- 2 × 2 × 2 × 2 × 2

Explore
Can you make every number just by multiplying prime numbers?

Exercise 1.1

1 Work out the product of 4, 6 and 2.

2 a Write the factors of 18 and 30 using this Venn diagram.
   b What is the highest common factor (HCF) of 18 and 30?

Factors of 18	Factors of 30

3 a List the first 8 multiples of 9 and 12.
   b What is the lowest common multiple (LCM) of 9 and 12?

4 a Copy and complete this factor tree to find all the prime factors of 90.

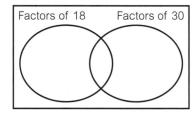
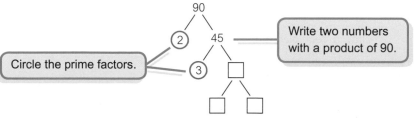

Write two numbers with a product of 90.

Circle the prime factors.

Key point
You can write a number as a product of prime number factors. This is called **prime factor decomposition**.

   b Write down the **product** of the prime factors.
   90 = 2 × 3 × ☐ × ☐
   Discussion Draw a different factor tree for the number 90. Does it matter which two factors you choose first?

Q4b Literacy hint
Product means multiplication of.

5 Write each number as a product of its prime factors.
   a 32   **b** 75   **c** 54   **d** 36
   Discussion How can you use the **prime factor decomposition** of 36 to quickly work out the prime factor decomposition of 72? What about 18?

Topic links: Long multiplication, Venn diagrams

1

6 Write each number as a product of its prime factors.

   a **i** 225

      ii 450

   b **i** 140

      ii 420

Q6a ii hint

$450 = 225 \times \square$

Investigation   **Reasoning**

  1 Write 48 and 336 as a product of their prime factors.

  2 Explain how you can tell by looking at the prime factor decomposition that 48 divides exactly into 336.

  3 Use your answers to part 1 and part 2 to write down the answer to 336 ÷ 48. Use a calculator to check your answer.

  4 Use prime factor decomposition to test whether these divisions have exact answers.

      If they have, write down the answer. Check your answers with a calculator.

      a 840 ÷ 56   **b** 576 ÷ 64   **c** 594 ÷ 108   **d** 468 ÷ 39

  5 Write two division questions of your own that have exact answers. Test them on a partner to see if

      they can work out the answer using prime factor decomposition, not a calculator.

---

7 **Problem-solving** Here are some prime factor decomposition cards.

1·6

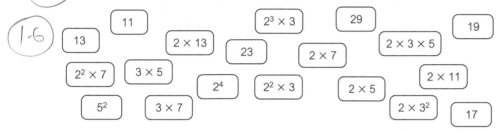

| 11 | $2^3 \times 3$ | 29 | | 19 |

| 13 | 2×13 | 23 | 2×7 | $2 \times 3 \times 5$ |

| $2^2 \times 7$ | 3×5 | 2^4 | $2^2 \times 3$ | 2×5 | 2×11 |

| 5^2 | 3×7 | | 2×3^2 | 17 |

The cards represent the numbers from 10 to 30.

Two of the cards are missing.

What is the prime factor decomposition on the missing cards?

Worked example

Find the highest common factor of 90 and 252.

$90 = 2 \times 3^2 \times 5$

$252 = 2^2 \times 3^2 \times 7$

> Write each number as a product of prime factors.

Factors of 90   **Factors of 252**

5 3^2 7

2

2^2

> Draw a Venn diagram.
> 2^2 is a factor of 252 but only
> 2 is a factor of 90 *and* 252.

HCF is $3^2 \times 2 = 9 \times 2$

       $= 18$

> Multiply the common prime factors together.

Key point

You can use prime factor decomposition to find the HCF of two or more numbers.

---

8 Use prime factor decomposition to find the HCF of each pair of numbers.

   a 60 and 84

   b 90 and 210

   c 42 and 105

   d 99 and 165

9 Problem-solving Kyle works out that the HCF of two numbers is $2^2 \times 3^2 = 36$.

What two numbers might Kyle have been using?

Discussion What method did you use to solve this problem?

10 Reasoning

a Write the prime factors of 12 and 18 in this Venn diagram.

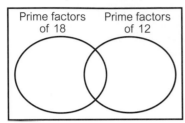

Prime factors of 18   Prime factors of 12

b Write 36 as a product of prime factors.

c The lowest common multiple (LCM) of 12 and 18 is 36.
Show how you can use the Venn diagram from part **a** to work out the LCM of 12 and 18.

Discussion What method did you use to answer part **c**?

11 Reasoning Use prime factor decomposition to show that the LCM of 21 and 45 is 315.

Q11 hint

Draw a Venn diagram.

12 Use prime factor decomposition to find the LCM of each pair of numbers.

a 8 and 36

b 18 and 66

c 28 and 42

d 30 and 75

13 STEM / Problem-solving Two weather satellites pass over the London Eye at 11 am. It takes one satellite 100 minutes to orbit the Earth and it takes the other satellite 120 minutes to orbit the Earth. At what time will both of the satellites next pass over the London Eye at the same time?

Q13 Strategy hint

Work out the LCM first.

14 Explore Can you make every number by just multiplying prime numbers?

Choose some sensible numbers to help you explore this situation. Then use what you've learned in this lesson to help you answer the question.

15 Reflect Write down your own short definition for each of these mathematics words.

• Prime

• Factor

• Decomposition

Use your definitions to write down (in your own words) the meaning of prime factor decomposition.

Q15 hint

Compose means to make or create something. What do you think decompose means?

Explore

Reflect

Active Learn   Delta 2, Section 1.1

1.2 Laws of indices

CONFIDENCE

You will learn to:
- Work out the laws of indices for positive powers
- Show that any number to the power of zero is 1
- Use the laws for indices for multiplying and dividing.

Why learn this?
Knowing the rules for indices can speed up complicated calculations that scientists, engineers and doctors need to do.

Fluency
What is the missing power?
- $3 \times 3 \times 3 \times 3 \times 3 = 3^\square$
- $4 \times 4 \times 4 = 4^\square$
- $5 \times 5 \times 5 \times 5 \times 5 \times 5 \times 5 = 5^\square$
- $16 = 4^\square$
- $25 = 5^\square$
- $27 = 3^\square$

Explore
What expressions will simplify to 9^6?

Exercise 1.2

1 Work out
   a $\dfrac{2 \times 2}{4 \times 5}$ b $\dfrac{4 \times 9}{6 \times 2}$ c $\dfrac{8 \times 5}{6 \times 4}$

2 Work out
   a 4×4^2 b $5^2 \times 5$ c $3^2 \times 3^2$ d $2^2 \times 2^3$

 3 Work out
   a 2^6 b 3^5 c 10^7 d 5^4

4 **Reasoning** Penny works out
   $2^2 \times 2^3$
   $2 \times 2 \times 2 \times 2 \times 2 = 2^5$
   How can you quickly find $2^2 \times 2^3$ without writing all the 2s?

5 Write each product as a single power.
   a $3^4 \times 3^2$ b $4^3 \times 4$ c $5^4 \times 5^2$ d $7^3 \times 7^3$
   e $4^8 \times 4^6$ f $3^9 \times 3$ g 6×6^{12}

6 **Problem-solving** Tam multiplies three powers of 8 together.
   $8^\square \times 8^\square \times 8^\square = 8^{15}$
   What could the three powers be if
   a all the powers are different
   b two of the powers are the same
   c all three powers are the same?

7 **Reasoning**
   a i Work out $\dfrac{4 \times 4 \times 4 \times 4 \times 4}{4 \times 4 \times 4}$ by cancelling. Write your answer as a power of 4.
     ii Copy and complete $4^5 \div 4^3 = 4^\square$
   b Copy and complete $2^5 \div 2^2 = \dfrac{2^5}{2^2} = \dfrac{2 \times 2 \times 2 \times 2 \times 2}{2 \times 2} = 2^\square$
   c Work out $5^4 \div 5^3$
   Discussion How can you quickly find $4^8 \div 4^3$ without writing all the 4s?

Warm up

Q3 hint
Use the x^y button on your calculator.

Q4 hint
Look at the indices in the question and the answer.

Key point
When you multiply numbers written as powers of the same number, you add the indices.

Q5 Literacy hint
A single power means one number with a power. For example, 5^7.

Q5b hint
$4 = 4^1$

8 Write each as a single power.

   a $6^8 \div 6^2$ **b** $5^7 \div 5^3$ **c** $9^9 \div 9^8$

   d $2^9 \div 2^4$ **e** $4^{15} \div 4^9$ **f** $12^5 \div 12$

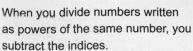
9 **Problem-solving** Su divides two powers of 3.

   $3^{\square} \div 3^{\square} = 3^2$

   What could the two numbers be if

   a both numbers are greater than 3^{20}

   b both numbers are smaller than 3^{20}

   c the power of one number is double the power of the other number?

10 **STEM** The diameter of Saturn is approximately 2^{17} km. The diameter of the dwarf planet Ceres is approximately 2^{10} km. How many times larger is the diameter of Saturn than the diameter of Ceres?

Q10 hint

$2^{10} \times \square = 2^{17}$

11 **Reasoning** Write each as a single power.

   a $(2^4)^2$ **b** $(5^2)^2$ **c** $(3^2)^3$ **d** $(6^2)^4$

   Discussion How can you find the values of parts **a**–**d** using the indices?

12 Write each of these as a single power.

   a $(4^3)^4$ **b** $(7^2)^5$ **c** $(3^6)^3$ **d** $(8^5)^7$

13 **Reasoning** **a** Write each as a single power.

     i $2^5 \times 2^3$ **ii** $3^5 \times 3^3$ **iii** $p^5 \times p^3 = p^{\square}$

   b Copy and complete this general rule for any number p, with positive integer powers a and b. $p^a \times p^b = p^{\square + \square}$

   c Write each as a single power. **i** $2^5 \div 2^3$ **ii** $3^5 \div 3^3$ **iii** $p^5 \div p^3$

   d Copy and complete this general rule for any number p, with positive integer powers a and b. $p^a \div p^b = p^{\square - \square}$

   e Copy and complete **i** $(2^5)^3 = 2^{\square}$ **ii** $(3^5)^3 = 3^{\square}$ **iii** $(p^5)^3 = p^{\square}$

   f Copy and complete this general rule for any number p, with positive integer powers a and b. $(p^a)^b = p^{\square \times \square}$

Q13 hint

A general rule is a rule that works for any numbers. Using letters shows that any number can be substituted.

14 **Reasoning**

   a **i** Work out the answers to these divisions: $\dfrac{5}{5}$ $\dfrac{7}{7}$ $\dfrac{12}{12}$ $\dfrac{100}{100}$ $\dfrac{3^4}{3^4}$ $\dfrac{9^5}{9^5}$

     ii What do you notice about dividing a number by itself? Test with a few more numbers.

   b **i** Copy and complete this pattern.

      $\dfrac{9^5}{9^1} = 9^4$ $\dfrac{9^5}{9^2} = 9^3$ $\dfrac{9^5}{9^3} = 9^{\square}$ $\dfrac{9^5}{9^4} = 9^{\square}$ $\dfrac{9^5}{9^5} = 9^{\square}$

     ii What do you notice about your answers to $\dfrac{9^5}{9^5}$ in part **a** **i** and part **b** **i**?

     iii Complete this statement: 'Any number to the power of zero = $\square$'.

   Discussion $2^0 = 1$. Does this mean that 4^0 is twice as big?

15 Write each calculation as a single power.

   a $\dfrac{4^2 \times 4^8}{4^3}$ **b** $\dfrac{7^{12}}{7^2 \times 7^6}$ **c** $\dfrac{5^6 \times 5^6}{5^7 \times 5}$

Q16a Strategy hint

Start by writing each number as a power of 2.

16 **Problem-solving** Write each calculation as a single power.

   a $16 \times 32 \times 8$ **b** $\dfrac{4^9}{64}$ **c** $\dfrac{27 \times 81}{3^2}$

17 **Explore** What expressions will simplify to 9^6?

   Choose some sensible numbers and use what you've learned in this lesson to help you explore this situation.

Q18 hint

Look back at this lesson. Can you find questions where you were spotting a pattern? Where else in mathematics have you used pattern spotting?

18 **Reflect** Lana says, 'Mathematics is often about spotting patterns.'

   Do you agree with Lana? Explain.

   Why does it help to spot patterns in mathematics? Explain.

1.3 STEM: Powers of 10

You will learn to:
- Use and understand powers of 10
- Use the prefixes associated with powers of 10
- Understand the effect of multiplying and dividing by any integer power of 10.

Why learn this?
A byte is a unit of digital information stored on a computer. A megabyte is 10^6 bytes and a gigabyte is 10^9 bytes.

Fluency
$10^2 \times 10^3 = 10^\square$
$10^4 \times 10 = 10^\square$
$10^7 \div 10^5 = 10^\square$
$10^8 \div 10^2 = 10^\square$

Explore
How many photographs can you store on a 1 terabyte server?

Exercise 1.3: Powers of 10

1 Match each blue number to the equivalent red value.

$10^2 \quad 10^4 \quad 10^3 \quad 10^5$
$1000 \quad 100\,000 \quad 100 \quad 10\,000$

2 Work out
  a 4.5×10 **b** 2.36×1000 **c** 0.843×100 **d** $1.45 \times 10\,000$
  e $270 \div 10$ **f** $4685 \div 1000$ **g** $35 \div 100$ **h** $450 \div 10\,000$

> **Key point**
> Each of the headings in the place-value table is a power of 10. This is because we have a *dec*imal system (*dec* = 10).

3 Copy and complete this place-value table.

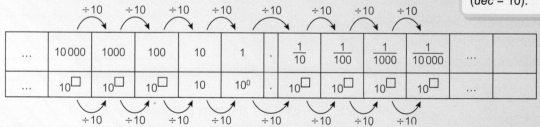

4 STEM
  This table shows the **prefixes** for powers of 10.

Prefix	Letter	Power	Number
tera	T	10^{12}	1 000 000 000 000
giga	G	10^9	1 000 000 000
mega	M	10^6	1 000 000
kilo	k	10^3	1000
deci	d	10^{-1}	0.1
centi	c	10^{-2}	0.01
milli	m	10^{-3}	0.001
micro	μ	10^{-6}	0.000 001
nano	n	10^{-9}	0.000 000 001
pico	p	10^{-12}	0.000 000 000 001

> **Key point**
> Some powers of 10 have a name called a **prefix**. Each prefix is represented by a letter. The prefix for 10^6 is mega (M) as in megabyte (MB).

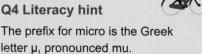

> **Q4 Literacy hint**
> The prefix for micro is the Greek letter μ, pronounced mu.

a Add the prefixes to your place-value table in Q3.

b A gram (g) is a unit of mass. How many grams are in a kilogram (kg)?

c A joule (J) is a unit of energy. How many joules are in a megajoule (MJ)?

d A watt (W) is a unit of power. How many watts are in a gigawatt (GW)?

5 STEM Convert

a 4 kg to g   b 2.4 MJ to J   c 12.5 GW to W

6 STEM How many times bigger is

a a millimetre than a nanometre   b a gigawatt than a megawatt

c a kilojoule than a joule   d a megagram than a kilogram?

Discussion What other name do we use for a megagram?

Worked example

The average distance of Venus from the Sun is 1.08×10^8 km.
Write this distance as an ordinary number.

> First write 10^8 as an ordinary number.

$1.08 \times 10^8 = 1.08 \times 100\,000\,000 = 108\,000\,000$ km

7 STEM The table shows information about some different planets.

Name of planet	Diameter of planet (km)	Average distance from Sun (km)
Mercury	4.9×10^3	5.79×10^7
Earth	1.28×10^4	1.5×10^8
Saturn	1.2×10^5	1.427×10^9

a Copy the table. Write all the distances as ordinary numbers.

b Which planet has the greatest diameter?

c Which planet is closest to the Sun?

Discussion How can you answer parts **b** and **c** without writing the distances as ordinary numbers?

8 STEM / Problem-solving The Space Shuttle had a lift-off mass of 1.1×10^5 kg. How many tonnes is this?

> **Q8 hint**
>
> 1 tonne = 1000 kg

9 STEM The table shows the dimensions of some small organisms.

Name of organism	Length	Width
dust mite	0.42 millimetres	0.25 millimetres
bacteria	2 micrometres	0.5 micrometres
virus	0.3 micrometres	15 nanometres

> **Q9 Literacy hint**
>
> The **dimensions** of an object are its measurements.

a Write all the **dimensions** in metres.

b Which organism has the greatest length?

c Which organism has the smallest width?

Discussion How can you answer parts **b** and **c** without writing the dimensions as ordinary numbers?

10 STEM / Reasoning An atom is the smallest object that we can see with an electron microscope. The width of an atom is about 0.1 nanometres.
What is this distance in millimetres?

11 Explore How many photographs can you store on a 1 terabyte server?
What have you learned in this lesson to help you answer this question?
What other information do you need?

12 Reflect After this lesson Jemma says, 'I understood this lesson well because it's all about place value.' Look back at the work you have done this lesson. How has place value helped you? What other maths skills have you used in this lesson?

1.4 Calculating and estimating

You will learn to:

* Calculate with powers
* Round to a number of significant figures.

Why learn this?
The organisers of sporting events often round the number of spectators to estimate the income from ticket sales.

Fluency
What is
2^3
2^4
2^5
2^6?

Explore
When is it a good idea to round numbers?
When is it not a good idea?

CONFIDENCE

Warm up

Exercise 1.4

1 Simplify

  a $5^2 \times 5^4$ **b** $\dfrac{8^5}{8^3}$ **c** $\dfrac{7^4 \times 7^6}{7^7}$

2 Work out

  a -4×-4 **b** -7×-7 **c** $(-3)^2$ **d** $(-10)^2$

3 Use rounding to estimate the answers.

  a $97 \div 4$ **b** 12.3×10.2 **c** $18.6 \div 5$

4 Evaluate $\dfrac{2 \times 3^9}{3^7}$

  $\dfrac{2 \times 3^9}{3^7} = 2 \times 3^\square$

  $\phantom{\dfrac{2 \times 3^9}{3^7}} = 2 \times \square$

  $\phantom{\dfrac{2 \times 3^9}{3^7}} = \square$

5 Work out

  a $\dfrac{5 \times 2^{12}}{2^9}$ **b** $\dfrac{3^2 \times 4^4}{4^3}$ **c** $\dfrac{2 \times 5^3 \times 5^5}{5^4}$ **d** $\dfrac{6^{15} \times 10}{6^7 \times 6^6}$

6 **Problem-solving** Work out $\dfrac{2^8 \times 16 \times 32 \times 7}{8 \times 2^{10}}$

7 **Reasoning** Sophie and Rasheed both work out the same calculation. Here is what they write.

Sophie
| $32 - (-5)^2 = 32 - -25$ |
| $= 32 + 25$ |
| $= 57$ |

Rasheed
| $32 - (-5)^2 = 32 - +25$ |
| $= 32 - 25$ |
| $= 7$ |

Who is correct? Explain the mistake that the other one has made.

Key point
You can simplify expressions containing powers to make calculations easier.

Q4 Literacy hint
Evaluate means 'work out the value'.

Q4 hint
Simplify the powers of 3, $\dfrac{3^9}{3^7} = 3^\square$, then multiply by 2.

Q6 Strategy hint
Write as many numbers as possible as powers of 2.

8 Sort these cards into matching pairs.

$14 + 4^2$

$14 - 4^2$

$14 + (-4)^2$

$14 - (-4)^2$

$25 - 2^2 - 6^2$

$25 - (-2)^2 + 6^2$

$25 - 2^2 + (-6)^2$

$25 - 2^2 - (-6)^2$

Discussion What method did you use?

Investigation Reasoning

1 a Work out **i** $(2 × 5)^2$ **ii** $2^2 × 5^2$
  b Work out **i** $(2 × 5)^3$ **ii** $2^3 × 5^3$
2 What do you notice about your answers to Q1?
3 a Write a rule for calculating the power of the product of two numbers.
    Check this rule works using two numbers of your own.
  b Will this same rule work for three or more numbers?
4 a Work out **i** $(10 ÷ 2)^2$ **ii** $10^2 ÷ 2^2$
  b What do you notice about your answers to part **a**?
5 Write a rule for calculating the power of the division of two numbers.
    Check this rule works using two numbers of your own.
6 a Work out **i** $(3 + 4)^2$ **ii** $3^2 + 4^2$
  b What do you notice about your answers to part **a**?
Discussion Is there a rule for calculating the power of the sum or difference of two numbers?

Investigation Q5 hint

Make sure the second number divides exactly into the first, and that the power is greater than 2.

9 Work out

a $\dfrac{(3 × 4)^2}{2^2 × 3}$

b $\dfrac{(3 × 4)^3}{2^2 × 9}$

c $\dfrac{32 × 5^3}{(5 × 4)^2}$

d $\dfrac{(6 × 2 × 8)^2}{4^3 × 3}$

Q9a hint

$\dfrac{(3 × 4)^2}{2^2 × 3} = \dfrac{3^2 × 4^2}{2^2 × 3} = \dfrac{3 × \cancel{3} × \cancel{4}^2 × \cancel{4}^2}{\cancel{2} × \cancel{2} × \cancel{3}} = \ldots$

Worked example

Round these numbers to the given number of **significant figures**.

a 42.038 (4 s.f.)
b 0.05713 (3 s.f.)
c 21561 (2 s.f.)

When the next digit is 5 or above, round the previous digit up. Here the fifth significant figure is an 8, so round the 3 up to a 4.

a 42.04

The fourth significant figure is 3, so leave the third digit as 1.

b 0.0571

c 22000

2 and 1 are the first 2 significant figures. The third is 5, so round the 1 up to 2.

Key point

You can round numbers to a given number of **significant figures (s.f.)**. The first significant figure is the one with the highest place value. It is the first non-zero digit in the number, counting from the left.

10 Round these numbers to the given number of significant figures.
  a 47.368 (4 s.f.)
  b 0.00662 (1 s.f.)
  c 579452 (2 s.f.)

Topic links: Negative numbers, Volume, Range, Order of operations

Subject links: Science (Q15)

11 Estimate the answer to each calculation by rounding each number to 1 significant figure.

   a 37×492

   b 6230×26

   c $897 \div 28$

   d $45\,239 \div 183$

Q11a hint

$40 \times 500 = \square$

12 ~~Estimate the answer to each calculation by rounding each number to 1 significant figure.~~

   a $\dfrac{(1.2 + 3.5)^2}{1.8^3}$

Work out ans

(1.5) used in D2

   b $\dfrac{(27 - 14)^3}{7.3^2}$

   c $\dfrac{(3.3^2 \times 2)}{(2.3 + 4.2)^2}$

   d $\dfrac{(786 - 529)^2}{7.4^2}$

Q12a hint

$\dfrac{(1.2 + 3.5)^2}{1.8^3} \approx \dfrac{5^2}{8}$

What number is a multiple of 8 and close to 5^2? Use this to estimate the final answer.

Q12 Literacy hint

$\approx$ means approximately equal to.

13 The diagram shows a cuboid.

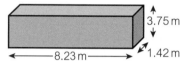

3.75 m

8.23 m   1.42 m

   Work out the volume of the cuboid.

   Give your answer in m^3 correct to 3 s.f.

14 **Problem-solving** Sarita starts with a whole number.

   She rounds it to 2 significant figures.

   Her answer is 670.

   a Write down two different numbers she could have started with.

   b What is the largest number she could have started with?

   c What is the smallest number she could have started with?

15 **STEM** The table shows the diameters of five planets.

Planet	Mercury	Venus	Earth	Mars	Uranus
Diameter (km)	4878	12104	12756	6794	51118

   a Round each diameter correct to 1 s.f.

   b Work out an estimate of the range in diameters.

16 **Real** A football stadium seats 42785.

   The average price of a ticket is £32.

   Estimate the total money taken from ticket sales for one match.

17 **Explore** When is it a good idea to round numbers?

   When is it not a good idea?

   Look back at the maths you have learned in this lesson.

   How can you use it to answer this question?

18 **Reflect** Look back at Q12.

   Use a calculator to work out the exact answer to each part.

   How can your estimate help you check your calculator answer?

Master
P1

CHECK

Strengthen
P13

Extend
P17

Test
P21

1 Check up

Log how you did on your
Student Progression Chart.

Prime factors

1 Draw a factor tree for the number 72.

2 Write 300 as a product of its prime factors.

3 Use prime factor decomposition to find
   a the highest common factor of 135 and 180
   b the lowest common multiple of 32 and 40.

Laws of indices

4 Write each calculation as a single power.
   a $3^4 \times 3^3$ **b** $5^2 \times 5$ **c** $6^7 \times 6^2 \times 6^9$ **d** $2^6 \div 2^2$
   e $5^8 \div 5$ **f** $(3^4)^2$ **g** $4^3 \div 4^3$

5 Evaluate $\dfrac{3 \times 2^9}{2^6}$

6 Work out
   a $(-5)^2$ **b** $30 - 3^2 - (-4)^2$ **c** 6^0

7 Write each calculation as a single power.
   a $\dfrac{6^4 \times 6^5}{6^3}$ **b** $\dfrac{2^5 \times 2^2}{2 \times 2^3}$ **c** $27 \times 3 \times 9$

8 Which two calculations give the same answer?
   A $(2 \times 5)^2$ B 2×5^2 C $2^2 \times 5^2$ D $2^2 \times 5$

9 Evaluate $\dfrac{(3 \times 2)^3}{2 \times 18}$

10 Copy and complete these statements.
   $a^x \times a^y = a^{\square}$ $a^x \div a^y = a^{\square}$ $(a^x)^y = a^{\square}$

Powers of 10

11 a Complete this table of prefixes.

Prefix	Power of 10	Number
giga	$10^{\square}$	
mega	$10^{\square}$	
kilo	$10^{\square}$	1000
deci	$10^{\square}$	
centi	$10^{\square}$	
milli	$10^{\square}$	0.001
micro	$10^{\square}$	

   b Match the cards that show the same value.

50 000 milligrams	5000 kilograms	5 grams

0.005 kilograms	5 megagrams	500 decigrams

12 Write these numbers in order of size, starting with the smallest.

4.6×10^4, $8.9 \div 10^5$, 2.1×10^5, $2.4 \div 10^7$

Significant figures

13 Round these numbers to the given number of significant figures.

    a 129.288 (4 s.f.)

    b 0.000397 (1 s.f.)

    c 696 332 (2 s.f.)

14 Estimate the answer to each calculation by rounding each number to one significant figure.

    a 42×579

    b $8241 \div 19$

15 The average monthly charity donation is £11.50 per person. Estimate the total amount of money donated to charity each month by 32 476 people.

16 How sure are you of your answers? Were you mostly

    😞 **Just guessing**   😐 **Feeling doubtful**   🙂 **Confident**

What next? Use your results to decide whether to strengthen or extend your learning.

Reflect

Challenge

17 a Choose your own numbers to make these calculations correct.

    $5^\square \times 5^\square = 5^{18}$

    $5^\square \div 5^\square = 5^{18}$

    $(5^\square)^\square = 5^{18}$

    b Repeat part **a** using different numbers.

18 Ellen is working out the prime factor decomposition of a number. She draws this factor tree.

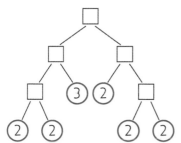

1·6

    What is Ellen's number?

19 Hassan writes a number as a product of its prime factors like this:

$2^3 \times 3 \times 7^2$

What number did Hassan start with?

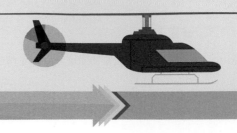

1 Strengthen

You will:
• Strengthen your understanding with practice.

Prime factors

1 Write each product using index notation (powers).
The first one has been done for you.

a $11 \times 11 \times 11 \times 7 \times 7 \times 7 \times 7 \times 2 = 11^3 \times 7^4 \times 2 = 2 \times 7^4 \times 11^3$

b $2 \times 2 \times 2 \times 2 \times 5 \times 5 \times 3$

c $5 \times 5 \times 5 \times 5 \times 5 \times 3 \times 3 \times 3 \times 2 \times 7$

> **Q1a hint**
>
> Write the factors in numerical order: 2s, then 7s, then 11s.

2 a Copy and complete the factor tree for the number 630 until you end up with just prime factors.

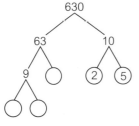

> **Q2a hint**
>
> Choose an easy factor pair to start with (630 = 63 × 10).
> 2 and 5 are prime factors of 630.

b Use index notation to write 630 as the product of its prime factors.

3 Use a factor tree to write each number as a product of its prime factors.

a 92

b 160

c 156

d 195

e 441

> **Q3a hint**
>
> 92 is an even number, so start by dividing by 2.

> **Q3d hint**
>
> 195 is an odd number, so try dividing by 3 or 5.

4 This is how Yona works out the HCF of 12 and 30.

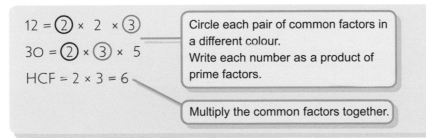

Circle each pair of common factors in a different colour.
Write each number as a product of prime factors.

Multiply the common factors together.

Work out the HCF of each pair of numbers.

a 32 and 36

b 45 and 72

c 132 and 180

> **Q4 hint**
>
> First work out the prime factor decomposition.

Topic links: Negative numbers, Order of operations

Subject links: Science (Power of 10 Q3, 4)

5 This is how Simon works out the LCM of 12 and 30.

$12 = ②×②×③$ — Circle one factor at a time from the first number and if it appears in the second number cross it off.

$30 = ✗ × ✗ × ⑤$ — Circle any factors that are not crossed off from the second number.

$LCM = 2 × 2 × 3 × 5 = 60$ — Multiply all the circled factors together.

Work out the LCM of each pair of numbers.

a 27 and 45　　**b** 36 and 54　　**c** 135 and 225

Q5 hint

First find the prime factor decomposition.

Laws of indices

1 Copy and complete this table showing the powers of 4.

4^0	4^1	4^2	4^3	4^4
	4	16		

×4　×4　×4　×4

2 Write each calculation as a single power.

a $3^2 × 3^5 = 3^{□+□} = 3^□$　　　**b** $4^3 × 4 = 4^{3+□} = 4^□$

c $9^6 × 9^3 = 9^{□+□}$　　　**d** $5^4 × 5^5 × 5^2$

Q2a hint

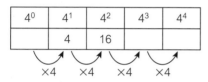

$$3^2 × 3^5 = \underbrace{3×3}_{2} × \underbrace{3×3×3×3×3}_{5}$$
$$\underbrace{}_{□}$$

3 Write each calculation as a single power.

a $4^6 ÷ 4^3 = 4^{□-□} = 4^□$　　　**b** $3^5 ÷ 3 = 3^{□-□} = 3^□$

c $7^7 ÷ 7^5$　　　**d** $9^{12} ÷ 9^4$

Q3a hint

$$4^6 ÷ 4^3 = \frac{\overbrace{4×4×4×4×4×4}^{6}}{\underbrace{4×4×4}_{3}}$$

4 Write each calculation as a single power.

a $(4^3)^2 = 4^3 × 4^3 = 4^□$　　　**b** $(3^2)^5 = 3^2 × 3^2 × 3^2 × 3^2 × 3^2$

c $(6^4)^2$　　　**d** $(8^5)^6$

5 Copy and complete these statements.

$2^4 × 2^3 = 2^{□+□}$　　　$2^x × 2^y = 2^{□+□}$　　　$n^x × n^y = n^□$

$2^4 ÷ 2^3 = 2^{□-□}$　　　$2^x ÷ 2^y = 2^{□-□}$　　　$n^x ÷ n^y = n^□$

$(2^4)^3 = 2^{□×□}$　　　$(2^x)^y = 2^{□×□}$　　　$(n^x)^y = n^□$

Q5 hint

Write the answers in terms of x and y.

6 Copy and complete this table showing the powers of 2.

2^0	2^1	2^2	2^3	2^4	2^5	2^6	2^7
	2	4					

×2　×2　×2　×2　×2　×2　×2

7 Work out

a i $\dfrac{2^8}{2^5}$　　**ii** $\dfrac{3 × 2^8}{2^5}$　　**b i** $\dfrac{5^6}{5^4}$　　**ii** $\dfrac{5^6 × 4}{5^4}$

Q7aii hint

$$\frac{3 × 2^8}{2^5} = 3 × \frac{2^8}{2^5}$$

8 a Work out

　i $(-3)^2$　　**ii** $(7)^2$　　**iii** $(-7)^2$

b Work out

　i $(-4)^2$　　**ii** $20 + (-4)^2$　　**iii** $20 - (-4)^2$

Q8 hint

Negative × negative = □

9 Write each calculation as a single power.

a $\dfrac{8^6 \times 8^5}{8^4} = \dfrac{8^\square}{8^4} = 8^\square$

b $\dfrac{3^7 \times 3^4}{3^6 \times 3} = \dfrac{3^\square}{3^\square} = 3^\square$

c $\dfrac{6^2 \times 6^5}{6^6}$

d $\dfrac{10^4 \times 10^7}{10 \times 10^5}$

10 Write each calculation as a single power.

a $64 \times 4 \times 8 = 2^\square \times 2^\square \times 2^\square = 2^{\square + \square + \square} = 2^\square$

b $27 \times 81 \times 9 =$

c $\dfrac{3^{10}}{9 \times 27} = \dfrac{3^{10}}{3^\square \times 3^\square} = 3^{10 - \square - \square} = 3^\square$

Q10 hint

Use the powers of 2 from your table in Q6.

Powers of 10

1 Copy and complete

a kilo (k) = 10^3 = 1000

b mega (M) = 10^6 = $\square$

c giga (G) = 10^9 = $\square$

Key point

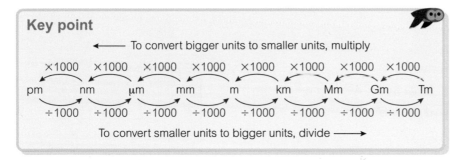

To convert bigger units to smaller units, multiply

| ×1000 | ×1000 | ×1000 | ×1000 | ×1000 | ×1000 | ×1000 | ×1000 |

pm   nm   μm   mm   m   km   Mm   Gm   Tm

÷1000   ÷1000   ÷1000   ÷1000   ÷1000   ÷1000   ÷1000   ÷1000

To convert smaller units to bigger units, divide ⟶

Literacy hint

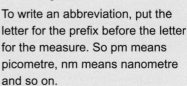

To write an abbreviation, put the letter for the prefix before the letter for the measure. So pm means picometre, nm means nanometre and so on.

2 Convert

a 6.5 Tm to km

b 0.014 m to nm

c 50 000 nm to mm

d 2200 km to Mm

e 0.000 0006 Gm to mm

Q2a hint

$6.5 \times 1000 \times 1000 \times 1000 = \square$

3 Convert

a 5 kilojoules (kJ) to joules (J)

b 0.021 megawatts (MW) to watts (W)

c 270 000 l to ml

d 720 μg to mg

4 STEM

a Safia's computer processor has a speed of 6.1 megahertz (MHz). What is its speed in kilohertz (kHz)?

b The wavelength of a red light is 690 nm. Convert this length to μm.

Significant figures

1 Copy these numbers. Circle the first significant figure. Write down its value.

a 23.56   **b** 0.0781   **c** 56 810   **d** 0.8843

Q1 hint

②3.56   20

0.0⑦81   7 hundredths

2 Write these numbers correct to 1 significant figure.

  a ②85   **b** 38.25   **c** 2481

  d 365 570   **e** 0.044 23   **f** 0.000 578

3 Round these numbers to the given number of significant figures.

  a 63 689 (2 s.f.)   **b** 63.559 (3 s.f.)

  c 0.825 (2 s.f.)   **d** 0.007 3301 (3 s.f.)

4 Round each number in these calculations to 1 significant figure. Then estimate the answer to the calculation.

  a 57 × 324   **b** 42 × 685   **c** 357 × 4386

  d 2186 ÷ 38   **e** 785 ÷ 17   **f** 42 559 ÷ 815

5 The average weekly wage of the staff at a factory is £286.50. The factory employs 2158 staff. Estimate the factory's total weekly wages bill.

> **Q2a hint**
>
> Circle the first significant figure. It's in the 100s column, so round to the nearest 100.

> **Q3a hint**
>
> Circle the second significant figure. What place-value column is it in?

> **Q4a hint**
>
> ⑤7 → 60 ③24 → 300 60 × 300 = ☐

> **Q5 hint**
>
> Round to 1 significant figure.

Enrichment

1 Use the numbers from the cloud to complete these calculations. You can only use each number once.

$7^{\square} \times 7^{\square} = 7^{\square}$

$7^{\square} \div 7^{\square} = 7^{\square}$

$(7^{\square})^{\square} = 7^{\square}$

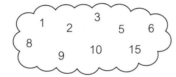

2 It takes Aisha 84 seconds to run one lap of an athletics track. It takes Brenda 96 seconds to run one lap of the athletics track. They set off from the start line at the same time.

  a After how many seconds will they cross the line together for the first time? (Assume they keep running at the same speed.)

  b They set off at 2 pm. At what time will they cross the line together for the first time? Give your answer in hours, minutes and seconds.

  c When they cross the line together for the first time,

    i how many laps will Aisha have run

    ii how many laps will Brenda have run?

One lap is 400 m.

  d When they cross the line together for the first time,

    i how far will Aisha have run

    ii how far will Brenda have run?

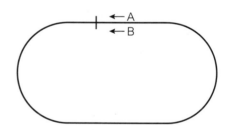

3 **Reflect** Lynda says, 'Working with indices is all about adding, subtracting, multiplying and dividing.'

Look back at the questions you answered in these strengthen lessons. Describe when you had to:

  • add   • subtract   • multiply   • divide

Do you agree with Lynda's statement? Give some examples to explain why.

Reflect

1 Extend

You will:

• Extend your understanding with problem-solving.

1 Problem-solving / Reasoning Here is the prime factor decomposition of a number.

The number is less than 100.

$\square = 2^2 \times \square \times 7$

What is the number? Explain how you made your decision.

Q1 hint

Start by working out $2^2 \times 7$

2 Problem-solving Work out the missing numbers in this prime factor decomposition.

1.6

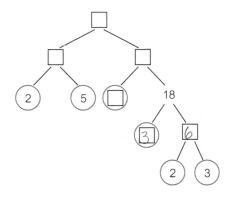

$\square = 2^3 \times 3^{\square} \times \square$

3 Reasoning

D3
1.1

a Is $(-2)^2 \times (-2)^3$ equal to $(-2)^5$? Explain.

b Is $(-3)^5 \div (-3)^2$ equal to $(-3)^3$?

c Write with a single power.

   i $(-4)^4 \times (-4)^6$

   ii $(-7)^8 \div (-7)^3$

Q3a,b hint

Show your working.

4 Reasoning The area of this square is 2^6 cm^2.
What is the length of one side?

2^6 cm^2

Write your answer as a power of 2.

5 a Work out the prime factor decomposition of these numbers.

#D2
1.6

   i 165

   ii 180

   iii 210

b What is the HCF of 165, 180 and 210?

c What is the LCM of 165, 180 and 210?

6 Copy and complete this table of prefixes.

Prefix	Letter	Power	Number
tera	T	10^{12}	1 000 000 000 000
giga	G	10^{9}	
mega	M	$10^{\square}$	
kilo	k	10^{3}	1000
deci	d	10^{-1}	0.1
centi	c	10^{-2}	0.01
milli	m	$10^{\square}$	
micro	μ	10^{-6}	0.000001
nano	n	$10^{\square}$	0.000000001
pico	p	10^{-12}	

7 Use the table in Q6 to work out these conversions.
  a 1 kilogram (kg) = $\square$ g
  b 1 megajoule (MJ) = $\square$ J
  c 1 gigatonne (Gt) = $\square$ t
  d 1 terawatt (TW) = $\square$ W
  e 1 decilitre (dl) = $\square$ l

Q7e hint

1 decimetre = 0.1 m

8 Write these quantities using an appropriate prefix.
  a 3.4×10^{-2} grams
  b 10.19×10^{-6} metres
  c 8×10^{12} joules
  d 2.5×10^{6} grams

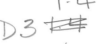

9 Convert
  a 23 s to ds
  b 900 cl to l

10 Copy and complete these calculations.
  a $3^3 \times 3^{\square} = 3^{10}$
  b $7^9 \times 7^{\square} = 7^{15}$
  c $5^4 \times 2^3 \times 5^{\square} \times 2^{\square} = 5^{10} \times 2^7$

11 Write each of these as a product of primes.
  a $6^3 \times 2^5 \times 3^2$
  b $5^4 \times 10^5 \times 2^6$
  c $6^4 \times 18^3 \times 9^7$

Q11a hint

First write 6^3 as $(2 \times 3)^3$.

12 Evaluate these. Give each fraction in its simplest form.
  a $\dfrac{12 \times 3^{10}}{3^{13}}$
  b $\dfrac{15 \times 5^7}{5^9}$
  c $\dfrac{2 \times 8^9}{8^{10} \times 3}$
  d $\dfrac{20 \times 4^{12}}{4^7 \times 4^9}$

Q12a hint

$\dfrac{12 \times 3^{10}}{3^{13}} = \dfrac{12}{3^3}$

13 Use the formula $F = mg - 3t^2$ to work out the value of F when
  a $m = 5$, $g = 8$ and $t = 5$
  b $m = 7$, $g = 10$ and $t = -2$

14 **Problem-solving** The numbers in this diagram follow this rule.

Work out the missing numbers in the diagram.

Q14 hint

$7 \times 8 + 20 = \square^2$

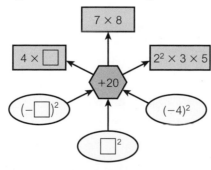

15 Use the formula $m = \sqrt{3h^2 - k^2}$ to work out the value of m when

   a $h = 4.7$ and $k = 3.5$. Give your answer correct to 3 s.f.

   b $h = 79$ and $k = -12$. Give your answer correct to 2 s.f.

16 Evaluate

   a $\dfrac{(2 \times 4)^3}{8 \times 4} = \dfrac{8^3}{8 \times 4} =$

   b $\dfrac{(5 \times 3)^2}{9 \times 5} = \dfrac{15^2}{3 \times 3 \times 5} = \dfrac{15 \times 15}{3 \times 15} =$

   c $\dfrac{24 \times 6^3}{(3 \times 4)^2} = \dfrac{24 \times 6 \times 6 \times 6}{12^2} =$

> **Q16a hint**
>
> Cancel before multiplying $\dfrac{{}^{1}\!8 \times {}^{2}\!8 \times 8}{{}^{1}\!8 \times {}^{1}\!4}$
>
> to make the calculation easier.

17 In this spider diagram, the four calculations give the answer in the middle.
Work out the missing numbers.

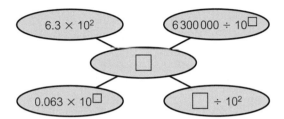

6.3×10^2 $6\,300\,000 \div 10^{\square}$ $\square$ $0.063 \times 10^{\square}$ $\square \div 10^2$

D3 1–2 or 1·3

18 STEM A computer processor chip is 15 nm long.
How many will fit in a container 10 µm long?

19 The table shows the approximate population and area of five countries.

1·4

   a Copy the table, writing all the numbers as ordinary numbers.

D3 ?

   b The population density of a country is calculated using this formula

$$\text{population density} = \frac{\text{population of country}}{\text{area of country}}$$

Country	Population	Area (km²)
China	1.36×10^9	9.57×10^6
Hong Kong	7.11×10^6	1.05×10^3
Iceland	3.17×10^5	1.00×10^5
USA	3.19×10^{10}	9.16×10^6
Vietnam	9.34×10^7	3.10×10^5

   Calculate the population density of each country in the table.
Give your answers to the nearest whole number.

   c Which country has

     i the highest population density

     ii the lowest population density?

> **Q19b Literacy hint**
>
> The population density is the number of people per square kilometre.

20 Real The table shows the number of children and adults in the different countries of the UK in 2012.

Country	England	Scotland	Wales	Northern Ireland
Number of children	10 130 226	914 671	556 552	382 141
Number of adults	43 363 503	4 398 929	2 517 515	1 441 693

Source: StatsWales

   a Estimate the answer to each of these questions by rounding the numbers in the table to 1 significant figure.

     i What is the mean number of children in the 4 countries in the UK in 2012?

     ii What percentage of the total population in England in 2012 were children?

   b Use a calculator to work out the accurate answers to part **a**.

   c How good were your estimates? Were they close to your accurate answers?

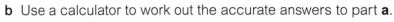

Topic links: Using formulae, Mean, Percentages

Subject links: Computing (Q18), Geography (Q19, Q20), Science (Q6–9)

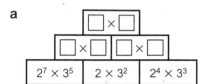

21 Work out each of these. Give your answer in its simplest form, as a mixed number or a fraction.

a $\dfrac{(2 \times 5)^2}{15 \times 2^3}$ **b** $\dfrac{(3 \times 7)^3}{21 \times 14}$ **c** $\dfrac{6 \times 5^2}{(4 \times 3)^3}$ **d** $\dfrac{(3 \times 2 \times 4)^3}{9 \times (6 \times 2)^2}$

D2 **22 Problem-solving** In these multiplication pyramids, the number in a brick is the product of the two bricks below it.
Work out the missing entries. Write each answer in index form.

a

	$\square \times \square$	
$\square \times \square$		$\square \times \square$
$2^7 \times 3^5$	2×3^2	$2^4 \times 3^3$

b

	$4^{20} \times 5^{15}$	
$\square \times \square$	$4^{12} \times 5^9$	
$\square \times \square$	$4^3 \times 5^5$	$\square \times \square$

c Make your own multiplication pyramid like the ones above, for a partner to work out.

23 Reasoning Use your answers from Q22 to help you copy and complete these general rules.

a $x^a \times y^b \times x^c \times y^d = x^\square \times y^\square$

b $\dfrac{x^a \times y^b}{x^c \times y^d} = x^\square \times y^\square$

Investigation   D3
                                                                1.1   **Problem-solving**

1 Copy and complete these number patterns.

a $2^2 = 4$ **b** $2^2 = 4$
$2^2 + 2^2 = \square\ 8$ $2^3 = \square\ 8$
$2^2 + 2^2 + 2^3 = \square\ 16$ $2^4 = \square\ 16$
$2^2 + 2^2 + 2^3 + 2^4 = \square\ 32$ $2^5 = \square$
$2^2 + 2^2 + 2^3 + 2^4 + 2^5 = \square$ $2^6 = \square$

2 What do you notice about the answers to part **1a**?
3 What do you notice about the answers to part **1a** and **b**?
4 Write down the missing numbers in this statement.
$2^2 + 2^2 + 2^3 + 2^4 + 2^5 + 2^6 = \square = 2^\square$
5 Use your answer to part 4 to write down the answer to $2^1 + 2^2 + 2^3 + 2^4 + 2^5 + 2^6$
6 Copy and complete
$2^1 + 2^2 + 2^3 + 2^4 + 2^5 + 2^6 = 2^\square - 2$
$2^1 + 2^2 + 2^3 + 2^4 + 2^5 + 2^6 + 2^7 = 2^\square - 2$
$2^1 + 2^2 + 2^3 + 2^4 + \ldots + 2^x = 2^\square - 2$

> **Investigation hint**
>
> Compare $2^1 + 2^2 + 2^3 + 2^4 + 2^5 + 2^6$
> with $2^2 + 2^2 + 2^3 + 2^4 + 2^5 + 2^6$

24 Reflect Look back at the questions you answered in these lessons. Find a question that you could not answer straight away, or that you really had to think about.
• Why couldn't you immediately see what to do?
• How did this make you feel?
• Did you keep trying or did you give up?
• Did you think you would get the answer correct or incorrect?
Write down any strategies you could use when answering challenging questions. Compare your strategies with others.

Master
P1

Check
P11

Strengthen
p13

Extend
p17

TEST

1 Unit test

Log how you did on your
Student Progression Chart.

1 Write each number as a product of prime factors.
   a 76   **b** 648

2 Write each calculation as a single power.
   a $8^5 \times 8^4$ **b** $3^{11} \times 3$ **c** $9^3 \times 9^7 \times 9^6$
   d $7^7 \div 7$ **e** $12^{10} \div 12^5$ **f** $(6^3)^6$

3 Write each calculation as a single power.
   a $(-3)^5 \times (-3)^2$ **b** $(-8)^7 \times (-8)^3$

4 **a** Work out the prime factor decomposition of
      i 144   **ii** 180
   b Work out the HCF of 144 and 180.

5 Ardem has two lights.
   One flashes every 15 seconds, the other flashes every 42 seconds.
   They start flashing at the same time.
   After how many seconds will they next flash at the same time?

6 **a** Calculate the HCF of 180, 189 and 600.
   b Calculate the LCM of 180, 189 and 600.

7 Evaluate $\dfrac{2 \times 5^7}{5^4}$

8 **a** Arrange these cards into their correct groups.
      Each group must have one card of each colour.

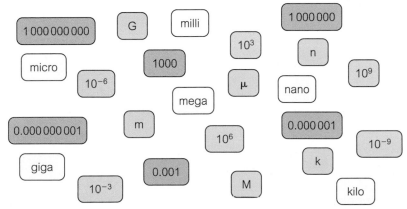

   b Convert
      i 9 GJ to joules   **ii** 13 kW to walls   **iii** 8.5 Ms to seconds

9 Write each of these as a product of primes.
   a $5^3 \times 2^5 \times 10^2$ **b** $3^3 \times 15^3 \times 5^6$

10 Work out
   a $(-7)^2$ **b** $10^2 - (-2)^2 - (3)^2$

11 Use the formula $F = mg - 3t^2$ to work out the value of F when
   a $m = 4$, $g = 6$ and $t = 2$ **b** $m = 6$, $g = 11$ and $t = -4$

12 Round these numbers to the given number of significant figures.

 a 27695 (3 s.f.)   b 7.98226 (4 s.f.)   c 0.00673 (1 s.f.)

13 Estimate the answer to these calculations by rounding each number to 1 significant figure.

 a 632 × 87   b 2875 ÷ 58

14 The table shows the value of sales in an antique shop each day for one week.

Monday	Tuesday	Wednesday	Thursday	Friday
£1670	£986	£437	£2185	£785

Estimate the mean value of the sales for the week. Show all your working.

15 Work out each calculation as a single power.

 a $\dfrac{15^3 \times 15^8}{15^6}$ b $\dfrac{4^7 \times 4}{4^2 \times 4^4}$ c $25 \times 5 \times 125$ d $\dfrac{2^{10}}{32 \times 8}$

16 Which calculation does not give the same answer as the others?

 A $(3 \times 4)^2$ **B** 3×4^2 **C** $3^2 \times 4^2$ **D** 12^2

17 Evaluate

 a $\dfrac{(7 \times 4)^2}{8 \times 14}$ b $\dfrac{6 \times 15}{(3 \times 5)^3}$

18 Match each red card to the correct blue card.

A $(m^p)^q$	**D** m^{p-q}
B $m^p \times m^q$	**E** m^{p+q}
C $m^p \div m^q$	**F** m^{pq}

Challenge

19 STEM The table shows the number of days it takes four of the planets in our solar system to orbit the Sun.

Planet	Number of days to orbit the Sun	Prime factor decomposition
Mercury	88	88 =
Earth	365	365 =
Uranus	30700	30700 =
Neptune	60200	60200 =

 a Copy and complete the table.

 Assume that on one day, all four planets are in alignment with the Sun.

 b How many days will it be before these planets are aligned with the Sun again?

  i Uranus and Neptune
  ii Earth and Uranus
  iii Uranus and Mercury
  iv Mercury and Neptune

 c Which two planets will take the longest time to align with the Sun again?

 d How many days will it be before Uranus, Mercury and Neptune are aligned with the Sun again?

> **Q19b hint**
>
> Draw a diagram of the Sun and the four planets.

20 Reflect Which of the questions in this Unit test took the shortest time to answer? Why?

Which question needed the most thought to answer? Why? Source: StatsWales

Reflect

2 Working with powers

MASTER   Check P33   Strengthen P35   Extend P39   Test P43

2.1 Simplifying expressions

You will learn to:
- Simplify expressions involving powers and brackets
- Understand the meaning of an identity.

CONFIDENCE

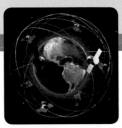

Why learn this?
Scientists simplify expressions involving powers to calculate when and where two objects will collide.

Fluency
All these expressions simplify to $12x$.
What are the missing terms or numbers?
- $8x + \square$
- $\square - 8x$
- $\square \times 4x$
- $\dfrac{24x}{\square}$

Explore
What does the expression $x\wedge3*x\wedge2$ mean in a spreadsheet program?

Exercise 2.1

1 Simplify
  a $3x + 5x$
          b $8y + 2z + 2y + 9z$
  c $7t + 5g - 2g - 5t$
          d $8h + 9j - 15h$
  e $3x^3 + x^2 - x^3$

Warm up

2 Copy and complete this addition pyramid.
Each brick is the sum of the two bricks below it.

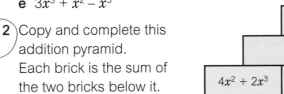

3 Expand
  a $5(x + 7)$
          b $-2(a + 3)$

4 Simplify
  a $2a \times 5a$
          b $4m \times 3m \times 2m$

5 **Real** A sculptor makes two cubes out of concrete. The smaller cube has side length x cm.
The larger cube has a side length 3 times the length of the smaller cube.
  a Write an expression, in terms of x, for the side length of the larger cube.
  b Write an expression for the volume of each cube.
  c Write an expression for the total volume of concrete needed for both cubes. Write your expression in its simplest form.
  d Use your answer to part **c** to work out the total volume of concrete needed for both cubes when $x = 10$ cm.

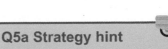

Q5a Strategy hint
Sketch both cubes and label the lengths of their sides.

Topic links: Perimeter, Volume of cube

6 Write an expression for each perimeter. Write your answer in its simplest form.

a
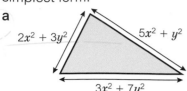
$2x^2 + 3y^2$ $5x^2 + y^2$ $3x^2 + 7y^2$

b
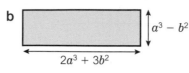
$a^3 - b^2$ $2a^3 + 3b^2$

7 a Add together two of the expressions linked by lines.
b Repeat part **a** in as many different ways as you can.
c Add all three expressions together.

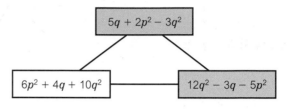
$5q + 2p^2 - 3q^2$
$6p^2 + 4q + 10q^2$ $12q^2 - 3q - 5p^2$

Worked example

a Work out $4(x + 5) + 3(x - 6)$.

$4(x + 5) + 3(x - 6)$

$= 4x + 20 + 3x - 18$ —— Expand the brackets.

$= 7x + 2$ —— Collect like terms.

b Work out $6(p + 2) - 2(p + 1)$.

$6(p + 2) - 2(p + 1)$ —— Expand the brackets. Multiply terms in the second bracket by -2.

$= 6p + 12 - 2p - 2$

$= 4p + 10$ —— Collect like terms.

8 Expand and simplify
a $3(x + 5) + 4(x - 2)$ **b** $5(m - 4) - 3(m + 1)$ **c** $2(y + 5) - 2(y - 1)$
d $2(x + 5) - (3x - 2)$ **e** $3(2x + 4) + 2(x - 3)$ **f** $4(3x - 5) - 3(2x - 1)$

9 a Write an expression for the area of the larger rectangle.
b Write an expression for the area of the smaller rectangle.
c Write an expression for the shaded area.

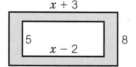
$x + 3$
5 $x - 2$ 8

> **Key point**
>
> An **equation** has an equals (=) sign. It is true for particular values.
> For example $2x + 5 = 11$ is only true for $x = 3$.
> The **identity** symbol ($\equiv$) shows that two expressions are always equivalent.
> For example $x + x + 5 \equiv 2x + 5$.

10 Reasoning The = and $\equiv$ signs are not printed in these statements. Decide if each one is an **equation** or an **identity**.
a $3m + 6 \square 21$
b $x + x + x + x \square 4x$
c $5 \times r \times r \square 5r^2$
d $6n^2 \square 13n + 5$
e $9y + 9 \square 2y + 7y + 4 + 5$
f $5 \times p \times p + 3 \times p - 2 \square 5p^2 + 5p + 2$

11 Reasoning a Show that $2^2 + 2^2 \equiv 2^3$.
b Is $x^2 + x^2 \equiv x^3$ true for all values of x? Explain your answer.

> **Q11a hint**
> Work out the value of both sides.

12 Explore What does the expression $x\verb|^|3*x\verb|^|2$ mean in a spreadsheet program?
Is it easier to explore this question now you have completed the lesson?
What further information do you need to be able to answer this?

13 Reflect Write a definition, in your own words, for each of these mathematics words.
• Expand
• Simplify
Compare your definitions with others in your class.
Can you improve your definitions?

> **Q13 hint**
> Look back at questions where you were asked to expand and simplify. What did you do?

Explore

Reflect

2.2 More simplifying

You will learn to:
- Use the index laws in algebraic calculations and expressions
- Simplify expressions with powers.

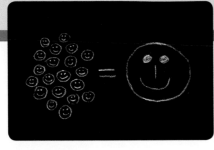

Why learn this?
Solving equations becomes much easier when you can simplify first.

Fluency
What is the value of
- 3^0
- 5^0
- 7^1
- 10^0?

Explore
What is the area of this shape?

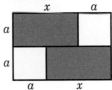

Exercise 2.2

1 Write each expression as a single power.

  a $3^2 \times 3^3$ **b** $5^3 \times 5$ **c** $4^5 \div 4^2$

  d $(2^2)^3$ **e** $x \times x$

2 Simplify

  a $2x \times 2x$ **b** $5a \times 4b$ **c** $\dfrac{6t}{3}$

3 Reasoning

  a Simplify

   i $2^4 \times 2^5$ **ii** $3^4 \times 3^5$ **iii** $x^4 \times x^5$

  b Write a rule to explain what you do to indices when you multiply powers of the same **variable**.

  c Copy and complete.

   i $2^5 \div 2^3 = \dfrac{2^5}{2^3} = \dfrac{2 \times 2 \times 2 \times 2 \times 2}{2 \times 2 \times 2} = 2^\square$

   ii $x^5 \div x^3 = \dfrac{x^5}{x^3} = \dfrac{x \times x \times x \times x \times x}{x \times x \times x} = x^\square$

  d Write a rule to explain what you do to indices when you divide powers of the same variable.

  e Simplify

   i $(2^3)^5$ **ii** $(3^3)^5$ **iii** $(x^3)^5$

  f Write a rule to explain what you do to indices when you raise the power of a variable to another power.

> **Key point**
> A **variable** is a letter that represents a number.

4 Simplify

  a $x^7 \times x^9 = x^\square$ **b** $z^{12} \div z^4 = z^\square$ **c** $(v^4)^2 = v^\square$

5 Work out the missing power.

  a $y^2 \times y^\square = y^8$ **b** $n^\square \div n^3 = n^6$ **c** $(w^\square)^3 = w^{18}$

> **Q4a hint**
> $x^7 \times x^9 = x^{7+9} = x^\square$

Topic links: Index laws, Multiplication

6 Multiply each pair of expressions linked by a line.

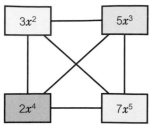

$$3x^2 \qquad 5x^3$$

$$2x^4 \qquad 7x^5$$

Worked example

Simplify

a $\dfrac{15x^3}{3x}$

$\dfrac{15x^3}{3x}$

$\dfrac{15}{3} = 5$ and $\dfrac{x^3}{x} = x^2$

$= 5x^2$

b $\dfrac{8a^3 \times 6a^2}{3a^3}$

$\dfrac{8a^3 \times 6a^2}{3a^3}$

$\dfrac{6}{3} = 2$

$\dfrac{a^3}{a^3} = 1$

$= 16a^2$

7 Simplify

a $\dfrac{12a^8}{4a^3} = 3a^\square$

b $\dfrac{25b^7}{5b^4}$

c $\dfrac{30n^3}{6n}$

d $\dfrac{18t^5}{3t^4}$

e $\dfrac{3p^5 \times 8p^3}{2p}$

f $\dfrac{5x^3 \times 6x}{3x}$

Q8 Strategy hint

Decide on the numbers first, then the powers of x.

8 Problem-solving Write two expressions that simplify to give $24x^5$. One expression must be a multiplication and the other a division.

9 Problem-solving This is part of Teri's homework. Her pen has leaked ink onto her page. Work out the numbers underneath the blobs of ink.

Simplify these.

a $\dfrac{5y^5 \times 9y^3}{3y^\blacksquare} = \blacksquare y^2$

b $\dfrac{4y^\blacksquare \times y^7}{6y^5} = 8y^4$

10 Simplify

a $(4x^2)^2 = 4^2 \times (x^2)^2 = \square x^\square$

b $(2y^3)^2$

c $(3z^4)^3$

d $\left(\dfrac{x^2}{4}\right)^3 = \dfrac{(x^2)^3}{4^3} = \dfrac{x^6}{\square}$

e $\left(\dfrac{y^4}{7}\right)^2$

f $\left(\dfrac{z^5}{3}\right)^3$

Discussion Which of these are the same?

$(4x^2)^2 \qquad -4x^4 \qquad -(4x)^4 \qquad (-4x^2)^2 \qquad 4x^4$

11 Decide if these are always true, sometimes true or never true for positive values of a, b, c and d.

For the statements that are always true, replace the equals sign (=) with an identity sign ($\equiv$).

For the equations that are sometimes true, state values that make them true.

a $x^a \times x^b = x^{ab}$

b $x^a \div x^b = x^{a-b}$

c $(x^a)^b = x^{a+b}$

d $y^c \div y^d = y^{d-c}$

e $(y^c)^d = (y^d)^c$

f $y^d \times y^c = y^{c+d}$

Q11 Strategy hint

Try different values for a, b, c and d.

12 Explore What is the area of this shape?

Is it easier to explore this question now you have completed the lesson? What further information do you need to be able to answer this?

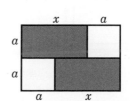

Q13 hint

Substitute $x = 2$ and $x = 3$ into each expression. Do you get the same or different answers? Why?

13 Reflect Lucy asks, 'Are the results of $x^2 \times x^2$ and $x^2 + x^2$ the same or different?' Answer Lucy's question, then explain your answer.

2.3 Expanding and factorising expressions

You will learn to:
- Write and simplify expressions involving brackets and powers
- Factorise an algebraic expression.

CONFIDENCE

Why learn this?
Scientists factorise expressions to solve equations to find forces, for example the force of a skier coming down a slope.

Fluency
- Which of these are like terms?

  $7x^3$ x^4 $9x^3$ $\dfrac{x^4}{2}$ $11x^2$ $-4x^2$

- What is the highest common factor of:
  8 and 12
  12 and $15x$?

Explore
How many expressions can be simplified to give $12x^2 + 24x$?

Exercise 2.3

1 Simplify
  a $5a \times 3b$
  b $2m \times 3m$
  c $4n \times -5n$
  d $7a^2 \times 2a^3$
  e $6p \times -5p^4$

2 Expand
  a $2(3x + 5)$
  b $4(3 - 2y)$
  c $y(y + 3)$
  d $2(x - 1)$
  e $3(10 + p)$
  f $s(10 - s)$

3 Expand
  a $x(x + 5)$
  b $y(8 + y)$
  c $p(2p - 5)$
  d $2q(6 - 3q)$

4 Joel was asked to factorise $12x - 16$ completely.
  His answer is $12x - 16 = 2(6x - 8)$
  Why is this not factorised completely?

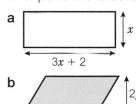

5 For each shape
  i write an expression for the area of the shape
  ii expand the brackets in your expression.

  a
  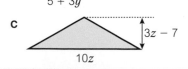
  x
  $3x + 2$

Q5a hint
$x(\square + \square)$

  b
  $2y$
  $5 + 3y$

  c

  $3z - 7$
  $10z$

Warm up

Topic links: Area of rectangle, parallelogram and triangle,
Surface area and volume of cuboid, HCF

6 Expand

    a $x(x^2 + 4x)$

    b $2x^3(7x^3 - 3x^2)$

    c $5x(x^3 + 2x^2 + 7)$

    d $x^2(x^2 - 5x + 7)$

Q6b hint

$2x^3(7x^3 - 3x^2) = \square x^\square - \square x^\square$

7 Expand and simplify

    a $2(a + 3b) + 5(a + b)$

    b $x(2x^2 + 5) + 3x(4x^2 + 7)$

    c $3(6 - 2y) + y^2(y - 8)$

    d $5t(t + 2) - 4t^3(t^2 - 2)$

Q7a hint

First expand the two brackets.
Then collect like terms.

8 **Reasoning** The diagram shows a cuboid.

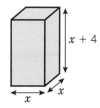

    a Write an expression for the volume of the cuboid.

    b Show that an expression for the surface area of
       the cuboid is $6x^2 + 16x$.

  Discussion For the volume does it matter in which order you
multiply the three lengths together?

Q8b Strategy hint

'Show that' means 'Show your
working'.

Investigation   **Reasoning**
Start with 2 sticks x cm long. Cut y cm off the end of each stick.

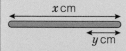

You can arrange the 4 pieces into a rectangle like this.

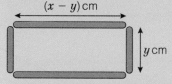

1 Write a simplified expression for the perimeter and for the area of the rectangle.

2 Now start with 4 sticks x cm long and cut y cm off the end of each stick.
   Arrange the pieces to make a rectangle. You don't have to use all the pieces.

   a How many different rectangles can you make?

   b How many different expressions are there for the area and for the perimeter?

   c Work out the perimeter and area of each rectangle when $x = 30$ cm and $y = 10$ cm.

---

9 Write the **highest common factor** of each pair.

    a x^2 and x^3

    b p^2 and p

    c y^5 and y^2

    d $8z^3$ and $4z$

    e $10m^5$ and $15m^3$

    f pq and p^2q^2

Q9a hint

$x^2 = \boxed{x} \times \boxed{x}$
$x^3 = \boxed{x} \times \boxed{x} \times x$

Worked example

Factorise $18x^2 - 24x$ completely.

$18x^2 - 24x = 6x(3x - 4)$ ⟵ The **HCF** of $18x^2$ and $24x$ is $6x$.

Check:

$6x(3x - 4) = 18x^2 - 24x$ ⟵ $6x \times 3x = 18x^2$ and $6x \times -4 = -24x$

Key point

To **factorise** an expression completely, take out the **highest common factor (HCF)** of its terms.

10 Factorise
    a $15x^3 - 3x$
    b $32x + 16x^2$
    c $15x + 21x^2$
    d $3x^3 + 6x$
    e $y^2 - 7y^4$
    f $3y^5 + 15y^3$
    g $12y^4 - 4y^3$

11 **Reasoning** For each question, which is the odd one out, A, B or C?
    Explain why.
    a A $8x(x^2 + 9x + 4)$ B $12x(2x^2 + 6x + 2)$ C $24x(x^2 + 3x + 1)$
    b A $y^2(3y + 1)$ B $y(3y^2 + y)$ C $3y(y^2 + 1)$
    c A $-z^3(3z^2 + 6z - 9)$ B $z^3(6z - 3z^2 + 9)$ C $z^3(9 + 6z + 3z^2)$

12 **Problem-solving / Reasoning**
    a Show that both of these statements are identities.
       i $4x^3 + x(3x^2 + 7x) \equiv 7x^2(x + 1)$
       ii $2b(b^2 + 3b) - b(b^2 + 8b) \equiv 2b^2(b - 1) - b^3$
    b Work out the missing numbers from this identity.
       $\square y(y^3 - 3) - 2y(2y^3 - \square) \equiv 2y(y^3 + 3) - 2y$

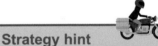

Q12a Strategy hint

Expand the left-hand side and rewrite it as the right-hand side.

13 **Problem-solving** This expression has been factorised completely.
    $\square x^2 \square + \square\square y^3 = 6\square y^3(2\square + \square\square)$
    Fill in possible missing terms.

14 **Explore** How many expressions can be simplified to give
    $12x^2 + 24x$?
    Look back at the maths you have learned in this lesson.
    How can you use it to answer this question?

15 **Reflect**
    a Write a definition, in your own words, of highest common factor.
    b Use your definition to explain, in your own words, what factorising is.
    c How did the definition you wrote in part **a** help you to write the definition in part **b**?

2.4 Substituting and solving

You will learn to:
- Substitute integers into expressions
- Construct and solve equations.

CONFIDENCE

Why learn this?
Engineers substitute negative values into expressions when calculating the speed of trains as they are slowing down.

Fluency
Which of these expressions is the correct expression for the perimeter of this rectangle?

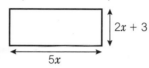

$2x + 3$

$5x$

A $7x + 3$ B $10x^2 + 15x$
C $14x + 6$ D $20x$

Explore
How long does it take a car to slow down to enter a speed restriction area?

Exercise 2.4

1 Work out the value of these expressions when $x = 4$ and $y = 5$.
   a $3x + 8$ **b** $2xy$
   c $6(x + y)$ **d** $y^2 - x^2$

2 Solve
   a $3x + 8 = 23$ **b** $5 = 20 - 5x$ **c** $8x + 3 = 3x + 33$
   d $7(x + 8) = 3(x - 4)$ **e** $5x^2 = 500$

3 Square A has area x cm². Square B has area $(x + 3)$ cm².
The area of square B is four times the area of square A.
   a Write an equation using the information given.
   b Solve the equation to find the value of x.

[handwritten: $x + 3 = 4x$, $x = 1$]

Key point
A **linear expression** is one where the highest power is 1.
For example, $2x + 5$ and $a + 2b$ are linear expressions, but $2x^2 + 5$ is not a linear expression.

4 Find the value of these **linear expressions** when $x = 8$, $y = 5$ and $z = -3$.
   a $4x + 3z$ **b** $2(x + 3) + y + x$
   c $5(y - z) - 2x$ **d** $3(x + y) - 2(y + z)$

Q4a hint
$4x + 3z = 4 \times 8 + 3 \times -3$

5 For each shape
   a write an expression for the perimeter of the shape
   b simplify the expression
   c work out the perimeter when $a = 3$ and $b = -2$.

A

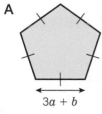

$3a + b$

B

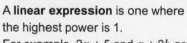

$4a + 3b$

$5a - 2b$

Discussion Is it possible to work out the perimeter of the rectangle when $a = 2$ and $b = -4$?

[handwritten: $5(3a + b) = 15a + 5b$]

Warm up

6 These two shapes have the same area. Work out the value of x.

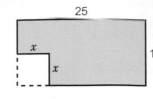

25

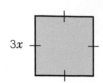

3x

10

$\frac{8}{9}x^2 = 250 - x^2$

$10x^2 = 250$

$x = \sqrt{25} = 5$

Q6 hint

Write expressions for the areas.

7 Substitute $x = 3$, $y = 4$ and $z = -2$ into
   a $3x(x + y)$
   b $z^2(z + x^2)$
   c $2x(5 + z) + y^2$.

Q7b hint

$(-2)^2 \times (-2 + 3^2)$

8 **STEM** A formula you can use to work out the distance, s, a car has travelled in metres is

$$s = ut + \frac{1}{2}at^2$$

where: u is the starting speed in metres per second
         a is the acceleration in metres per second²
         t is the time in seconds.

Work out the distance the car has travelled when
   a $u = 0$, $a = 2$ and $t = 10$
   b $u = 13$, $a = 3$ and $t = 4$
   c $u = 25$, $a = -4$ and $t = 8$.
Discussion What does it mean when $u = 0$?

9 **Problem-solving / Reasoning** The diagram shows a cuboid and a cube.
The volume of the cuboid is greater than the volume of the cube.

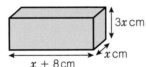

3x cm

x cm

$x + 8$ cm

2x cm

$(x + 8) . x . 3x$

$3x^3 + 24x^2 > 8x^3$

$24x^2 > 5x^3$

$24 > 5x$

$x < 4.8$

   a Write an expression, in its simplest form, for the difference between the volume of the cuboid and cube.
   b Use your expression to calculate this difference when
      i $x = 1$ **ii** $x = 2$
      iii $x = 3$ **iv** $x = 4$.
   c Explain why it is not possible for x to be an **integer** greater than 4.

Q9 Literacy hint

An **integer** is a whole number.

Worked example

Solve the equation $4(2a - 1) = 32 - 3(2a - 2)$.

$4(2a - 1) = 32 - 3(2a - 2)$

$8a - 4 = 32 - 6a + 6$ — Multiply out the brackets. Take care with the minus signs.

$8a - 4 = 38 - 6a$ — Collect like terms on the right-hand side. $32 + 6 = 38$

$8a + 6a = 38 + 4$ — Rearrange to get like terms on both sides.

$14a = 42$

$a = \frac{42}{14} = 3$ — Simplify and then solve.

Topic links: Writing expressions, Perimeter of shapes, Volume of cube and cuboid, Area of composite shapes

Subject links: Science (Q8)

10 Solve

    a $3(x + 5) = 37 - 2(x + 1)$

    b $6(2y + 1) = 46 - 4(3y - 2)$

    c $4(3z - 7) = 65 - 3(4z - 9)$

    d $2(2x + 9) = 4x + 3 - 5(6 - x)$

11 **Problem-solving**

    a In this diagram the green shapes have the same area.

> **Q11 Strategy hint**
>
> Write an expression for the area of each shape.

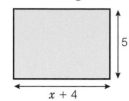
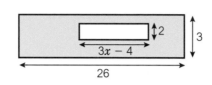

    Work out the value of x.

    b In this diagram the yellow shapes have the same area.

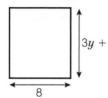
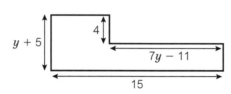

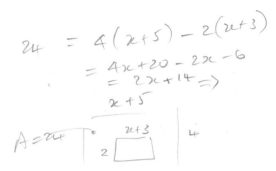

    Work out the value of y.

12 **Problem-solving** A rectangular piece of card measuring 4 cm by $(x + 5)$ cm has a rectangular hole cut out of it. The hole measures 2 cm by $(x + 3)$ cm. The area of card left over is 24 cm².

    a Work out the value of x.

    b Work out the dimensions of the original piece of card and the hole.

> **Q12 Strategy hint**
>
> Draw a diagram.

Investigation   **Problem-solving**

Use the values $a = 6$, $b = 8$, $c = -4$, $d = -3$ to write three expressions that will give an answer of

a 19   **b** 26   **c** −30   **d** −42

For example, $\frac{ab}{2} + c - 1$ is one expression that gives an answer of 19.

At least one of your expressions for each number should involve a square or square root.

Ask a partner to check your expressions are correct.

---

13 **Explore** How long does it take a car to slow down to enter a speed restriction area?

    Is it easier to explore this question now you have completed the lesson? What further information do you need to be able to answer this?

14 **Reflect** Safiya says, 'When solving equations, I always check that my solution is correct. If it isn't, first I check my check! Then, I cover my original working and try to solve the equation again.'

    Did you check your solutions to the questions in this lesson?

    If so, what did you do to check?

    What is your strategy if you get an incorrect solution?

    Compare your strategy with others in your class.

Master
P23

CHECK

Strengthen
P35

Extend
P39

Test
P43

2 Check up

Log how you did on your
Student Progression Chart.

Simplifying and substituting into expressions

1 Simplify

  a $4x^2 + 6x^2$

  b $8a^2 - 2b^2 - 4b^2 + 3a^2$

  c $9y + 12y^2 + 2y - 7y^2$

2 Copy these statements. Write the correct sign $=$ or $\equiv$ in each empty box.

  a $2x + 5 \;\Box\; x + 7 + x - 2$

  b $2x + 1 \;\Box\; 4x - 3$

3 Find the value of each linear expression when $x = 3$, $y = -2$ and $z = 4$.

  a $5x + 2y$

  b $6(y + z)$

  c $3(z + 1) + x - y$

  d $4(2z + y) - 3(z - y)$

4 Substitute $x = -1$, $y = -3$ and $z = 5$ into

  a $y^2(z + x^2)$

  b $2xy + z(z + 2y)$

Index laws

5 Simplify

  a $x^3 \times x^2$

  b $\dfrac{y^{12}}{y^2}$

  c $(z^3)^2$

6 Simplify

  a $5x^4 \times 6x^2$

  b $\dfrac{12b^3}{6b}$

  c $(3p^4)^2$

  d $\dfrac{2p^2 \times 6p^4}{3p^3}$

  e $\left(\dfrac{n^3}{5}\right)^2$

Expanding and factorising

7 Expand

  a $x(x^2 + 2x)$

  b $3x^2(2x - 4)$

  c $x^2(3x^2 + 2x - 1)$

8 Expand and simplify

    a $4(x + 3) + 7(x - 1)$

    b $x(x - 6) - x(4x - 2)$

    c $x(3x^2 + 4) + 2x(5x^2 + 9)$

9 Show that this identity is true.

    $5x^3 + x^2(3x - 4) \equiv 4x^2(2x - 1)$

10 Factorise completely

    a $6x^2 + 18x$

    b $8y^3 - 2y^4$

    c $16xy - 8x^2y^2$

Solving equations

11 Solve $2(x + 7) = 28 - 3(6 - x)$.

12 In this diagram the blue shapes have the same area.

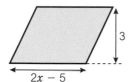 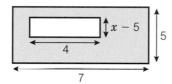

    Work out the value of x.

13 **How sure are you of your answers? Were you mostly**

    😟 **Just guessing**   😐 **Feeling doubtful**   🙂 **Confident**

    What next? Use your results to decide whether to strengthen or extend your learning.

Reflect

Challenge

14 a Choose your own numbers to complete these identities.

    $\square y^{\square} \times \square y^{\square} \equiv 20y^{12}$

    $\square y^{\square} \div \square y^{\square} \equiv 6y^{12}$

    $(\square y^{\square})^{\square} \equiv \square y^{12}$

    b Repeat part **a** using different numbers.

15 a Work out the missing terms from this expression that has been factorised.

    $\square x^2y + \square y^2 + 9\square = 3x\square(\square + 4y + \square)$

    b Is there only one answer to this problem?

    Explain your answer.

16 Work out the whole number values of a and b when $ab = -24$ and $a + b = -2$.

Master
P23

Check
P33

STRENGTHEN

Extend
P39

Test
P43

2 Strengthen

You will:

- Strengthen your understanding with practice.

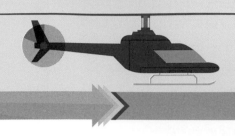

Simplifying and substituting into expressions

1 Copy and complete

   a $2x^2 + 3x^2 = \square x^2$

   b $7t^3 - 2t^3$

   c $5y^4 + 6y^4 - 2y^4$

> **Q1a hint**
>
> How many x^2 are there altogether?

2 Sort these terms into three groups of like terms.

$$-12y^3 \qquad -y \qquad -y^2$$
$$6y \qquad y^3 \qquad 2y^2$$
$$11y^2$$
$$-7y \qquad 3y$$
$$5y^2 \qquad 4y^3$$

3 Ryan uses this method to simplify $7y + 5y^2 + 3y - 8y^2$.

> $\boxed{7y} \boxed{+ 5y^2} \boxed{+ 3y} \boxed{- 8y^2}$
>
> $7y + 3y = 10y$
>
> $5y^2 - 8y^2 = -3y^2$
>
> Answer: $10y - 3y^2$

> **Q3a hint**
>
> Copy the expression. Circle like terms in different colours.

Simplify

   a $8x + 2x^2 + 4x + 3x^2$

   b $4a^2 + 3b^2 - b^2 - a^2$

   c $9p^3 - 6n^2 - 4n^2 + 2p^3$

   d $2v^3 + 7 + 5v - 2v + 2v^3 - 3$

> **Q4a hint**
>
>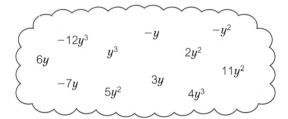
>
> $4 \times 6 = 24$
>
> $+2 \times 5 = 10$
>
> $-3 \times -3 = 9$
>
> Add together: $24 + 10 + 9 = \square$

4 Find the value of each linear expression when $x = 6$, $y = -3$ and $z = 5$.

   a $4x + 2z - 3y$

   b $4z - 2x + y$

   c $4(x + 2) + 5y - z$

   d $3(z + 3x) - 3(z - y)$

> **Q4c hint**
>
> Always work out brackets first.
>
> $4\boxed{(x + 2)} + 5y - z$
>
> $6 + 2$

5 Find the value of each expression when $a = -4$ and $b = 8$.

   a $a + b^2 = \square + 8^2 = \square + \square =$

   b $3a^2 - b = 3 \times (\square)^2 - \square =$

   c $10b + a^3$

   d $(b - a)^2$

> **Q5b hint**
>
> The square of a negative number is positive.

6 Find the value of each expression when
$x = -2$, $y = -4$ and $z = 3$.

  a $y^2(5z - 3x^2)$

  b $z(xy + x^2)$

  c $z^2 - yz + xz$

  d $3(z - x)^2 - 5y$

Q6a hint

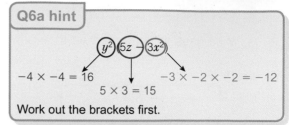

$-4 \times -4 = 16$ $-3 \times -2 \times -2 = -12$

$5 \times 3 = 15$

Work out the brackets first.

Index laws

1 Simplify

  a $x^4 \times x^3$

  b $y^2 \times y^5$

  c $z^8 \times z$

Q1a hint

$$x^4 \times x^3 = \underbrace{x \times x \times x \times x}_{4} \times \underbrace{x \times x \times x}_{3}$$

2 Simplify

  a $x^6 \div x^2$

  b $y^5 \div y^2$

  c $z^8 \div z^3$

Q2a hint

$$x^6 \div x^2 = \frac{\overbrace{x \times x \times x \times x \times x \times x}^{6}}{\underbrace{x \times x}_{2}}$$

3 Simplify

  a $(x^3)^2$

  b $(y^2)^4$

  c $(z^5)^3$

Q3a hint

$$(x^3)^2 = \underbrace{(x \times x \times x)}_{3} \times \underbrace{(x \times x \times x)}_{3}$$

$3 \times 2 = \square$

4 Mia uses this method to simplify $6y^2 \times 3y^4$ and $\dfrac{6y^5}{3y^2}$

$\textcircled{6}y^2 \times \textcircled{3}y^4$ $\dfrac{6y^5}{3y^2}$

$6 \times 3 = 18$ $\dfrac{6}{3} = 2$

$y^2 \times y^4 = y^6$ $\dfrac{y^5}{y^2} = y^3$

Answer: $18y^6$ Answer: $2y^3$

Simplify

  a $2x^3 \times 3x$ **b** $4y^4 \times 5y^3$

  c $6p^2 \times 3p^5$ **d** $9q \times 8q^7$

  e $\dfrac{16a^6}{8a^2}$ **f** $\dfrac{12b^4}{4b^3}$

  g $\dfrac{15b^9}{15b^5}$ **h** $\dfrac{10b^7}{5b}$

Q4a hint

Multiply the numbers first. Then multiply the variables (letters).

Q4e hint

Divide the numbers first. Then divide the variables (letters).

5 Copy and complete

  a $(5x^3)^2 = 5x^3 \times 5x^3 =$

  b $(4m^5)^3$

  c $(3n^3)^4$

  d $\left(\dfrac{x^3}{2}\right)^2 = \dfrac{x^3}{2} \times \dfrac{x^3}{2} = \dfrac{\square}{\square}$

  e $\left(\dfrac{w^6}{6}\right)^2$

Expanding and factorising

1 Miko uses the grid method to expand $y^2(2y - 9)$.

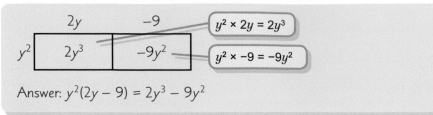

$y^2 \times 2y = 2y^3$

$y^2 \times -9 = -9y^2$

Answer: $y^2(2y - 9) = 2y^3 - 9y^2$

Expand

a $x^2(x + 3)$

b $y^2(y - 5)$

c $2x^3(x - 4)$

d $3y^2(2y^2 + 4y)$

2 Expand and simplify

    a $3(x + 2) + 5(x + 1)$

    b $4(a + 3) + 2(a - 1)$

    c $x(x - 1) + x(x + 8)$

    d $3a(a + 2) - 5a(a - 1)$

> **Q2a hint**
>
> Expand each bracket, then collect like terms.
>
>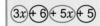

3 Use this checklist to decide if a statement is an equation or an identity.

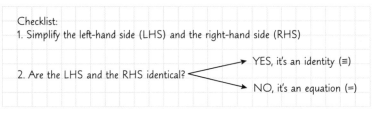

Checklist:
1. Simplify the left-hand side (LHS) and the right-hand side (RHS)

2. Are the LHS and the RHS identical?
→ YES, it's an identity ($\equiv$)
→ NO, it's an equation ($=$)

Copy these statements. Write the correct sign $=$ or $\equiv$ in each empty box.

    a $3x + 2 \;\square\; x + 5 + 2x - 3$

    b $5x + 7 \;\square\; 27$

    c $8p^2 \;\square\; 2p \times 4p$

    d $t + t + t + 8 + 3 \;\square\; 3t + 11$

    e $3x - 9 \;\square\; 2x + 6$

    f $5(x + 3) \;\square\; 3x + 2x + 20 - 5$

4 Copy and complete the workings to show that these identities are true.
The first one has been started for you.

    a $2x^3 + 3x^2(4x - 1) \equiv 7x^2(2x - 1) - 2x^2$

$$\text{LHS} = 2x^3 + 3x^2(4x - 1) \qquad\qquad \text{RHS} = 7x^2(2x - 1) + 4x^2$$
$$= 2x^3 + 12x^3 - 3x^2 \qquad\qquad\qquad\quad = 14x^3 - 7x^2 + 4x^2$$
$$= \qquad\qquad\qquad\qquad\qquad\qquad\qquad =$$

    b $3y(y^2 - 5y) + y^2(3 - 2y) \equiv y^2(y - 9) - 3y^2$

5 Factorise completely

    a $2x^2 + 8x^3$

    b $36d - 30d^4$

    c $6q^3 - 14q^2$

    d $27u^3 + 36u^2$

    e $5b^2 - 50b$

    f $36mn + 8m^2n^2$

> **Q5a hint**
>
> • Look at the numbers. What is the highest common factor?
> • Look at the variables. Is there a letter that appears in every term? If yes, what is its lowest power?

Solving equations

1 Solve

  a $6(x + 5) = 44 - 2(4 - 2x)$

  b $2(3x - 13) = 40 - 3(x + 4)$

  c $7(x + 1) = 8x + 7 - 2(3x - 5)$

  d $4(3 + 5x) = 16x + 56 - 4(2x - 1)$

2 a Write an expression for the area of the parallelogram.

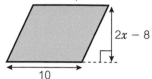

  b **i** Work out the area of the whole large purple rectangle.

    ii Write an expression for the area of the small white rectangle.

    iii The white rectangle is cut out of the purple rectangle.

    Write an expression for the purple area that is left.

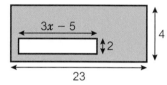

  c The two purple areas from parts **a** and **b** are equal.

  Write an equation to show this.

  d Solve your equation to work out the value of x.

Enrichment

1 **Reasoning** Here are four cards.

$3x^2 + 5y^3 - 2z$	$15x^2 - 12y^3 + 8z$	$3y^3 - z - 7x^2$	$7z + 13x^2 - 4y^3$

  a Show that the mean of these expression cards is $6x^2 - 2y^3 + 3z$.

  b When $x = 2$, $y = 1$ and $z = 3$

    i work out the value of each card

    ii calculate the mean of the four values

    iii check the mean by working out the value of the expression in part **a**

    iv work out the range of the four values.

2 a Substitute for values of x from -4 to 4 in $y = \sqrt{16 - x^2}$

x	-4	-3	-2	-1	0	1	2	3	4
y									

  b Plot the graph of the coordinates in the table.

  c What shape have you drawn?

3 **Reflect** Carla says, 'Algebra is just like arithmetic really, but you use letters when you don't know a number.'

Is Carla's explanation a good one?

Explain your answer.

Q1 Strategy hint

Step 1: Expand the brackets on the right hand side of =, and simplify if you can.

Step 2: Expand the brackets on the left hand side of =, and simplify if you can.

Step 3: Solve the equation.

Step 4: Substitute your value of x into the original equation to check.

Q2a hint

Area of parallelogram
= base length × perpendicular height

Q2c hint

Answer to part **a** = answer to part **b iii**

Q2 hint

Join the points with a smooth curve.

Reflect

2 Extend

You will:
- Extend your understanding with problem-solving.

1 **STEM / Modelling** You can use this formula to calculate the energy,
E (joules), in a moving object
$$E = \tfrac{1}{2}mv^2$$
where m = mass of object (kg) and v = speed (metres per second, m/s).
Work out the speed, v, of the object when
   a $E = 125$ and $m = 10$
   b $E = 450$ and $m = 16$
   c $E = 1134$ and $m = 7$

2 **Reasoning** Here are a regular pentagon and octagon.
   a Write an expression using brackets for the perimeter of
      i the pentagon   **ii** the octagon.
   b Write an expression, in its simplest form, for the total
      perimeter of the two shapes.
   c Write an expression, in its simplest form, for the
      difference in the perimeters of the two shapes when
      i the perimeter of the pentagon is greater than the perimeter of
         the octagon
      ii the perimeter of the octagon is greater than the perimeter of the
         pentagon.
   d Explain what you notice about your two answers to part **c**.

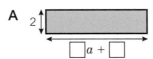

$4p^2 + 3pq - 2q^2$

$3q^2 - pq - 4p^2$

3 **Reasoning** Each rectangle has an area of $12a + 36$.
   a Factorise $12a + 36$ in three
      different ways to work out the
      length and width of the three
      rectangles.
   b **i** Which rectangle has dimensions
         that result in the complete
         factorisation of $12a + 36$?
      ii How could you use the diagrams in part **a** to answer part **b i**?
   c Which rectangle do you think has
      i the greatest perimeter
      ii the smallest perimeter?
      Explain your answers.
   d Write an expression for the perimeter of each rectangle.
   e For $a = 2$
      i work out the dimensions of each rectangle and check they have
         the same area
      ii work out the perimeter of each rectangle and check your
         answers to part **c**.

A 2 [ ] $a +$ [ ]

B [ ] [ ] $a +$ [ ]

C 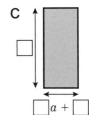 [ ] $a +$ [ ]

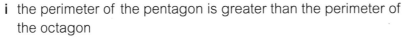
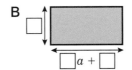

Topic links: Negative numbers, Mean, Range, Perimeter of shapes,
Area of a rectangle, Angles in a triangle and kite, Prime factorisation

4 Reasoning **a** Show that this statement is **not** true.
$15a^3 + 6a(3 - 2a^2) \equiv 3a(a^2 + 7)$
b How can you change the right-hand side of the statement to make it true?

Q4b hint

What do you need to change in the expression $3a(a^2 + 7)$, so it simplifies to the same as the LHS?

5 Factorise completely
a $5ab + 10bc - 25ac$
b $48x^2y - 72y^2 + 120x$
c $65pt + 39ty - 13yx - 52xp$

6 Factorise completely
a $16y^3 + 20y^2 + 24y$ **b** $12x^2 + 6xy - 2x$
c $18x^2y - 6x^2y^2 + 30xy^2$ **d** $60p^2q^3r^4 - 210p^3q^4r^5 + 54p^5q^4r^3$

7 Problem-solving Both of these expressions have been factorised completely. Work out the missing terms.
a $6xy - 12x^2 + \square x^2 \square = 3\square(2y - 4\square + 5xy)$
b $6\square b + 14a^2\square - 12\square b^2 = 2\square b(3a + 7 - 6a\square)$

Q8b hint

Work out the value using z and x before taking the square root.

8 Find the value of each expression when $x = -2$, $y = -4$ and $z = 3$.
a $3(z - x)^2 - 5y$

b $\sqrt{z^3 + x}$

c $\sqrt{y^2 - 7} + x^2$

d $\dfrac{2z^2 - x}{5}$

e $\dfrac{xy - 7y}{z}$

Q8d hint

Always work out the numerator and the denominator first, before dividing.

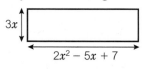

9 Problem-solving The diagram shows two rectangles. The red rectangle is larger than the yellow rectangle.

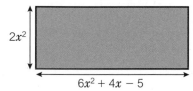

Write an expression to show the difference in the areas of the rectangles.

Q9 hint

Write your expression in its simplest form.

10 Problem-solving
a Match each algebraic expression with the correct value, given the variables in the table below.

a	b	c	d	e	f	g	h	i
4	-3	-6	36	-8	-12	9	-5	13

b One answer card has not been used.
Write an expression for this answer card.
You must use at least three of the letters from the table and your expression must include a power or a root.

$5a + 6b - c^2$ 2

$\sqrt{d} + h^2$ -9

$\dfrac{g^2 + b^2}{2h}$ -34

$f - 2\sqrt{d} + i$ 60

$\dfrac{abc}{d} - e^2$ -26

$\sqrt[3]{e} + a^2 + \dfrac{d}{b}$ -62 31

11 Reasoning Huron is substituting values into the expression $5xy^2 + y^3 + z^2$.
The values he uses for x, y and z are always negative.
Can the value of the expression ever be positive?
Explain your answer.

Q11 Strategy hint

Substitute different negative number values for x, y and z into the expression.

12 Find the value of each expression when $a = \frac{1}{2}$ and $b = \frac{3}{4}$.

   a $a^2 - b^2$ **b** $2ab^2$

13 Problem-solving / Reasoning

The diagram shows an isosceles triangle ABC.

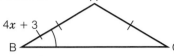

   a Write an expression for the size of
      i angle BCA
      ii angle BAC.

   b Write an equation using the fact that angle BAC = 5(3x − 2) and your answer to part **a ii**.

   c Solve your equation to find the value of x.

   d Work out the sizes of the angles in the triangle. Explain how to check your answers are correct.

Q13a hint

Angle BAC = 180 − 2 × angle ABC

14 Problem-solving / Reasoning

The diagram shows a kite ABCD.

   a Write an expression for the size of
      i angle BCD
      ii angle ADC.

   b Write an equation using the fact that angle ADC = 4(2x − 9) and your answer to part **a ii**.

   c Solve your equation to find the value of x.

   d Work out the sizes of the angles in the kite. Explain how to check your answers are correct.

Q14a hint

What is the total of the angles in a kite?

15 Problem-solving The ages of four friends are:

Adrian	Beth	Carl	Deeba
$y + 1$	$2y + 1$	$6y$	$12y + 7$

Twice Beth's age plus Carl's age is the same as Deeba's age take away three times Adrian's age.

Work out the age of each of the four people.

Q15 Strategy hint

Start by using the information given to write an equation that includes brackets.

16 Problem-solving Ludmilla substitutes $m = -5$ and $n = 3$ into this expression. $(2m)^2 + mn - p^2$

She gets an answer of 4.

What value does she use for p?

17 Copy and complete this multiplication pyramid.

Each brick is the product of the bricks below it.

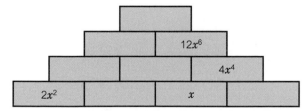

18 Work out

   a $w^3 \times w^7 \times w^2$ **b** $\dfrac{z^8 \times z^4}{z^5}$

   c $\dfrac{d^{12}}{d^2 \times d^4}$ **d** $\dfrac{9s^3 \times 2s^7}{6s^2}$

   e $\dfrac{(4b)^3}{(2b)^2 \times (2b)^2}$ **f** $(n^3)^3 \times (n^2)^2 \times n$

19 Problem-solving The three boxes contain terms involving the letter y.

A $8y^6$ $9y^5$ $12y^8$ $6y^7$

B $6y^3$ $10y^6$ $8y^9$ $12y^5$

C $4y^6$ $2y^5$ $5y^6$ $3y^7$

a Choose one term from each box and simplify $\dfrac{\text{A term} \times \text{B term}}{\text{C term}}$.

b Repeat part **a** two more times using different terms each time.

c Which terms from each box will give the answer with the smallest power of y?
   What is this answer?

d Which terms from each box will give the answer with the greatest power of y?
   What is this answer?

20 Problem-solving In this spider diagram, the six expressions are all equal to the expression in the middle.

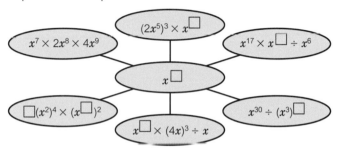

Copy and complete the spider diagram.

21 Problem-solving a Match each rectangular yellow expression card to the correct circular blue simplified card.

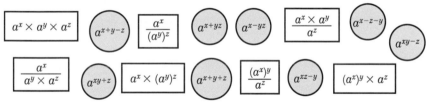

b There is one blue card left over. Write the rectangular yellow expression card that goes with this circular blue card.

Investigation   Reasoning

1 In the expressions below, x can be any positive or negative whole number.
   The letters a and b can be any positive whole numbers, with a being greater than b.
   Choose values for x, a and b that make these statements true.
   a $x^a \times x^b < (x^a)^b$ b $x^a \times x^b > (x^a)^b$
   c $x^a \div x^b < (x^a)^b$ d $x^a \div x^b > (x^a)^b$

2 What are the only values of x that you can use to make these statements true?

3 Choose values for a and b to show these statements are true.
   a $x^a \times x^b = (x^a)^b$ b $x^a \div x^b = (x^a)^b$ c $x^a \times x^b = x^a \div x^b$

---

22 Reflect What do you find easier: working with expressions, equations or identities?
Explain why.

2 Unit test

Log how you did on your Student Progression Chart.

1 Simplify

   a $12y^2 - 7y^2$

   b $2x + 5x^3 + 3x - 4x^3$

   c $4d^3 - 2 + 3d^3 - 1 + 2d^2$

2 Simplify

   a $x^7 \times x^3$

   b $\dfrac{y^{15}}{y^5}$

   c $(z^2)^5$

   d $m^9 \times m^4 \times m^2$

   e $\dfrac{b^4 \times b^5}{b^2}$

3 Expand

   a $p(p^3 + 2p)$ **b** $2m^2(m - 4)$

   c $2y^2(3y^2 - 2y + 7y^3)$ **d** $3x(8 + 4x - 8x^2)$

4 Expand and simplify

   a $p(8p + 3) + 2p(3p + 5)$

   b $3v(5v + 2u - 8) + 5v(4 - 2v)$

5 Which of these are identities?

   a $3x + 2x + 5 - 2 = 5x + 3$

   b $y + y + y + 6 = 3 + 6y$

   c $2 \times p + 4 \times p - 3 \times 5 = 3(2p - 5)$

6 Show that this identity is true.

   $3y(5y^2 + 4y) + 2y^2(1 + 3y) \equiv 7y^2(3y + 2)$

7 Factorise completely

   a $7y^2 + 28y$

   b $9x - 21x^3$

   c $12w^3 + 20w^2 - 32w$

8 The formula $v^2 - u^2 = 2as$ is used to model a moving object, where

     u = starting speed (m/s)

     v = final speed (m/s)

     a = acceleration (m/s²)

     s = distance travelled (m).

   A car stops at some traffic lights. It then accelerates at 2.3 m/s² until it reaches a speed of 13.6 m/s. Find the distance, s, that it has travelled since stopping at the lights. Give your answer correct to 1 decimal place.

9 Find the value of each expression when $x = 6$, $y = -5$ and $z = 8$.

   a $3(z + 2) + 2y$

   b $4(x - y) - 3(x + y)$

10 Find the value of each expression when $a = 4$, $b = -2$ and $c = 5$.

a $2c^2 + abc$

b $a(c + b)^2 - 2a^2$

c $\sqrt{b^2 + 3a}$

d $\dfrac{ac - 6b}{a}$

11 Solve $2(x - 5) = 48 - 4(x + 1)$

12 In this diagram the orange shapes have the same area.

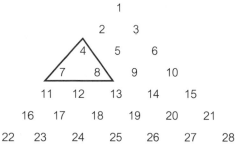

a Work out the value of x.

b What is the area of the orange rectangle?

13 Simplify

a $7y^5 \times 3y^3$

b $\dfrac{35b^{10}}{7b^2}$

c $(2g^3)^2$

d $\left(\dfrac{q^3}{3}\right)^3$

e $\dfrac{x^5 \times x^3}{x^7}$

Challenge

14 A red triangle is placed over three numbers in this number grid as shown.

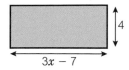

```
            1
        2       3
       4     5       6
      7     8      9     10
    11    12    13    14    15
  16   17    18    19    20    21
22   23    24    25    26    27    28
```

Using the numbers in the red triangle, this calculation has been done:

top × bottom right − top × bottom left = $4 \times 8 - 4 \times 7 = 32 - 28 = 4$

a Move the red triangle over three different numbers in the grid and do the same calculation. What do you notice?

b Repeat part **a** for three different numbers in the grid.

c The top number in the triangle is in row r. The top number is x.

  i Write expressions for the bottom left and bottom right numbers in terms of x and r. Simplify your expression.

  ii Compare your simplified expression to your answers to parts **a** and **b**. What do you notice? Write your findings as a rule.

15 Reflect Think back to when you have struggled to answer a question in a maths test.

a Write two words that describe how you felt.

b Write two things you could do when you struggle to answer a question in a maths test.

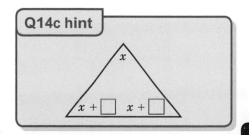

Q14c hint

Q15 hint

Look back at questions in this test or previous tests as a reminder.

Reflect

3.1 Plans and elevations

You will learn to:
- Use 2D representations of 3D solids.

CONFIDENCE

Why learn this?
Architects create drawings to show the side and front views of planned new buildings.

Fluency
Draw accurately
- a square with side length 3 cm
- an isosceles triangle with base length 4 cm and height 5 cm
- this circle.

5 cm

Explore
What would some famous landmarks look like if photographed from above?

Exercise 3.1

1 For each solid, write
  i the shapes of the faces
  ii the name of the solid.

a 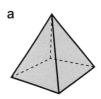 b 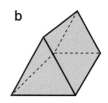 c 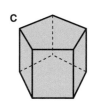 d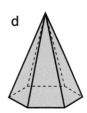

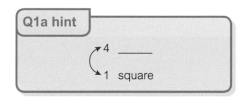

Q1a hint

4 _____
1 square

2 What 3D solid does each net make?

a 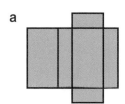 b 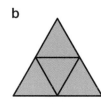 c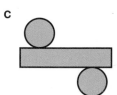

3 Sketch a net for each solid.
Label the lengths.

a
2 cm
2 cm 2 cm

b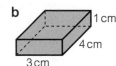
1 cm
4 cm
3 cm

c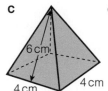
6 cm
4 cm 4 cm

d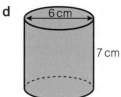
6 cm
7 cm

Warm up

4 Here are two views of the same cuboid.
The second is drawn on isometric paper.

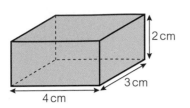

2 cm
3 cm
4 cm

Draw these solids on isometric paper.

a
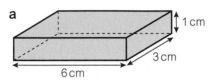
1 cm
3 cm
6 cm

b
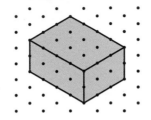
5 cm
2 cm
2 cm

c
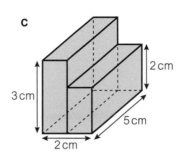
2 cm
3 cm
5 cm
2 cm

Worked example

Draw the **plan**, the **front elevation** and the **side elevation** of this cuboid on squared paper.

5 cm
2 cm
3 cm

Use a ruler.
Measure accurately.
Label lengths.

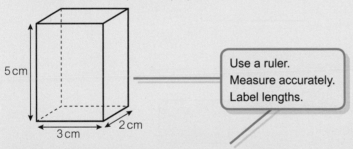

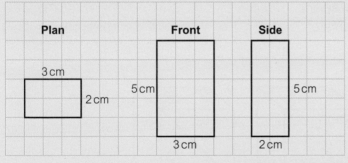

Plan   Front   Side
3 cm
2 cm
5 cm   5 cm
3 cm   2 cm

Key point

The **plan** is the view from above the object.
The **front elevation** is the view of the front of the object.
The **side elevation** is the view of the side of the object.

Plan
Side
Front

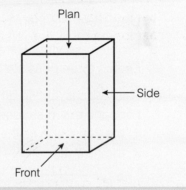

5 Draw the plan, the front elevation and the side elevation of each solid on squared paper.

a
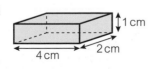
1 cm
4 cm   2 cm

b

5 cm   7 cm
2 cm

c
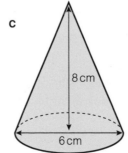
8 cm
6 cm

6　These solids are made from centimetre cubes.
　　Draw the plan, front elevation and side elevation of each solid on squared paper.

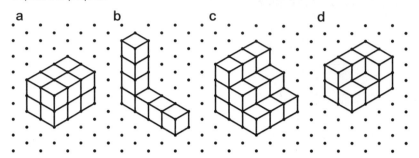

a　　　　b　　　　c　　　　d

　　Discussion What do you notice about your answers to shapes A and D? Why does this happen?

7　**Problem-solving** Here are the plan, front and side elevations of an irregular 3D solid.
　　Use cubes to make the solid.
　　Then draw it on isometric paper.

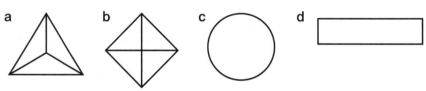

Plan　　　　Front　　　　Side

8　Here are the plan views of some solids.
　　What could each one be?

a　　　　b　　　　c　　　　d

　　Discussion Is there more than one answer?

9　**Problem-solving** Here is the side elevation of a 3D solid.
　　Sketch three possible 3D solids it could belong to.

10　This cube is 'cut' in different ways along the red line.
　　For each cut in shapes A to D, what is the name of
　　i　the 2D shape of the new faces?
　　ii　the new 3D solid(s) created?

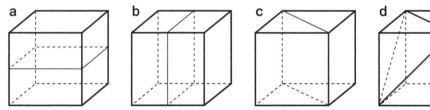

a　　　　b　　　　c　　　　d

11　**Explore** What would some famous landmarks look like if photographed from above?
　　Look back at the maths you have learned in this lesson.
　　How can you use it to answer this question?

12　**Reflect** Look back at Q6.
　　Draw the plan, front and side elevations for a unique solid shape.
　　Is it possible to draw two distinct solids that look the same on isometric paper?

> **Q12 Literacy hint**
>
> Unique means that there can't be a different solid with the same plan, front and side elevations.
> Distinct means different.

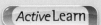

Explore

Reflect

3.2 Surface area of prisms

You will learn to:
- Sketch nets of 3D solids
- Calculate the surface area of prisms.

Why learn this?
Design engineers have to calculate surface area because it affects the speed of a racing car.

Fluency
Describe the faces of this solid.

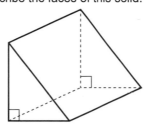

Explore
Why do African elephants have larger ears than Asian elephants?

Exercise 3.2

1 Calculate the area of each shape.

a
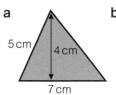
5 cm   4 cm   7 cm

b
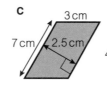
2 cm   80 mm

c
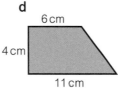
3 cm   7 cm   2.5 cm

d
6 cm   4 cm   11 cm

Q1 hint
First make sure that all measurements are in the same unit. Remember to write units cm² or mm² in your answers.

2 For each solid
  i sketch the net
  ii calculate the surface area.

a
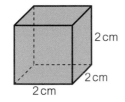
2 cm   2 cm   2 cm

b
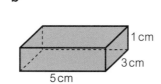
1 cm   3 cm   5 cm

Key point
A **prism** is a solid with the same **cross-section** throughout its length. A **right prism** is a prism where the cross-section is at right angles to the length of the solid.

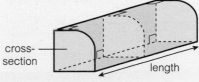

cross-section   length

The cross-section can be any flat shape.

3 a Which of these solids look like **right prisms**?

A   B   C   D   E   F

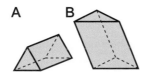   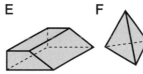

b What shapes are their **cross-sections**?

4 The diagram shows a triangular prism and its net.
  a Copy the net.
     Write the missing lengths.
  b Calculate the area of each shape in the net.
  c Calculate the total surface area of the prism.
  Discussion Are any of the faces congruent? Is there a quicker way to find the surface area of the net?

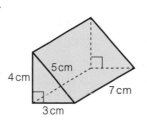
4 cm   5 cm   7 cm   3 cm

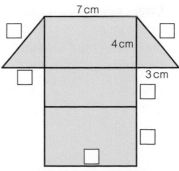
7 cm   4 cm   3 cm

Warm up

5 For each solid
  i sketch the net   **ii** calculate the total surface area.
  a   **b**

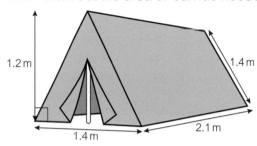

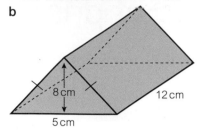

6 Real Work out the area of canvas needed to make this tent.

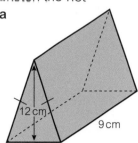

7 Problem-solving The diagram shows a foldaway camping bowl.
It has four sides in the shape of congruent trapezia.
The bottom of the bowl is square.
Work out the total surface area of the outside of the bowl.

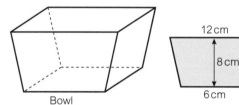

Bowl

8 Problem-solving These two solids have the same surface area.
Work out the value of x.

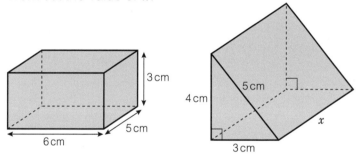

9 Explore Why do African elephants have larger ears than Asian elephants?
Look back at the maths you have learned in this lesson.
How can you use it to answer this question?

10 Reflect Siobhan says, 'A right prism always has two end faces that are exactly the same'.
Katrin says, 'The faces that aren't end faces are always rectangles'.
Omar says, 'It is called a **right** prism because the end faces and other faces are always at **right** angles to each other.'
Jason says, 'The shape of the end faces always give the prism its name'.
Are they all correct?

> **Q10 hint**
>
> Look carefully at the pictures of the right prisms you identified in Q3.

Topic links: Area of 2D shapes, Surface area of a cuboid   *Active* Learn   Delta 2, Section 3.2

3.3 Volume of prisms

You will learn to:
* Calculate the volume of right prisms.

Why learn this?
Landscape gardeners use volume to work out the amount of soil needed in gardens.

Fluency
* How many cm³ in
  6 m*l*   2 *l*?
* What is the formula for the volume of a cuboid?
* Which of these units is used for volume?
  mm³ cm² m³ cm³ m²

Explore
What volume of water do you need to fill a swimming pool?

Exercise 3.3

1 Calculate the area of each shape.

Q1 hint
Make sure all measurements are in the same unit.
Remember to write units cm² or mm² in your answers.

a

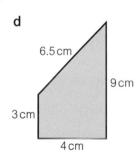
3 cm   2.5 cm   6 cm

b

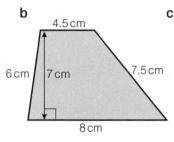
4.5 cm   6 cm   7 cm   7.5 cm   8 cm

c

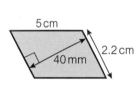
5 cm   40 mm   2.2 cm

d

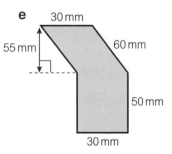
6.5 cm   9 cm   3 cm   4 cm

e

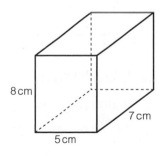
30 mm   55 mm   60 mm   50 mm   30 mm

2 The diagram shows a cuboid.

  a Work out the volume of the cuboid.

  The cuboid is cut along the red line to make two congruent triangular prisms.

  b Use your answer to part **a** to work out the volume of each triangular prism.

  c Work out the area of the triangular face of each prism.

  Discussion Harry says, 'The volume of a triangular prism is the area of the triangular face times the length.' Is he right?

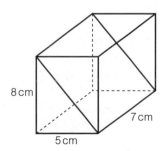
8 cm   7 cm   5 cm   8 cm   7 cm   5 cm

Warm up

3 For each triangular prism, work out
   i the cross-sectional area   **ii** the volume.

   a
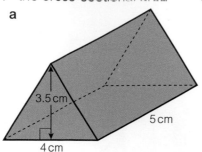
   3.5 cm
   5 cm
   4 cm

   b
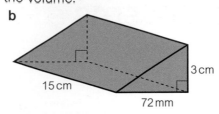
   3 cm
   15 cm
   72 mm

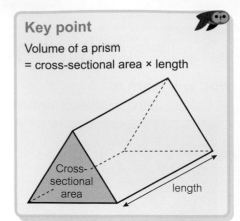
4 Calculate the volume of each prism.

   a
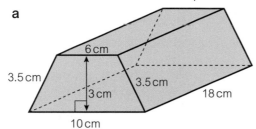
   6 cm
   3.5 cm
   3 cm
   3.5 cm
   18 cm
   10 cm

   b
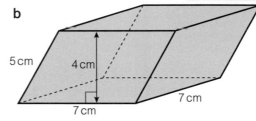
   5 cm
   4 cm
   7 cm
   7 cm

5 The volume of this prism is 84 cm³.
   Calculate the length marked x.

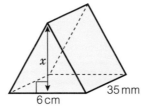
   x
   6 cm
   35 mm

6 **Problem-solving** This hexagonal prism glass
   has a **capacity** of 270 ml.
   The inside of the glass is 8 cm tall.
   a What is the area of the base of the inside
   of the glass?
   The edges of the hexagon are each
   3.5 cm long.
   b What is the surface area of the inside of the glass?

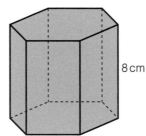
   8 cm

7 **Problem-solving** The volume of a 3D solid is 36 cm³.
   Sketch a possible solid and label its dimensions.
   Discussion How many possible answers are there?

8 This is the vertical cross-section of a diving pool.
   a Work out the area of the cross-section.
   The width of the pool is 15 m.
   b Calculate the volume of the pool in m³.
   c Calculate the capacity of the pool in litres.

   1.5 m
   20 m
   6 m
   9 m

9 **Explore** What volume of water do you need to fill a swimming pool?
   What have you learned in this lesson to help you answer this question?
   What other information do you need?

10 **Reflect** Maths is not the only subject where you use volume.
   Describe when you have used volume in science.
   In which ways is volume the same or different in science and in this
   maths lesson? Do you think volume means the same in all subjects?
   Explain.

3.4 Circumference of a circle

You will learn to:

- Name different parts of a circle
- Calculate the circumference
- Calculate the radius or diameter when you know the circumference.

CONFIDENCE

Why learn this?
Stadium designers use circumference when planning the curved portion of a running track.

Fluency
What is the perimeter of this shape?

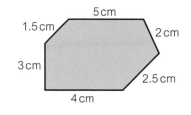

Explore
How long would it take to fly around the world?

Exercise 3.4

1 Write

  a 4.3275

    i to 1 decimal place   **ii** to 2 decimal places.

  b 9.367 m to the nearest centimetre

  c 7.453 cm to the nearest millimetre.

2 $C = 3d$. Work out the value of

  a C when $d = 6$ cm

  b C when $d = 1.5$ cm

  c d when $C = 33$ cm

  d d when $C = 7.5$ cm

3 a Draw a circle.

  b Mark the points O, P, Q, S on your diagram, where
- O is the **centre**
- OS is a **radius**
- PQ is a **diameter**

  c Write the letters of another line that is also a radius.

  d Colour the **arc** PS.

  e Mark any other point T on the **circumference**.

  f Does the picture show the diameter of a circle? Explain your answer.

4 a A circle has diameter 12 cm. What is its radius?

  b A circle has radius 4.2 cm. What is its diameter?

Key point

The **circumference** (C) is the perimeter of a circle. The centre of a circle is marked using a dot.
The **radius** (r) is the distance from the centre to the circumference.
The **diameter** (d) is a line from one edge to another through the centre.
An **arc** is part of the circumference.

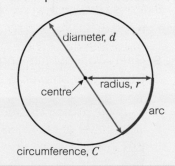

Warm up

5 Work out the circumference of each circle.
Round your answers to 1 decimal place and include the units
of measurement.

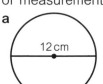

a   12 cm   b   4.3 cm   c   7 cm   d   2.9 cm

6 **STEM** Calculate the circumference of each circular object.
Round your answers to 1 decimal place.

   a The lens of a mobile phone camera with diameter 3.75 mm.

   b A Ferris wheel with diameter 30.7 m.

   c A crater on the Moon with radius approximately 173 km.

Q5 Strategy hint

Do you know the diameter or radius?
Which formula will you use?

7 For each circle, work out

   i the circumference of the whole circle

   ii the fraction of the whole circle shown in yellow

   iii the arc length of this part of the circle.

Round your answers to 1 decimal place.

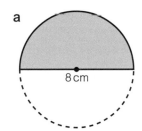 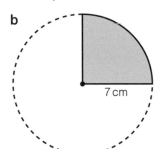

a   8 cm   b   7 cm

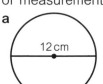

8 For each shape, work out

   i the length of the arc

   ii the perimeter of the whole shape.

Round your answers to 1 decimal place.

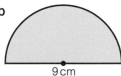

a   2.3 cm   b   9 cm

Q8 hint

The perimeter of a shape is the
distance around the edge of the
whole shape.

9 **Real** Work out the length of this race track.
Round your answer to 2 decimal places.

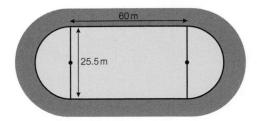

60 m   25.5 m

Q9 hint

The two curves join together to make
one circle.

Discussion What is the length in metres and centimetres?
Would it be sensible to round to 3 decimal places?

10 **Real** The second hand on a clock is 12 cm long.
How far does the tip of the second hand travel in

  a 60 seconds

  b 30 seconds

  c 5 seconds?

Give your answers to the nearest mm.

Q10 hint

The length of the second hand is
the _____ of the circle.

11 **Problem-solving** Noah says, 'The circumference of a circle
with radius 10 cm is double the circumference of a circle with
radius 5 cm.'
Is he right? Explain your answer.

12 **Problem-solving** Sunil needs two metal frames
like this to make an archway.
Work out the total length of metal required.
Round your answer to a sensible degree
of accuracy.

  Discussion How many decimal places do you
  have in your answer? What does this mean
  in m and cm?

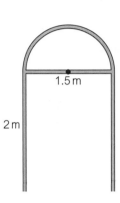

1.5 m

2 m

13 **Problem-solving / Real** At the Olympic opening ceremony,
there is a large light display of the five Olympic rings.
Each ring has radius 10 m.
Light bulbs are spaced every 50 cm around each ring.
How many light bulbs are there altogether?

14 A circle has circumference 24 cm.
Work out its diameter.
Round your answer to the nearest mm.

15 Work out the radius of a circle with circumference 150 m.
Round your answer to the nearest cm.

Q15 Strategy hint

Substitute the values you know into
the formula and rearrange.

16 **Explore** How long would it take to fly around the world?
What have you learned in this lesson to help you answer
this question?
What other information do you need?

17 **Reflect** Close your book and write down as many facts about
circles as you can.
Make sure you include all the ones you remember from this lesson.
Then open your book again and look back at the lesson.
Did you miss any facts? If so, add them to your list.
Did you make any spelling mistakes?
If so, correct them.

Explore

Reflect

3.5 Area of a circle

You will learn to:
- Calculate the area of a circle
- Calculate the radius or diameter when you know the area.

Why learn this?
Garden designers calculate the area of flower beds to work out how many plants they need.

Fluency
- Work out
  8^2 11^2 $\sqrt{49}$ $\sqrt{25}$
- Which of these units are used for area?
  cm^3 cm^2 mm mm^2 mm^3 km

Explore
How much would it cost to hire a circular dance floor for a school disco?

Exercise 3.5

1 $A = 4r^2$
Work out the value of
  a A when $r = 2$
  b A when $r = 5$
  c r when $A = 100$
  d r when $A = 9$

2 Substitute into each formula to work out the unknown quantity.
Round your answer to 1 decimal place.
  a $x = 4\pi$ **b** $A = 3.14r^2$ when $r = 9$ **c** $p = \sqrt{\dfrac{A}{3}}$ when $A = 60$

> **Q2a hint**
> Use the π key on your calculator.

3 Work out the area of each circle.
Round your answers to 1 decimal place and include the units of measurement.

a 4 cm **b** 2.5 m **c** 14 cm **d** 4.9 cm

> **Key point**
> The formula for the area, A, of a circle with radius r is $A = \pi r^2$

> **Q3c, d hint**
> First work out the radius of the circle.

4 Work out the area of each circular object.
Round your answers to 1 decimal place.
  a A chopping board with diameter 18 cm.
  b A Frisbee with radius 16.3 cm.
  c A coin with radius 19 mm.
  d A sumo wrestling ring with diameter 4.55 m.

> **Key point**
> A **sector** is the part of a circle enclosed by two **radii** and an arc.
>
>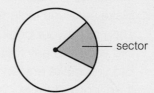
>
> sector
>
> Radii is the plural of radius.

5 This circle has radius 7 cm.
Work out the area of
  a the whole circle
  b the yellow **sector**
  c the red sector.
Round your answers to 1 decimal place.

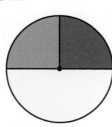

Topic links: Rounding, Fractions of an amount, Formulae

6 Work out the area of each shape.
Round your answers to 1 decimal place.

a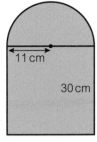
11 cm

b
4.7 cm

c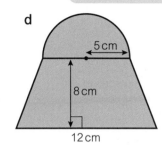
8.4 cm

7 Work out the area of each shape.
Round your answers to 1 decimal place.

Q7 hint

Divide each shape up into different parts.

a
11 cm
30 cm

b
6 cm

c
4 cm
3 cm

d
5 cm
8 cm
12 cm

8 Problem-solving Anil says, 'The area of a circle with radius 8 cm is double the area of a circle with radius 4 cm.'
Is he right?
Explain your answer.
Discussion What happens to the circumference when you double the radius? Does the same happen for area?

9 Real Copy and complete this table showing the cost of different pizzas.

Pizza diameter	Pizza area (1 d.p.)	Cost
8 inch		£5.99
10 inch		£7.99
12 inch		£9.99

Which pizza represents best value for money?
Explain your answer.

Q9 hint

How much of each pizza do you get for £1?

10 Work out the radius of each circle.
Round your answers to the nearest millimetre.

a
Area
83 cm²

b
Area
68.5 cm²

Q10a hint

$A = \pi r^2$
$83 = \pi \times r^2$
$r^2 = \frac{83}{\pi}$
$r = \square$

11 Problem-solving These diagrams show the area of part of a circle.
For each shape, work out the radius of the circle.

a
Area
16 m²

b
Area
7 cm²

Q11 hint

First work out the area of the whole circle. Round your answers for the radius to a sensible degree of accuracy.

12 Real / Reasoning A circular trampoline has an area of 20 m^2.

    a Calculate the radius of the trampoline to 1 decimal place.

    For safety, there must be at least a 1 m-wide free space beyond the edge of the trampoline, around the outside.

    b How wide must the total space be for the trampoline to safely fit?

    c The trampoline only just fits in a square garden.
    What is the area of the garden?

13 Real The diagram shows the dimensions of a running track.
What area of land is available for the field events inside the track?
Round your answer to the nearest square metre.

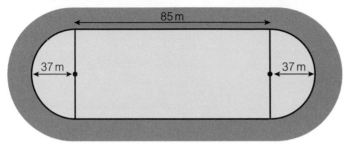

14 Work out the shaded area of each shape.
Round your answers to 1 decimal place.

a

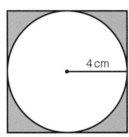

4 cm

b

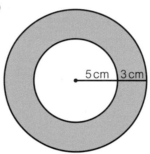

5 cm | 3 cm

> **Q14 Strategy hint**
> Work out the area of the larger shape and subtract the area of the smaller shape.

15 Real The top of a test tube rack is made from a piece of metal.
Six holes of diameter 15 mm are removed from the metal.
What is the area of the remaining metal?
Round your answer to 1 decimal place.

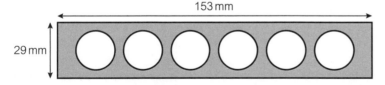

153 mm

29 mm

16 Explore How much would it cost to hire a circular dance floor for a school disco?
What have you learned in this lesson to help you answer this question?
What other information do you need?

17 Reflect Look back at Q11
List the steps you took to work out the answer.
Compare your steps with others in the class.

ActiveLearn   Delta 2, Section 3.5

MASTER

Check
P63

Strengthen
P65

Extend
P69

Test
P73

3.6 Cylinders

You will learn to:

• Calculate the volume and surface area of a cylinder.

CONFIDENCE

Why learn this?
The volume of the piston cylinders in a car engine tells us how powerful the car is.

Fluency
Work out
• 7^2 5^2 11^2 15^2
• $1 cm^3 = \square\ ml$
• $1 litre = \square\ cm^3$

Explore
What is the volume of beans in a tin?

Exercise 3.6

1 For each circle A and B, work out
  i the circumference
  ii the area.

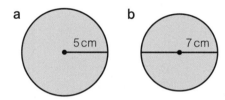

a

b

5 cm

7 cm

2 $V = 3a^2b$. Work out
  a V when $a = 4$ and $b = 2$
  b b when $V = 81$ and $a = 3$
  c a when $V = 98$ and $b = 2$

3 What is the volume of this right prism?

Area
8 cm²

12 cm

Warm up

 4 The diagram shows a cylinder and its net.

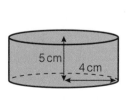

5 cm

4 cm

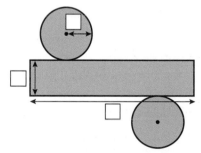

  a Copy the net. Work out and write the missing lengths.
  b Work out the area of each shape.
  c Add the areas together to work out the surface area of the cylinder.

Q4a hint

The rectangle wraps around the circle so the length of the long side must be the _____ of the ciircle.

5 a Copy this net and write the missing lengths.
  b Write an expression for the area inside each shape.
  c Write an expression for the total area.
    Total surface area of a cylinder = _____ + _____

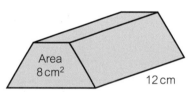

h

r

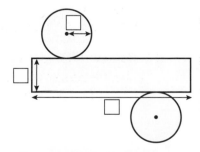

6 Work out the surface area of each cylinder.

a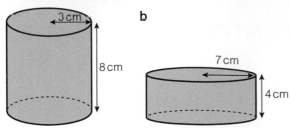
b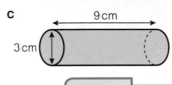

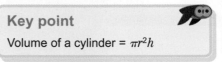

Key point

Surface area of a cylinder
$= 2\pi r^2 + 2\pi rh$

7 For each cylinder, work out
   i the area of a circular end   **ii** the volume of the cylinder.

Key point

Volume of a cylinder $= \pi r^2 h$

a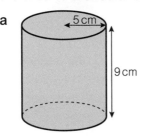
b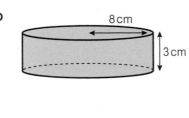
c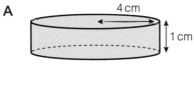

Q8 hint

The volume of a cylinder is the cross-sectional area multiplied by the length (or height).

8 STEM These three cylinders have the same volume.

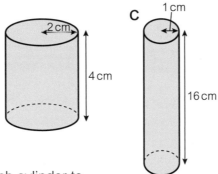

A   4 cm, 1 cm
B   2 cm, 4 cm
C   1 cm, 16 cm

a Which cylinder do you think will have the smallest surface area?
Explain your answer.
b Work out the surface area of each cylinder to check your answer to part **a**. Were you correct?

Discussion The amount of heat energy entering or leaving an object depends on its surface area. Explain why a tall, thin mug of tea will cool more slowly from its surface than a short wide one.

9 Modelling The inside of a saucepan has diameter 20 cm and height 13 cm.
The manufacturer claims the pan has a capacity of 4 litres.
Is the claim correct?
Explain your answer.

10 Explore What is the volume of beans in a tin?
Is it easier to explore this question now you have completed the lesson?
What further information do you need to be able to answer this?

11 Reflect Obinze says, 'You can't make a perfect net of a cylinder, they are all just approximations.'
Explain what he means. Do you agree?

Topic links: Squares and square roots, Rounding, Formulae

Subject links: Science (Q8)

ActiveLearn   Delta 2, Section 3.6

Explore

Reflect

3.7 Pythagoras' theorem

You will learn to:
- Use Pythagoras' theorem in right-angled triangles.

CONFIDENCE

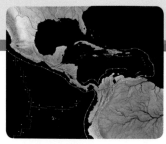

Why learn this?
Geologists use Pythagoras' theorem to help calculate the epicentre of an earthquake.

Fluency
- Work out
  3^2 4^2 5^2 12^2 13^2
- Which is the longest side in this triangle?

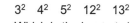

Explore
What size of wall space is needed for a 42-inch TV?

Warm up

Exercise 3.7

 1 Work out
  a $8^2 + 3^2$ **b** $2.7^2 + 9.1^2$ **c** $\sqrt{9^2 + 7^2}$ **d** $\sqrt{3.5^2 - 2.1^2}$

2 a Draw this triangle on centimetre squared paper.
  b Measure the lengths of the three sides to the nearest mm.
  c What is the length of the **hypotenuse**?

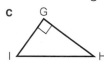

Key point
The longest side of a right-angled triangle is called the **hypotenuse**.

Discussion Darren says, 'The largest angle in a right-angled triangle will always be the right angle.'
Lea says, 'The hypotenuse will always be the side opposite the right angle.' Who is right?

3 Which side is the hypotenuse in each triangle?

a **b** **c** **d**

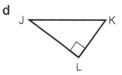

Investigation   Reasoning

1 Draw these triangles accurately on squared paper.
2 Measure the hypotenuse c.
3 Copy and complete this table.

	a	b	c	$a^2 + b^2$	c^2
X	4	3		$4^2 + 3^2 =$	
Y	12	5			
Z	8	6			

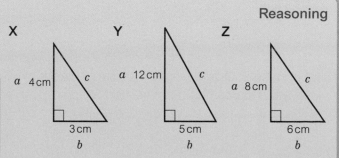

4 What do you notice about your answers in the last two columns?
5 Write a formula linking the shorter sides, a and b, and the hypotenuse, c.

Worked example

Work out the length of the hypotenuse of this right-angled triangle, to the nearest mm.

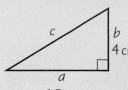

Sketch the triangle. Label the hypotenuse c and the other sides a and b.

$c^2 = a^2 + b^2$

$c^2 = 6.5^2 + 4^2$

Substitute $a = 6.5$ and $b = 4$ into the formula for Pythagoras' theorem, $c^2 = a^2 + b^2$

$c^2 = 42.25 + 16 = 58.25$

$c = \sqrt{58.25} = 7.632168...$

Use a calculator to find the square root.

The length of the hypotenuse is 7.6 cm to the nearest mm.

Round to the nearest mm.

Discussion Does it matter which way round you label the sides a and b?

Key point

Pythagoras' theorem shows the relationship between the lengths of the three sides of a right-angled triangle.

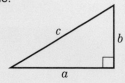

$c^2 = a^2 + b^2$

 4 Use **Pythagoras' theorem** to work out the missing length of each right-angled triangle.
Round your answers to the nearest mm.

a   7 cm   4 cm

b 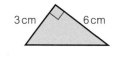   3 cm   6 cm

c 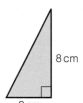   8 cm   2 cm

 5 **Real** To meet safety requirements, a wheelchair ramp must rise 1 m over a distance of 12 m.
How long must the ramp be?
Round your answer to the nearest centimetre.

Q5 Strategy hint

Sketch a diagram.

 6 **Problem-solving** Work out which of these triangles are right-angled triangles.

a   7 cm   10 cm   7 cm

b 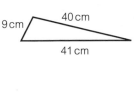   9 cm   40 cm   41 cm

c 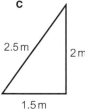   2.5 m   2 m   1.5 m

Q6 Strategy hint

First identify the hypotenuse of the triangle.
If $c^2 = a^2 + b^2$, then the triangle is a right-angled triangle.

 7 Work out the missing length in each right-angled triangle.
Round your answers to 1 decimal place.
The first one has been started for you.

a   9 cm   10 cm

$c^2 = a^2 + b^2$
$10^2 = 9^2 + b^2$
$100 - 81 = b^2$
$b = \sqrt{\Box}$

b 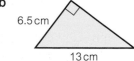   6.5 cm   13 cm

c 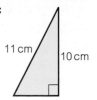   11 cm   10 cm

Q7 Strategy hint

Label the sides a, b, c.
Substitute into Pythagoras' theorem, $c^2 = a^2 + b^2$
Solve the equation.

Topic links: Squares and square roots, Rounding, Formulae

8 Problem-solving
Work out the area of this triangle.

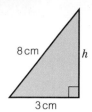

8 cm
h
3 cm

Q8 hint
Work out the height, h, first.

9 Problem-solving
Work out the area of this triangle.

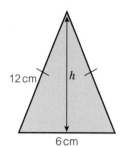

12 cm
h
6 cm

Q9 hint
Work out h using Pythagoras.

10 Real Andy sets the base of his ladder 0.8 m away from the base of his house. His ladder is 6.3 m long. How far up the wall will the top of his ladder touch?

Q10 Strategy hint
Sketch and label a diagram.

11 Problem-solving The diagram shows a square with side length 8 cm.
  a Work out the area of the square.
  b Calculate the length of the diagonal of the square.
  c Multiply the lengths of the two diagonals together.
     Compare your answer to part **a**.
     What do you notice?
  d Use your answer to part **c** to find the area of this square.

8 cm

8 cm

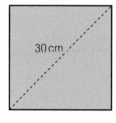

30 cm

12 Problem-solving
  a Use the triangle shown and Pythagoras' theorem to calculate the length AB.
  b Calculate the lengths of
     i CD
     ii EF
     iii GH.

13 Explore What size of wall space is needed for a 42-inch TV? What have you learned in this lesson to help you answer this question?
What other information do you need?

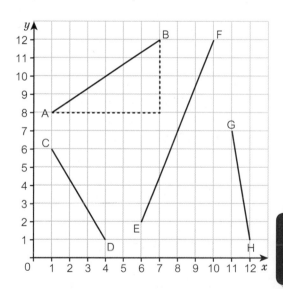

14 Reflect Look at the worked example.
List the steps to solve the problem in your own words.
Use pencil in case you wish to change them or add more steps later.
Look back at Q5.
Do your steps work to solve this problem? If not, change them.
Look back at Q8 and do the same.
Now compare your steps with others in your class.
Have you missed out any steps? If so, change them.

Q14 hint
You could write – Step 1: label the sides of the triangle, a, b, c (hypotenuse)

Explore

Reflect

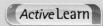

Master
P45

CHECK

Strengthen
P65

Extend
P69

Test
P73

3 Check up

Log how you did on your
Student Progression Chart.

Circumference and area of circles

1 For each circle in parts **a** and **b**, calculate
   i the circumference   **ii** the area.
   Round your answers to 2 d.p.

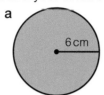

a 6 cm   **b** 11 cm

2 For this shape, calculate
   a the area   **b** the perimeter.
   Round your answers to 2 d.p.

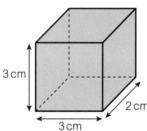

9.2 cm

Working with 3D solids

3 Draw this solid on isometric paper.

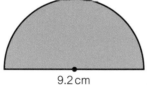

3 cm
3 cm
2 cm

4 Draw the plan, front elevation and side elevation of each solid on
   squared paper.

a

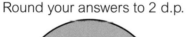

2 cm
3 cm
4 cm

b

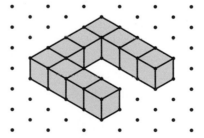

5 Sketch the 3D solid that has these elevations and plan.

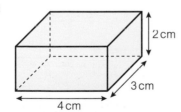

side   front   plan

6 Work out the surface area and volume of this triangular prism.

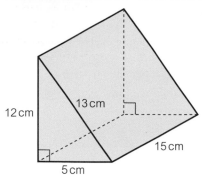

12 cm 13 cm 15 cm 5 cm

7 For this cylinder, work out
   a the volume
   b the surface area.
   Round your answers to 2 d.p.

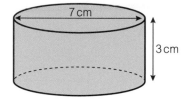

7 cm 3 cm

Pythagoras' theorem

8 Work out the missing length in each right-angled triangle.

a

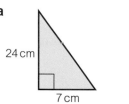

24 cm 7 cm

b

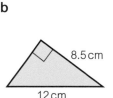

8.5 cm 12 cm

9 How sure are you of your answers? Were you mostly

   😟 **Just guessing**   😐 **Feeling doubtful**   🙂 **Confident**

   What next? Use your results to decide whether to strengthen or extend your learning.

Challenge

10 How many different 3D solids can you make with volume 4 cm³?
   Sketch the plan and front and side elevations of each solid.
   Are any of your solids rotations of each other?

> **Q10 hint**
>
> Use four 1 cm cubes.
>
>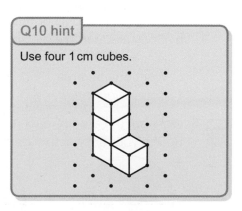

Master
P45

Check
P63

STRENGTHEN

Extend
P69

Test
P73

3 Strengthen

You will:
* Strengthen your understanding with practice.

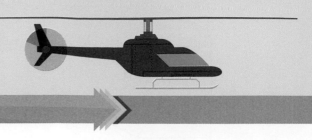

Circumference and area of circles

1 Write the length of radius and diameter of each circle.

a

5 cm

b

16 cm

Q1 hint

r for radius   **D** for diameter

2 Use your calculator to work out
a π **b** $4 \times \pi$ **c** 7π **d** $2\pi \times 5$ **e** $\pi \times 6^2$
Write your answers to 1 decimal place.

Q2 hint

Use the π key on your calculator.

3 Circumference, $C = \pi \times$ diameter
a What is the diameter of this circle?
b Copy and complete $C = \pi \times \square$
c Work out the circumference.
   Round your answer to 1 decimal place.

7 cm

4 a Copy and complete these statements.
   i diameter $= \square \times$ radius
   ii $\pi \times$ diameter $= \pi \times \square \times$ radius
   iii $\pi d = \square \pi r$
b Work out the circumference
   of each circle.
   Round your answer to
   1 decimal place.

i

6.5 cm

ii

17 cm

Q4b hint

Circumference $= 2\pi r$
Circumference $= \pi d$

5 The area of a circle, $A = \pi \times$ radius^2
a What is the radius of this circle?
b Copy and complete
   $A = \pi \times \square^2$
c Work out the area.
   Round your answer to 1 decimal place.

5 cm

6 Work out the area of each circle.
   Round your answer to 1 decimal place.

Q6b hint

First work out the radius.
Area $= \pi r^2$

a

3.4 cm

b

9.2 cm

7 **a** What fraction of a circle is this shape?
 b Work out the area of the whole circle.
 Round your answer to 1 decimal place.
 c Work out the area of the sector shown.
 d Work out the circumference of the whole circle.
 Round your answer to 1 decimal place.
 e Work out the length of the blue arc.
 f Work out the perimeter of the sector.

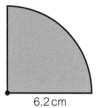
10 cm

Q7c hint

Use your answers to parts **a** and **b**.

Q7e hint

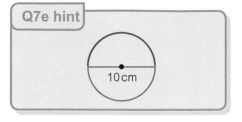
10 cm

8 For this shape, work out
 a the area
 b the perimeter.
 Round your answer to 1 decimal place.

6.2 cm

Q7f hint

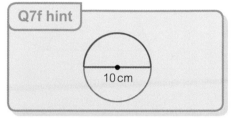
10 cm

9 Work out the area of this compound shape.
 Round your answer to 1 decimal place.

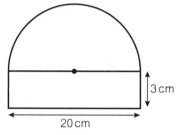
3 cm
20 cm

Q8 hint

Use the method in Q7.

Q9 hint

Divide the shape into a rectangle and a semicircle.

Working with 3D solids

1 Sketch all the faces of each solid. Label all the lengths.
 The first one has been started for you.

a
5 cm
3 cm
1 cm
4 cm

b
3 cm
4 cm

c
5 cm
4 cm   4 cm

a
5 cm
3 cm
1 cm
4 cm
3 cm

2 Draw the plan, front elevation and side elevation of each solid in Q1 on squared paper.

3 Work out the surface area of this triangular prism.

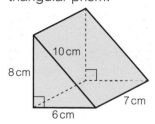
10 cm
8 cm
7 cm
6 cm

Q2 hint

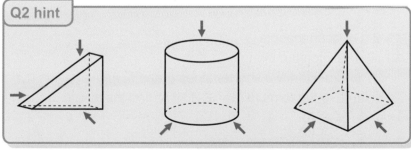

Q3 hint

Sketch each face. Work out the area of each face and add them together.

4 Work out the volume of the triangular prism in Q3.

5 Here is a triangular prism.

   a Sketch its cross-section.

   b Work out the area of the cross-section.

   c Work out the volume of the prism.

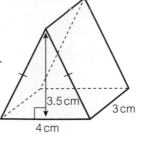

6 Here is a trapezoidal prism.

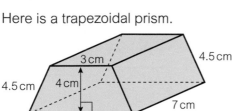

   a Sketch each face.
   Label the lengths.

   b Work out the area of each face.

   c Work out the total surface area.

 7 Here is a cylinder.

   a Sketch its faces.
   Label the lengths you know.

   b Work out the long length of the
   rectangle and label it.

   c Work out the area of each face.

   d Work out the total surface area of the cylinder.

   e Work out the volume of the cylinder.
   Round your answers to 1 d.p.

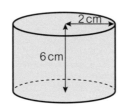

Q4 hint

Volume = cross-sectional area × length

You worked out this cross-sectional area in Q3.

Q5c hint

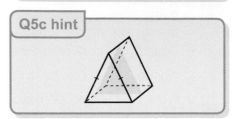

Q6a hint

How many faces are there?
Check you have sketched them all.

Q7b hint

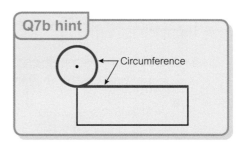

Circumference

Pythagoras' theorem

1 How long is the hypotenuse in each triangle?

a
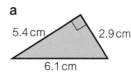

b
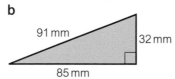

c
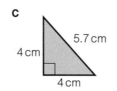

Q1 hint

The hypotenuse is the longest side of a right-angled triangle.

 2 For each triangle
   i sketch the triangle
   ii label the two shorter sides a and b, and label the hypotenuse c
   iii use the formula $c^2 = a^2 + b^2$ to find the length of the hypotenuse.

a
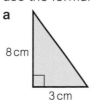

b
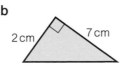

c
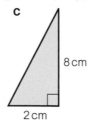

Q2a iii hint

$c^2 = a^2 + b^2$
$c^2 = 3^2 + 8^2$

3 Work out the length of the missing side in each right-angled triangle. The first one has been started for you.

Q3 hint
Follow the steps in Q2.

a

8 cm, 11 cm

b
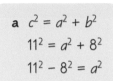
159 mm, 134 mm

c
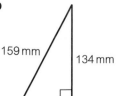
7.2 cm, 13 cm

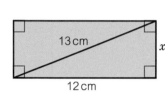
a $c^2 = a^2 + b^2$
$11^2 = a^2 + 8^2$
$11^2 - 8^2 = a^2$

4 Work out the area of each shape.

Q4 hint
Sketch each right-angled triangle and label the sides.
Use Pythagoras' theorem to first find the length labelled x.
Work out the area of the shape.

a
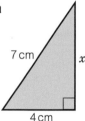
7 cm, x, 4 cm

b
13 cm, x, 12 cm

c
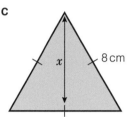
x, 8 cm

Enrichment

1 The diagram shows a smaller square inside a larger square.
  a Find the area of the smaller square.
   Try the two methods below.

   Method A Work out
   1 the length of one side of the larger square
   2 the area of the larger square
   3 the area of one triangle
   4 the area of the smaller square, using your answers to steps **2** and **3**.

   Method B Work out
   1 the length of x, using Pythagoras' theorem.
   2 the area of the smaller square, using your answer to step **1**.

  b Which method for working out the area of the smaller square did you prefer?
   Explain your answer.

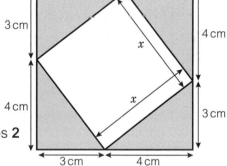
4 cm, 3 cm, 3 cm, 4 cm, 4 cm, 3 cm, x, x, 3 cm, 4 cm

Q1b hint
'Explain' means write a sentence that begins, for example,
'Method ☐, because _____.'

2 Reflect In these lessons you used these formulae:
Circumference = π × diameter
Area of a circle = π × radius^2
Volume of a prism = area of cross-section × length
Pythagoras' theorem $c^2 = a^2 + b^2$
Which formula was easiest to use? Explain.
Which formula was most difficult to use? Explain.
Discuss the formula you found most difficult with a classmate.
Ask them to explain to you a question they answered using this formula.

Reflect

3 Extend

You will:
- Extend your understanding with problem-solving.

1 A 1 cm by 1 cm square hole is cut through the centre of each face of this cube in all three directions.
Draw the plan, front elevation and side elevation.

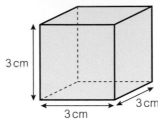

3 cm
3 cm
3 cm

 2 Work out the perimeter of each shape.
Round your answers to the nearest millimetre.

a

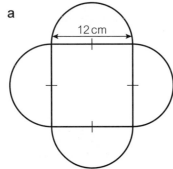

12 cm

b

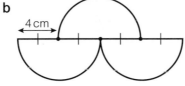

4 cm

Q2 hint

First work out the circumference of one semicircle.
Then work out the perimeter of the whole shape.

 3 The diagram shows a circle of radius 6 cm inside a square.
  a Calculate the area of the circle.
  b Calculate the area of the square.
  c What percentage of the square is shaded?
  d Repeat parts **a** to **c** for a radius of 4 cm.
Discussion What do you notice about your answers in parts **c** and **d**?

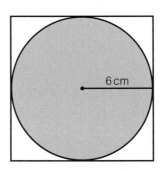

6 cm

4 Here is a circle.

7 cm

Lara says, 'The circumference is 14π and the area is 49π.'
  a Explain how she got her answers.
  b Now work out the circumference and area of this circle.
    Leave your answer in terms of π, as in part **a**.

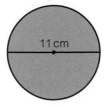

11 cm

Q4a hint

Write the calculations
$C = 2 \times \pi \times \square = \square\pi$
$A =$

Q4b hint

To write an answer in terms of π (pi), your answer should be $\square\pi$.
This gives an exact figure for area and circumference.

5 Problem-solving

a Mark a dot on the edge of a 2p coin and align it with the zero mark on a ruler.

b Roll the coin along the ruler to find the circumference of the coin.

c Use the circumference to estimate the diameter of the coin.

d Repeat parts **b** and **c**, but this time roll the coin 4 times.

Discussion Which method should give you a more accurate answer for the diameter of the coin?
Explain your answer.

e Measure the diameter of the coin.
Which method was the most accurate?

6 Real A trundle wheel clicks every time it travels 1 m.
Work out the diameter of the trundle wheel in centimetres to 1 decimal place.

7 Real / Modelling A penny-farthing bicycle has a large front wheel and a small back wheel. The radius of the front wheel is 74 cm.

a i How far does the wheel travel in one revolution?
Give your answer in metres to 1 decimal place.

ii How many revolutions will it go through when travelling 100 m?

Over the same distance, the back wheel rotates 108 times.

b i What is the circumference of the back wheel?
Round your answer to 1 decimal place.

ii What is the radius of the back wheel?
Round your answer to 1 decimal place.

> **Q6 hint**
>
> Use $C = \pi d$
> What is the circumference of the trundle wheel?

8 The diagram shows a square-based pyramid.

a Write the length of the distance x.

b Use Pythagoras' theorem to calculate ℓ, the slant height of the pyramid.

c Calculate the area of one triangular face of the pyramid.

d Calculate the area of the base of the pyramid.

e Calculate the surface area of the pyramid.

f Calculate the volume of the pyramid.

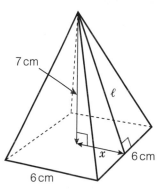

7 cm · ℓ · x · 6 cm · 6 cm

> **Key point**
>
> Volume of a pyramid
> $= \frac{1}{3} \times$ area of base $\times$ height

9 Modelling The diagram shows a car wheel.

a Work out the circumference of the wheel to the nearest cm.

On a journey to work and back, the wheel rotates 50 000 times.

b What is the total length of the journey?
Give your answer in kilometres to 1 decimal place.

47.5 cm

> **Q9b hint**
>
> 1 m = 100 cm
> 1 km = 1000 m

10 The diagram shows a regular hexagon.

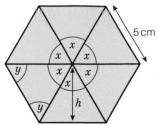

5 cm

a Copy and complete
$6x = \square$, so $x = \square$
b Copy and complete
$x + 2y = \square$, so $y = \square$
c What type of triangle are each of the six triangles?
d Use Pythagoras' theorem to calculate h, the perpendicular height of one triangle.
e Calculate the area of one triangle.
f Calculate the area of the hexagon.

11 a Find the radius of a circle with circumference 24 cm.
b Find the radius of a circle with area 54 cm².

12 Here is the outline of a circle and a sector with central angle 130°.

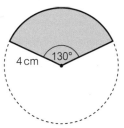

4 cm   130°

Work out
a the length of the arc
b the area of the sector.

13 For each shape, work out
i the arc length
ii the sector area.

a

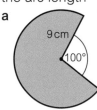

9 cm   100°

b

6 cm   50°

14 i Work out the surface area and volume of each triangular prism.

a

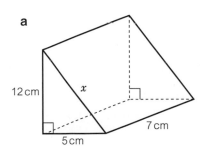

12 cm x 7 cm   5 cm

b

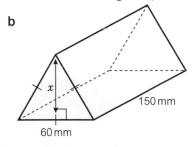

x 150 mm   60 mm

ii Which prism has the larger surface area and volume?

15 Problem-solving You drive 4 miles north and then 6 miles east. How far are you from your starting point, as the crow flies?

Q12a hint

What fraction of the whole circle is the sector?

Q14a hint

First use Pythagoras' theorem to calculate the length labelled x.

Q15 Literacy hint

'As the crow flies' means the shortest distance between two points.

Q15 hint

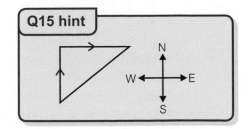

N   W   E   S

16 Problem-solving

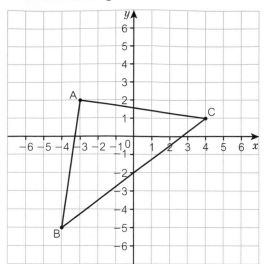

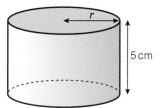

Q16 hint

Use Pythagoras' theorem to calculate the length of each line.

    a Calculate the length of the lines

      i AB

      ii BC

      iii AC

    b What type of triangle is ABC?

17 Real / Problem-solving The capacity of this cylindrical glass is 320 cm³.

    a Work out the internal radius of the glass. 4 of these glasses fit exactly in this box.

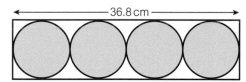

    b How thick is the glass? Round your answer to 2 decimal places.

18 Real A cake recipe asks for a 15 cm by 15 cm by 10 cm cuboid-shaped cake tin. You only have a circular tin, with diameter 16 cm and height 10 cm.

    Will this tin be suitable? Show your working to explain.

19 Each cylinder has a volume of 2000 cm³.

    Work out the missing length for each one.

    Round your answers to 2 decimal places.

    a   **b**

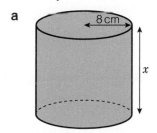
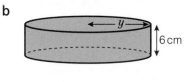

20 Reflect The Ancient Greeks had a famous problem: How to draw a square whose perimeter was equal to the circumference of a circle.

    They called the problem 'Squaring the circle'.

    Explain why squaring the circle exactly is impossible.

3 Unit test

Log how you did on your Student Progression Chart.

1 The diagram shows a cuboid.
Draw
  a the cuboid on isometric paper
  b the plan of the cuboid
  c the front elevation of the cuboid
  d the side elevation of the cuboid.

4 cm

6 cm

2 cm

2 For each circle, work out
  i the circumference
  ii the area.
  Round your answers to 2 decimal places.

a

2 cm

b

85 mm

3 For this semicircle, work out
  a the area
  b the perimeter.
  Round your answers to 2 decimal places.

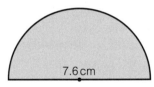

7.6 cm

4 The diagram shows a 3D object and its plan and elevations.
Which of A, B, C and D is
  a the plan
  b a side elevation
  c the front elevation?

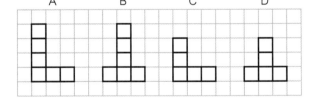

A   B   C   D

5 For each prism, work out
  i the volume   **ii** the surface area.

a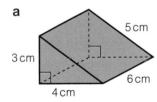

5 cm
3 cm
6 cm
4 cm

b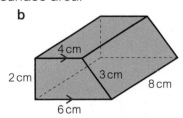

4 cm
2 cm
3 cm
8 cm
6 cm

6 Work out the missing length in each triangle.

a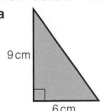

9 cm
6 cm

b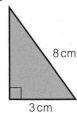

8 cm
3 cm

7 Calculate the radius of each circle. Round your answer to 2 decimal places.

a 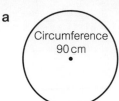 Circumference 90 cm

b Area 120 cm²

8 Work out the area of this triangle.

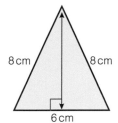

8 cm   8 cm

6 cm

9 Work out the length of the line AB in the diagram.

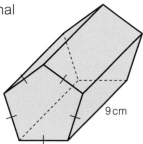

10 The volume of this pentagonal prism is 135 cm³.
  a Work out the area of the pentagon.
  b Work out the surface area of the prism.

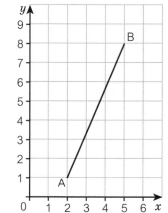

9 cm

11 For this cylinder, work out
  a the volume
  b the surface area.
  Round your answers to 2 decimal places.

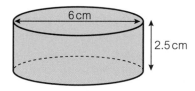

6 cm

2.5 cm

Challenge

12 a For each diagram A to C
  i write the length of the line labelled x
  ii write the length of the line labelled y
  iii work out the area of one circle
  iv work out the total area of the circles.
  b What can you say about the shaded area in each diagram?

A 12 cm
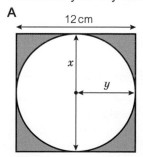
x
y

B 12 cm
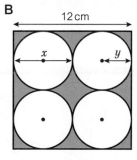
x y

C 12 cm
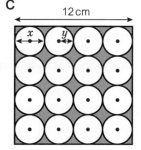
x y

13 Reflect This unit is about circles, prisms and Pythagoras.
  Which of these topics did you like best? Why?
  Which of these topics did you like least? Why?

4.1 Direct proportion

You will learn to:

- Recognise when values are in direct proportion
- Plot graphs and read values to solve problems.

Why learn this?
Some bills are charged in proportion to the time spent, and some are charged as a flat fee.

Fluency
1 yard ≈ 0.9 metres.
What are the missing lengths?
- 4 yards ≈ ☐ metres
- ☐ yards ≈ 8.1 metres
- 300 yards ≈ ☐ metres

Explore
How will different exchange rates affect the amount of money you can spend on holiday?

CONFIDENCE

Warm up

Exercise 4.1

1 a £1 = 170 Yen. How many Yen would you get for £12?
  b Two litres of juice cost £3.50. How much does 1 litre cost?
  c 300 g of bananas cost £1.80. How much does 1 kg cost?

2 200 g of sweets cost £1.

  a How much do 100 g of sweets cost?

  b How much do 500 g of sweets cost?

  c Copy and complete this table showing the cost of sweets.

Grams of sweets	0	100	200	300	400	500
Cost in £			1			

  d Draw a graph to show this information.
  Label the x-axis 'Grams of sweets' and the y-axis 'Cost in pounds'.
  Join the points in a straight line and give your graph a title.
  Discussion Where does the line cross the y-axis?

3 Which of these graphs show two quantities in **direct proportion** to another?

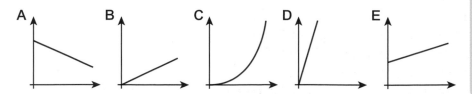

Key point

When two quantities are in **direct proportion**
- plotting them as a graph gives a straight line through the origin (0, 0)
- when one quantity is zero, the other quantity is also zero
- when one quantity doubles, so does the other.

4 Real / Problem-solving This graph can be used to convert approximately between inches (in) and centimetres (cm).

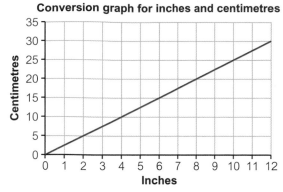

Conversion graph for inches and centimetres

a Are inches and centimetres in direct proportion?
b Copy and complete. 4 inches ≈ ☐ centimetres
c Copy and complete. 17 cm ≈ ☐ inches
d Which is longer, 6 inches or 14 centimetres?
e A car part needs to be exactly 5.3 inches long.
   How many centimetres is this?
Discussion Is a conversion graph a useful way to solve this problem?
f 15 inches ≈ ☐ cm.

Q4f hint

Convert 5 inches and multiply by 3.

5 STEM In a school science experiment, different masses are added to a spring and the extension is measured. The table shows some of the results.

Mass (g)	300	400	600
Extension (mm)	9	12	18

1000   too simple for D2 — could change values to make more complex? (decimals?)

1000   36mm

a Plot a line graph for these values.
b Are mass and spring extension in direct proportion?
A mass of 1000 g is added. The spring extension is 36 mm.
c When this point is added, does the graph still show direct proportion?

Q5a hint

Plot Mass up to 1000 g on the x-axis and Extension up to 40 mm on the y-axis. Use sensible scales.

6 STEM This is a conversion graph between degrees Celsius and degrees Fahrenheit.

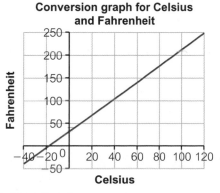

Conversion graph for Celsius and Fahrenheit

C/F context is used in C2 9.1 Q10 early?

a Use the graph to estimate
   i 30°C in degrees Fahrenheit   **ii** 100°F in degrees Celsius.
b What is the freezing point of water in degrees Fahrenheit?
c What is the boiling point of water in degrees Fahrenheit?
Discussion Are degrees Celsius and degrees Fahrenheit in direct proportion? Explain how you know.

Q6b, c hint

Find the freezing point and boiling point of water in degrees Celsius.

7 Keri is doing a DIY project. The cost of hiring a saw is shown on the graph.
  a How much would it cost Keri to hire the saw for 4 hours?
  b What is the cost per hour to hire the saw?
  Discussion How did you work out the cost per hour?
  c The store offers a daily fee of £59 if the customer pays in advance. After how many hours would this become the better value?

8 Match the description to the graph.
  a The total cost of a phone call for x minutes at 9p per minute.
  b The total cost of a phone call for x minutes at 35p per minute.
  c The total cost of a hotel phone call with a 50p connection fee and 12p per minute.
  d The total cost of a phone call for x minutes at 20p per minute.

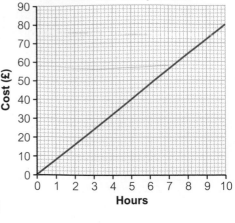

Saw hire cost per hour

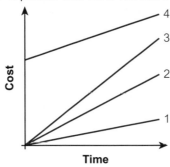

9 **Real** Which of these are in direct proportion?
  a Euros (€) and pounds (£)
  b The height of a person and their age up to 30
  c Cost and hours worked for an electrician.
  d Metres and yards

> **Q9 Strategy hint**
> Sketch or visualise a graph.

10 **Modelling** Face lotion costs £7 for 80 ml. The company plans to sell the lotion in different-sized bottles up to 200 ml.
  a Plot a line graph to show the price for up to 200 ml of lotion.
  b Are the price and volume in ml in direct proportion?
  Discussion Why don't companies usually price their goods like this?

> **Q10a hint**
> Plot the given values and two more points. Use a factor and a multiple of 80 ml.

11 **Explore** How will different exchange rates affect the amount of money you can spend on holiday?
  Is it easier to explore this question now you have completed the lesson? What further information do you need to be able to answer this?

12 **Reflect** Shane says, 'Straight-line graphs always show direct proportion.'
  a Look back at the work you have done this lesson, and find an example to prove Shane wrong.
  b Write a sentence to describe a graph showing direct proportion.

4.2 FINANCE: Interpreting financial graphs

You will learn to:

- Interpret graphs from different sources
- Understand financial graphs.

CONFIDENCE

Why learn this?

A company that makes sun cream can use previous years' weather graphs to predict how much sun cream they need to make next year.

Fluency

Write down a number that satisfies:

- at least 5
- no more than 7
- at most 18

Explore

How do stock-market traders use graphs to help make investment decisions?

Exercise 4.2: Interpreting financial graphs

1 Write down the coordinates of the points marked with letters.

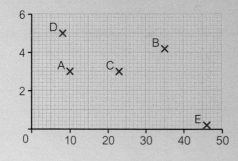

Warm up

2 **Finance / Problem-solving**

The graph shows two different phone plans.

a How much does it cost for 100 minutes on
   i Plan A   ii Plan B?

b What is the maximum amount you can pay on Plan B?

c What is the minimum amount you can pay on Plan A?

d At how many minutes is the largest difference between the cost on Plan A and B?

e For how many minutes of calls do both plans cost the same?

f On Plan C you pay £18 per month for unlimited calls.
Which plan should each person choose?

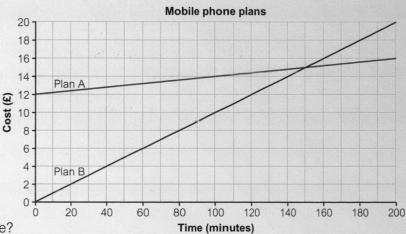

Mobile phone plans

	Average minutes of calls per month
Hannah	30
Jeff	200
Matt	160

3 Finance The graph shows the share price of a company in 2013.

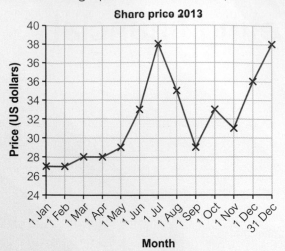

Key point

Line graphs can help you identify **trends** in the data. The trend is the general direction of the change, ignoring the individual ups and downs.

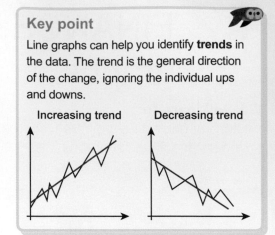

a Describe the overall **trend** in the share price during 2013.

b What was the difference in price from the start of 2013 to the end?

c On what two dates did the price reach a minimum before increasing again?

d On what two dates did the price reach a maximum before decreasing again?

e Ruth bought 160 shares at the beginning of March and sold them at the beginning of November. What was her **profit**?

Discussion Was the end of 2013 a good time to sell shares in this company?

Q3 Literacy hint

The **profit** is the buying price minus the selling price.

4 Finance The graph shows the income and expenditure for a town council.

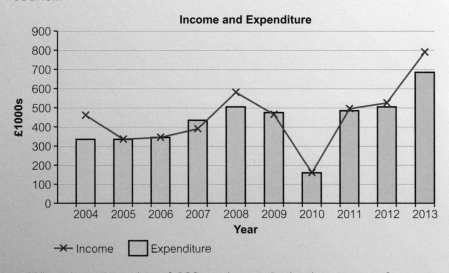

a What does the value of 300 on the vertical axis represent?

b In 2008 what was the total expenditure of the council?

c In which years was the income over £450 000?

d In which year did the council **overspend**?

e Describe the trend in the income
  i between 2008 and 2010
  ii between 2010 and 2013.

f Can you use the graph to estimate the income and expenditure in 2014?

Q4 Literacy hint

Overspending is when income is less than the amount spent.

Topic links: Averages, Pricing, Percentages

5 **Finance** The graph shows the percentage change in house prices in England and Wales since the beginning of 2000.

  a Describe the trend in house prices
    i between 2000 and 2002
    ii between 2002 and 2008
    iii between 2010 and 2012.

  b Robert bought a house at the beginning of 2005. Approximately what percentage did its value increase by the next year?

  c Approximately what was
    i the percentage increase in house prices between 2000 and 2013
    ii the percentage decrease between 2000 and 2008?

  d The average house price was £78 000 at the beginning of 2000.
    i What was the average house price at the end of 2013?
    ii What was the lowest average house price during these 13 years?
    iii What was the greatest house price during this period?

Discussion What year was the best year to buy a house? What about the worst year?

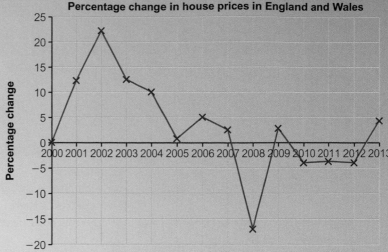

Percentage change in house prices in England and Wales

Source: Land Registry

Q5c hint

Compare the two values for 2000 and 2013.

Q5d i hint

Use your answer to part **c**.

6 **Finance / Modelling** The graph shows the cost of parking.

  a How much does 4 hours' parking cost?

  b How much does 6 hours' parking cost?

  c Steve paid £4 for parking. How long did he stay?

Discussion Can you tell exactly how long Steve stayed?

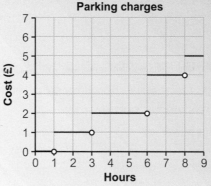

Parking charges

Q6 hint

The open circles show that the upper value of each graph line is not included in the interval.

7 **Finance / Modelling** The table shows prices for a smartphone data plan.

Data usage (MB)	Up to 100	101–300	301–500	501–800	801–1000	Over 1000
Cost (£)	Free	£1	£4	£8	£13	£15

Draw a graph to show the prices.

8 **Explore** How do stock-market traders use graphs to help make investment decisions?

Is it easier to explore this question now you have completed the lesson? What further information do you need to be able to answer this?

9 **Reflect** In this lesson you have used graphs to explore lots of real-life scenarios.

  a Write down one way that the graph has helped you answer questions.

  b Write down one thing you found difficult about using the graphs.

  c Compare your answers with your classmates.

Explore

Reflect

4.3 Distance–time graphs

You will learn to:
- Draw and interpret distance–time graphs
- Use distance–time graphs to solve problems.

CONFIDENCE

Why learn this?
Traffic cameras measure average speed by measuring the time taken to travel a set distance.

Fluency
A car travels at a constant speed of 60 km/h.
- What does 'constant speed' mean?

How far does the car go in
- 1 hour
- 3 hours
- $\frac{1}{2}$ hour?

Explore
What story does this distance–time graph tell you?

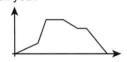

Exercise 4.3

Warm up

1 A train arrives into Cardiff Central from London Paddington at 1.25 pm. The train journey lasts 2 hours and 15 minutes. What time did the train leave London Paddington?

2 Write each time as a decimal.
a $\frac{1}{2}$ an hour
b 3 hours
c 2 and $\frac{1}{4}$ hours

3 Tony walks from home to the bank. On the way home he stops at the shops. The **distance–time** graph shows his journey.

Key point

A **distance–time graph** represents a journey. The vertical axis represents the **distance** from the starting point. The horizontal axis represents the **time** taken.

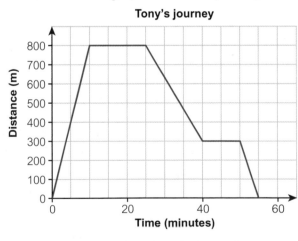

Tony's journey

a How far away is the bank from Tony's house?
b Does his distance from home change between 10 and 25 minutes?
c How long does Tony spend at the bank?
d How long does Tony spend at the shops on the way home?
e How long does it take Tony to get from his house to the bank?
f How long does it take Tony to get from the bank to his house?

Discussion What does a horizontal line mean on a distance–time graph?

Topic links: Measures, Decimals, Averages

Subject links: PE (Q8, 10)

4 Liam leaves home at 1 pm and jogs 7 km to his friend's house.
It takes him $\frac{3}{4}$ of an hour.
He spends 2 hours at his friend's house. He jogs 5 km further away
from home to his father's work. This takes him 30 minutes.
He waits 15 minutes for his father, and then they drive directly home.
Liam arrives home at 5 pm.
Draw a distance–time graph to show this information.

Q4 hint

Draw a horizontal axis from 1 pm to
5 pm with each square representing
15 minutes.
Draw a vertical axis from 0 km to
12 km with each square representing
1 km.

5 The distance–time graph shows the coach journey of a school trip.

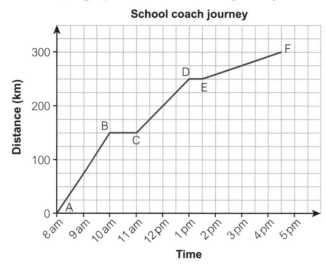

School coach journey

a How far is it from A to B?
b How long did it take the coach to travel from A to B?
c Calculate the average speed (km/h) from
  i B to C   **ii** C to D   **iii** E to F.
Discussion When was the coach travelling the fastest?
How can you tell this from the graph?

Key point
You can calculate **average speed**
if you know the **distance** and the
time.
$$\text{Speed} = \frac{\text{Distance}}{\text{Time}} \text{ or } S = \frac{D}{T}$$

6 Chris jogs 800 m in 15 minutes to his friend's house. He spends
1 hour at his friend's house, then walks home in 30 minutes.
a Sania and Karl sketch graphs to show Chris's journey.

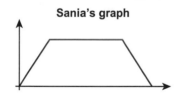
Sania's graph

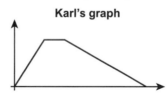
Karl's graph

Key point

Compound measures combine
measures of two different quantities.
Speed is a measure of distance
travelled and time taken. It can be
measured in metre per seconds
(m/s), kilometres per hour (km/h) or
miles per hour (mph).

They are both incorrect. Explain what is wrong with each graph.
b Sketch a more accurate graph for Chris's journey.

7 Michaela is travelling. She records her distance from home every hour.

Time	11 am	12 pm	1 pm	2 pm	3 pm	4 pm	5 pm
Distance from home (miles)	0	30	70	110	110	170	200

a Show this information on a graph.
b When did Michaela stop for a break?
c Michaela spent about 1 hour on a motorway.
  When do you think this was?
d Calculate Michaela's average speed between
  i 11 am and 2 pm   **ii** 1 pm and 5 pm.
Discussion Why is it an average speed?

Q7c hint

Compare the times spent in the
different stages.

8 Reasoning The distance–time graph shows Arthur's progress in his swimming race.

a Work out the speed of Arthur's swim for the first
   i 10 seconds
   ii 50 seconds.
b When was Arthur swimming fastest?
c How far did the Arthur swim in total?
d What was Arthur's average speed for the swim?

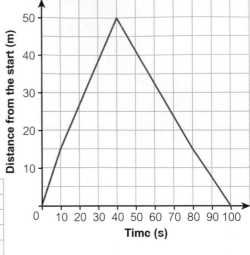

Arthur's swimming race

9 Train A travels from Bristol to Edinburgh.
Train B travels from Edinburgh to Bristol.

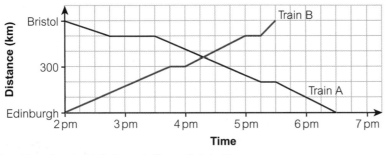

a How far is Edinburgh from Bristol?
b At what time do the trains pass each other?
c How far is each train from Edinburgh when they pass each other?
d What was the average speed of each train?

Discussion How can you tell that Train B had a faster average speed just by looking at the graph?

10 Athletes A, B and C take part in the London Marathon.
a How far is the race in kilometres?
b What time did Athlete C start the race?
c How long did each athlete take to complete the race?
d During the race Athlete B overtook Athlete C.
   i At what time did this happen?
   ii How far had they each run when this happened?

Discussion According to this graph, each runner was travelling at a constant speed. Do you think this is true?

11 Explore What story does this distance–time graph tell you?

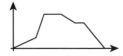

Is it easier to explore this question now you have completed the lesson? What further information do you need to be able to answer this?

12 Reflect You have seen lines like this on distance–time graphs:

A ╱   B ╲   C ─────

a Describe, in your own words, what each type of line tells you.
b What would lines A and B tell you if they were steeper?
c What would lines A and B tell you if they were less steep?
d Would there ever be a line like this on a distance–time graph? Explain.

for 9.2

4.4 Rates of change

You will learn to:
- Interpret graphs that are curved
- Interpret real-life graphs.

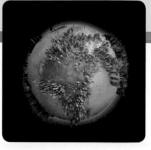

Why learn this?
Planners model the world's population by plotting graphs.

Fluency
Which person is travelling faster?

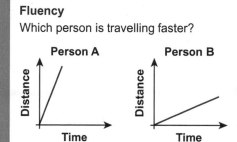

Person A   Person B

Explore
What will be the population of the world in 2050? In 2100?

Exercise 4.4

1 **Finance / Modelling** Gary invests some money in a savings account with a fixed rate of interest. The graph shows how his investment will grow.

  a How much money will he have after 5 years?

  b After how many years will he have £3000?

  c How much money did Gary invest?

  d How much was Gary's investment worth after 1 year?

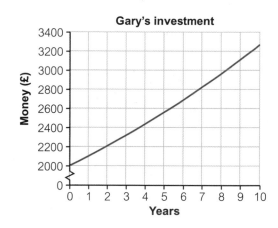

2 **Reasoning** **a** Match each race description to a graph.

  i Maddie starts off quickly and then runs more slowly.

  ii Sophie starts off slowly, then runs faster towards the finish.

  iii Beckie runs at a constant speed throughout the race.

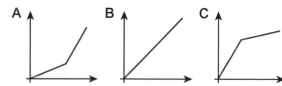

  b Two other students run in this race. Here are their graphs. Write a brief description of their races.

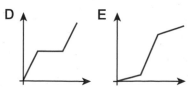

The table shows the depth of water as a pond fills up.

Time (minutes)	0	1	2
Depth (cm)	0	25	35

1 How much does the depth increase in
  a the first minute
  b the second minute?

2 When is the depth increasing faster?

3 Sketch a **rate of change graph** for filling the pool.

4 Draw an accurate graph to check your prediction.

5 Complete this sentence about your graph.
  The steeper the graph, the _____ the depth is increasing.

A solid object is dropped into the water.

6 What happens to the depth of water?

7 What does this look like on the graph?

> **Key point**
>
> A **rate of change graph** shows how a quantity changes over time.

---

3 The graph shows the depth of water in a bath.
  a In which three sections was water flowing into the bath?
  b At which two times was water flowing out of the bath?
  c At what time did a person get into the bath? Explain how you know.
  d How long was the person in the bath altogether?
  e Write a brief story to explain this graph.

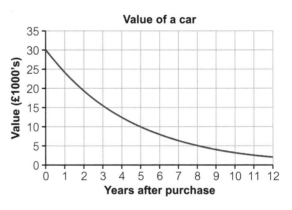

Depth of water

4 Finance / Modelling The graph shows the value of a car.
  a Estimate the price of the car when it is 4 years old.
  b Between which two years did the value change the most?
  c When is the car worth 50% of its original value?
  d Will the value of the car ever reach zero?
  Discussion Is this a realistic model for the value of a car?

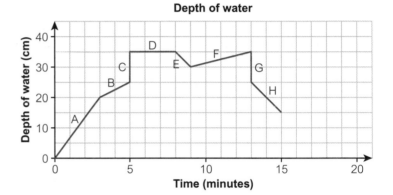

Value of a car

5 Water is poured into these two glasses at the same constant rate.
  a Which fills faster, glass 1 or glass 2?

  b Which graph shows the depth of water in each glass over time?

> **Key point**
>
> For a **linear relationship** the points on a graph form a straight line.
> When the points are not in a straight line, the relationship is **non-linear**.

Topic links: Ratios   **Subject links:** PE (Q2), Science (Q7), Geography (Q9)

6 Water is poured into this container at a steady rate.

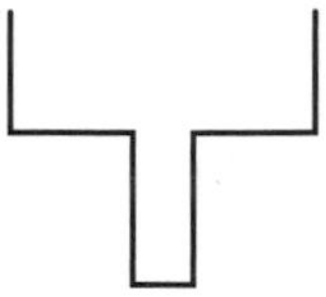

a Which fills faster, the wide part or the narrow part?

b Which graph shows how the depth of water in this container changes over time?

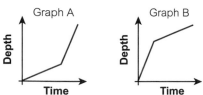

(handwritten: 9-1)

Graph A

Depth / Time

Graph B

Depth / Time

7 **Real / Modelling** Luke throws a ball straight up into the air. The table shows the ball's height above the ground on its way up.

Time (s)	0	1	2	3	4	5	6	7	8
Height (m)	1	38.1	65.4	82.9	90.6	88.6	76.6	54.9	23.4

a Draw a graph to show this information.

b Is the ball travelling at a constant speed? How can you tell?

c Why does the height not start from 0?

d Estimate the times when the height of the ball is 50 m.

e Why are there two times when the ball is at 50 m?

f Use the graph to estimate the time when the ball will hit the ground if Luke doesn't catch it.

Discussion Why is the graph a curve?

> **Q7a hint**
>
> Put Time on the horizontal axis and Height on the vertical axis.
> Plot the points and join them with a smooth curve.

8 These 4 containers are filled with water.

(handwritten: amended)

(handwritten: 9-1)

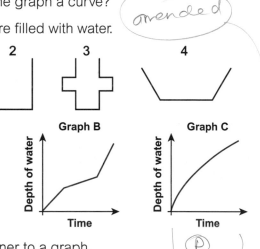

1   2   3   4

Graph A

Depth of water / Time

Graph B

Depth of water / Time

Graph C

Depth of water / Time

> **Q8 hint**
>
> Is the rate of water flow changing all the time? Is it getting slower or faster?

(handwritten: a Which graph shows DP?)
(handwritten: b Match it to container)

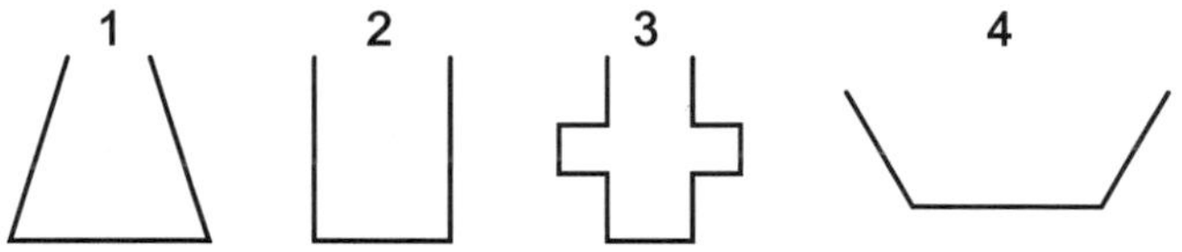

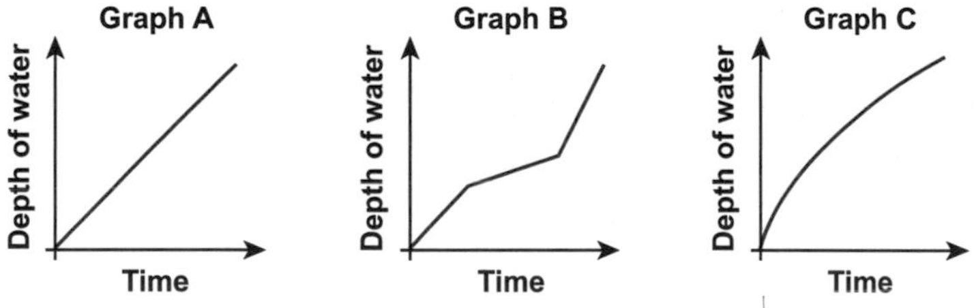

a Match each container to a graph.

b One container does not have a graph. Sketch a graph for that container.

9 **Explore** What will the population of the world be in 2050? In 2100? Is it easier to explore this question now you have completed the lesson? What further information do you need to be able to answer this?

10 **Reflect** Kayo says, 'Rates of change are like ratios. Ratios measure how many red beads there are for every blue bead. Speed measures how far you travel for *every* hour.

a Look back at the questions in this lesson. Do you agree with Kayo? Explain.

Jan says, 'Ratios compare similar things, like blue paint to yellow paint. Rates compare different things, like depth to time.'

b Do you agree with Jan? Explain.

c Write your own sentence, comparing ratios and rates of change.

Explore

Reflect

4.5 Misleading graphs

You will learn to:
• Understand when graphs are misleading.

Why learn this?
During an election campaign, parties present the same data in different ways to influence voters.

Fluency
What is missing from this pie chart?

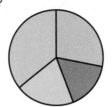

Explore
How can you draw a line graph to disguise falling sales figures?

Exercise 4.5

1 Each dual bar chart shows the number of text messages Marco sent and received each day.

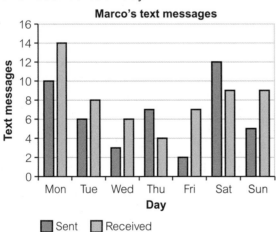

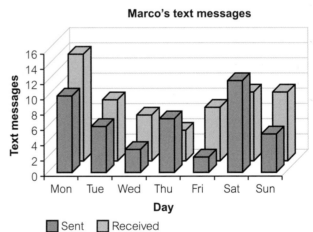

a On which day did Marco send the most text messages?
b How many more text messages did Marco receive than send on Tuesday?
c Over the whole week, did Marco send or receive more text messages?
Discussion Which chart did you use to answer each question?
Was one chart easier to read than the other?

2 Students were asked to choose their favourite dessert.
The pie chart shows the results.
Write 3 ways in which this pie chart is misleading.

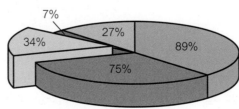

Topic links: Surveys, Pie charts, Percentages

Subject links: Computing (Q3)

3 Real / STEM The cost of 1 GB of data storage is shown on the graph.

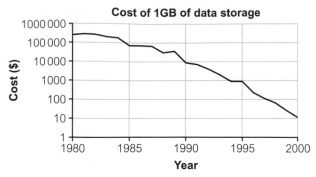

Cost of 1GB of data storage

a What is unusual about the vertical scale on the graph?
How do you get from one marked value to the next?

b Use the values in the table to draw a graph with a vertical scale of 0, 10 000, 20 000,…

Q3b hint

You could use a graph-plotting package to plot the graph.

Year	1980	1985	1990	1995	2000
Cost ($)	213 000	71 000	34 000	950	26

c Describe the trend in the price of data storage between 1980 and 2000.

Discussion Which graph shows the trend more accurately?

4 Finance These two graphs showing the same sales figures for Denise's clothing store.

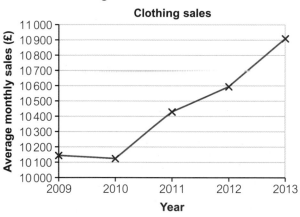

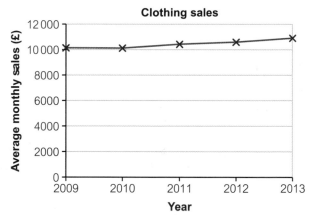

a Denise says, 'Sales are rising rapidly.' Which graph is she using?
b Her bank manager says, 'Sales are almost constant.'
Which graph is she using?
c What is the actual increase in sales between 2009 and 2013?
d Work out the percentage increase in sales between 2009 and 2013.

Discussion Do the figures show a large increase in sales?

Q4d hint

Percentage increase

$$= \frac{\text{actual increase}}{\text{original amount}} \times 100$$

5 Explore How can you draw a line graph to disguise falling sales figures?
Is it easier to explore this question now you have completed the lesson? What further information do you need to be able to answer this?

6 Reflect a List five ways in which graphs can mislead you.
You could begin with, 'It is misleading when the scale …'
b Why might a newspaper use misleading graphs?

Master
P75

CHECK

Strengthen
P91

Extend
P95

Test
P99

4 Check up

Log how you did on your
Student Progression Chart.

Direct proportion

1 a Copy and complete.

  i 10 miles ≈ ☐ km

  ii 5 km ≈ ☐ miles

  iii 1 mile ≈ ☐ km

  iv 80 km ≈ ☐ miles

 b Explain how the graph shows that miles and kilometres
   are in direct proportion.

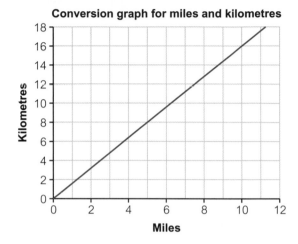

Conversion graph for miles and kilometres

2 The table shows the cost of hiring two different venues.

Hours	1	3	5
Venue A cost (£)	40	120	200
Venue B cost (£)	95	125	155

 a Copy the axes and draw the graphs for the two different venues.

 b Which line shows direct proportion, Venue A or Venue B?

 c Which is cheaper for 4 hours' hire?

 d For what number of hours' hire do both venues cost the same?

 e Which venue charges a booking fee? How much is it?

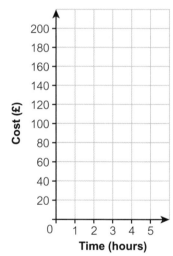

Distance–time graphs

3 Max drives from home to visit his brother.
  He stops on the way to buy pizza.

 a How far does Max live from his brother?

 b How long does Max spend buying pizza?

 c How long does Max spend at his brother's house?

 d On which part of the journey was Max travelling fastest?
   How can you tell?

4 Jasmine leaves home at 10 am and walks $\frac{1}{2}$ km to the bus stop.
  The walk takes her 15 minutes and she waits 5 minutes for the bus.
  The 5 km bus journey takes 20 minutes. She spends 2 hours in town.
  Her father takes her home in the car. She arrives home at 1:15 pm.
  Draw a distance–time graph to show Jasmine's journey.

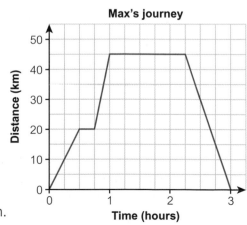

Max's journey

5 The graph shows the Langleys' journey to their holiday destination.
  a How far did they travel in total?
  b How many times did they stop for a break?
  c What was their average speed for the whole journey?

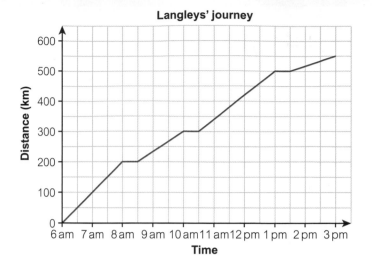

Langleys' journey

Real-life graphs

6 The graph shows the numbers of visitors (in millions) to three different theme parks.
  a Describe the trend in the numbers of visitors between 2009 and 2013 to
    i Park A
    ii Park C.
  b What was the difference in the number of visitors between
    i Park B and Park C in 2012
    ii Park A and Park B in 2010?

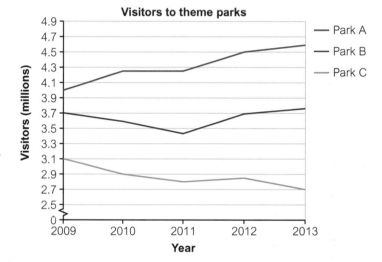

Visitors to theme parks

— Park A
— Park B
— Park C

7 Match the vase to the correct graph showing depth of water against time when the water flows at a constant rate.

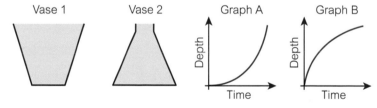

8 **How sure are you of your answers? Were you mostly**
  ☹ **Just guessing** 😐 **Feeling doubtful** ☺ **Confident**
  What next? Use your results to decide whether to strengthen or extend your learning.

Challenge

9 Here are the car hire costs for two companies.
  a Draw a graph for these costs.
  b Unlimited Cars charges a booking fee. How much is it?
  c Explain which company you should use for different numbers of days' hire.

Number of days	2	5	7
Cars Direct	£40	£100	£140
Unlimited Cars	£64	£100	£124

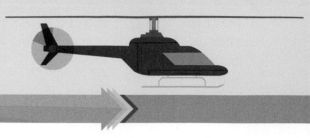

4 Strengthen

You will:
- Strengthen your understanding with practice.

Direct proportion

1 a Draw a pair of axes as shown.
  b Draw an straight-line graph through the origin.
  c Underneath your graph, copy and complete:
   When two quantities are in direct proportion, their graph
   is a s_____ l_____ through _____.

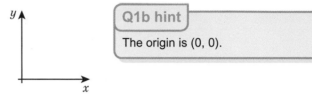

Q1b hint

The origin is (0, 0).

2 Real Which of these graphs show direct proportion?

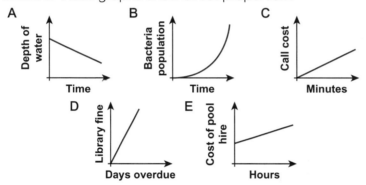

Q2 hint

Which graphs look like the graph you drew in Q1?

3 The graph shows the cost of hiring a roller-skating rink.
  a How much does it cost to hire the rink for 90 minutes?
  b How much does it cost to hire the rink for 1 hour?
  c Megan has £125. What is the maximum length of time she can hire the rink for?

Q3a hint

90

Q3c hint

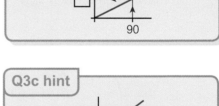

125

4 A gym offers two monthly membership plans.
   The table shows the costs for different numbers of visits.

Number of visits	2	5	7
Plan A	£15	£22.50	£27.50
Plan B	£8	£20	£28

  a Draw a pair of axes as shown.
  b Plot the points for Plan A.
  c Join the points with a straight line.
  d Draw the graph for Plan B.
  e Which plan shows direct proportion?
  f Which plan charges a fixed monthly fee? How much is this fee?
  g Copy and complete, filling in the missing number:
   For more than ☐ visits, plan A is cheaper.

Q4d hint

Follow the steps in parts **b** and **c**.

Q4f hint

How much do no visits cost? This is the fixed monthly fee.

Topic links: Converting currencies, Coordinates, Averages, Trends

Subject links: Geography (Real-life graphs Q4)

Distance–time graphs

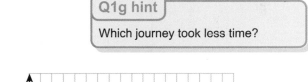

1 Sandra drives Harry to football practice, and then home again.

a Match each description to the part of the graph labelled A, B or C.
  i Driving home
  ii Driving to football practice
  iii At football practice.

b How many minutes is one square on the time axis?

c How long is Harry at football practice?

d How many kilometres is one square on the distance axis?

e How far away is football practice?

f Copy and complete, filling in the missing numbers.
On the way to football practice Sandra and Harry drove ☐ km in ☐ minutes.
On the way back they drove ☐ km in ☐ minutes.

g Did they drive faster on the way there or way back?

h Choose 'fastest' or 'slowest' to complete this sentence.
The steepest section shows the _____ speed.

> **Q1a iii hint**
>
> At football practice, the distance from home stays the same.

> **Q1g hint**
>
> Which journey took less time?

2 Debbie travelled by car to visit her mother for her birthday. She left home at 2 pm.
She drove 80 km in 1 hour 15 minutes.
She stayed at her mother's house for 1 hour 45 minutes and then drove directly home, arriving home at 6.15 pm.

a Copy the axes onto squared paper.

b Draw a distance–time graph to show Debbie's journey.

c Give your graph a title.

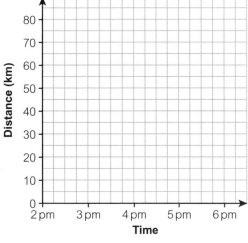

3 The Murphys' travel home after their holiday.

a How often did they stop on the journey?

b How many miles does one small square on the vertical axis represent?

c What is the total distance from holiday to home?

d How many minutes does one small square on the horizontal axis represent?

e What is the total time to travel home?
Write it as a decimal.

f Work out the average speed in miles per hour using the formula

$$\text{average speed} = \frac{\text{total distance in miles}}{\text{total time in hours}}$$

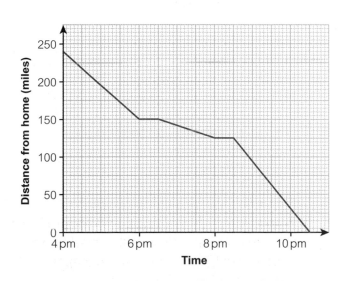

Real-life graphs

1 The graph shows the UK average house price since 2000.

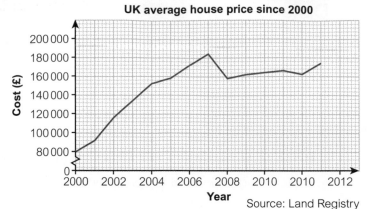

UK average house price since 2000

Source: Land Registry

  a How many squares on the horizontal axis represent 1 year?

  b What was the average house price in

  i 2002   **ii** 2005?

  c What does one small square on the vertical axis represent?

  d In which year was the average house price £130 000?

  e In which year did the average house price reach its maximum value?

Q1 Strategy hint

Before you answer questions about a graph

• read the title

• read the axes labels

• read the key

• look at the axes scales.

2 The graph shows the value of a bike.

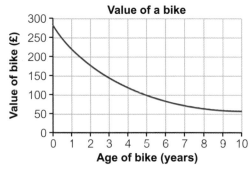

Value of a bike

  a What does one square on the vertical axis represent?

  b How much did the new bike cost?

  c Copy and complete this table.

Age of bike (years)	0	1	2	3	4	5	6	7	8	9	10
Cost (£)		220									

  d From your table, when did the value of the bike decrease the fastest?

  e How does the graph show this?

  f Will the value of the bike ever reach £0?

Q2e hint

The steepest section shows the _____ decrease.

Q2e hint

Imagine extending the graph. Will the line ever touch the horizontal axis?

3 The graph shows the percentage of adults in an American town who own a car.

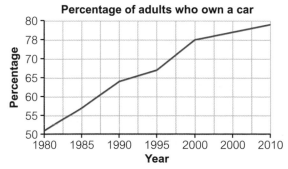

Percentage of adults who own a car

  a What percentage of adults owned a car in 1980?

  b What was the change in percentage of adults owning a car between 1990 and 1995?

  c In which 5-year period did car ownership increase the most?

  d Describe the trend in the percentage of adults who own a car.

  e Use the graph to estimate the percentage of adults who owned a car in 1992.

Q3b hint

change = 1995 percentage
        – 1990 percentage

Q3c hint

Make a table, as in Q2, or look for the steepest section of the graph.

Q3e hint

Choose 'increasing' or 'decreasing' to complete this sentence.
The percentage is _____.

4 The graph shows the average monthly maximum daytime and minimum night-time temperatures in Minehead.

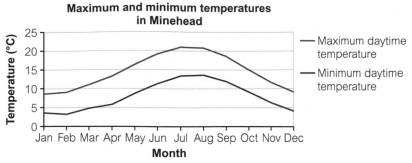

a Which colour graph line shows
   i maximum temperatures   **ii** minimum temperatures?

b In May, what was the average
   i maximum temperature   **ii** minimum temperature?

c Which month had the
   i highest maximum temperature   **ii** lowest minimum temperature?

d Which month had the largest difference between the maximum and minimum temperatures?

> **Q4d hint**
>
> Look on the graph for the biggest gap between the maximum and minimum lines.

Enrichment

1 The graphs show the conversion rates from British pounds to Chinese yuan, and from Chinese yuan to Indian rupees.

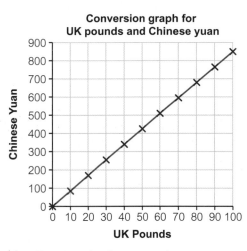 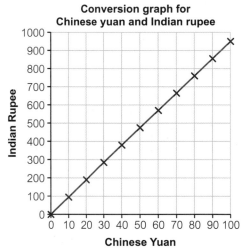

Use the graphs to convert
a £40 into Chinese yuan   **b** £440 in Chinese yuan
c 50 yuan into Indian rupees   **d** £20 into Indian rupees.

Susie goes on a trip. She changes £200 into Chinese yuan. She spends 700 yuan in China and then changes the remaining money into Indian rupees.

e How many rupees does she have?

f Susie has 800 rupees left at the end of her trip. How many pounds is this?

2 Reflect Look back at Q1 and Q2 on distance–time graphs.
   a Which do you find harder, reading from distance–time graphs or drawing distance–time graphs?
   b What makes it more difficult?
   c Write one thing about drawing distance–time graphs and one thing about reading distance–time graphs that you think you need more practice on.

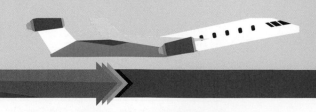

4 Extend

You will:
• Extend your understanding with problem-solving.

1 **Modelling** The graph shows the average rainfall and maximum temperature in the Gower Peninsula, Wales.

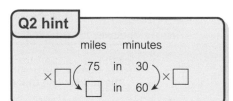

Gower Peninsula climate

■ Rainfall (mm) — Temperature (°C)

 a On average, which month is
  i the warmest   ii the driest?
 Reanna is planning a trip to the Gower Peninsula. She is considering going in either April or October.
 b Use the graph to work out the temperature in
  i April   ii October.
 c Use the graph to work out the rainfall in
  i April   ii October.
 Discussion In which month should Reanna go to the Gower Peninsula?

2 A racing car travels 75 miles in 30 minutes.
 a Calculate its average speed in miles per hour.
 b How far will it travel in 40 minutes?

Q2 hint

miles   minutes

×☐ ⟨ 75 in 30 ⟩ ×☐
    ☐ in 60

 3 **Modelling** Remy travelled from Newcastle to Cardiff for a meeting, a distance of 300 miles. His average speed on the way there was 50 mph and on the way back it was 60 mph. Remy's meeting lasted $1\frac{1}{2}$ hours.
 a Draw a distance–time graph to show this information.
 b Calculate Remy's average speed for the whole journey.

 4 Work out the average speed of each journey.
 a A plane travels 5530 km London to New York in 6 hours
 b A snail slides 1733 mm in 2 days
 c A golf ball travels 293 m in 11.2 seconds

Q5b hint

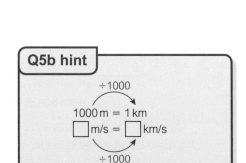

÷1000
1000 m = 1 km
☐ m/s = ☐ km/s
÷1000

5 An athlete runs 200 m in 24 seconds.
 Work out his speed
 a in metres per second
 b in kilometres per second
 c in kilometres per minute
 d in kilometres per hour.

6 **Problem-solving / Modelling** The diagram shows a distance–altitude map for a stage in a cycling race.
 a How many km was the stage?
 b What was the lowest altitude?
 c Which of the three climbs was the steepest?
 The stage takes 6 hours.
 d Sketch a possible distance–time graph for this stage.

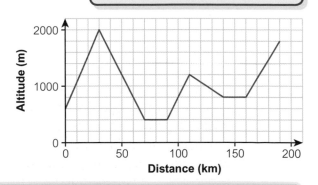

Topic links: Proportion, Percentages, Averages, Measures

Subject links: Geography (Q1, 7, 9, 10), Science (Q11, 16), PE (Q5, 6)

7 Modelling The Youngs are planning a Disney holiday and are choosing between Paris and Florida.

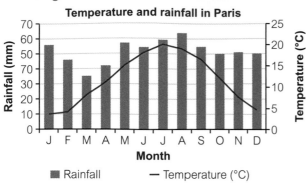

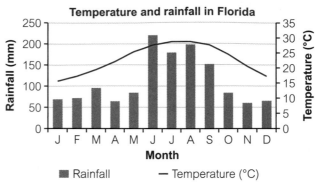

- **a** What is the temperature in August in
  - **i** Paris
  - **ii** Florida?
- **b** What is the rainfall in January in
  - **i** Paris
  - **ii** Florida?
- **c** Explain why the scales of these graphs make it difficult to compare the weather in Paris and Florida.
- **d** Hannah says, 'The graphs show that Florida is always warmer and wetter than Paris.' Is Hannah correct? Explain your answer.

8 a Plot two separate graphs for these tables of data.

i

Edge length of a cube (cm)	2	5	7	9
Volume of a cube (cm³)	8	125	343	729

ii

Radius of circle (cm)	1	5	7	11
Circumference of circle (cm)	$2\pi = 6.3$ (1 d.p.)	10π	14π	22π

> **Q8 hint**
>
> Work out the circumferences to 1 d.p.

b Are the two quantities in each graph in direct proportion?

9 STEM / Modelling The table shows the time difference between a lightning flash and the sound of thunder (seconds), and the distance to the storm (miles).

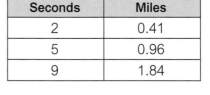

Seconds	Miles
2	0.41
5	0.96
9	1.84

- **a** Plot a graph to show the results.
- **b** Is the distance of the thunderstorm in direct proportion to the number of seconds it takes to hear it?

Sound travels 1 mile every 5.2 seconds.

- **c** Draw a line onto your graph to represent this.

Discussion How well can you model the distance of a storm using the speed of sound?

10 The graph shows the percentages of different age groups in the UK between 1911 and 2011

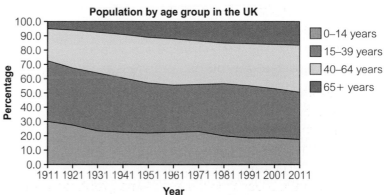

- **a** Approximately what percentage of the population was aged 0−14 years in
  - **i** 1911
  - **ii** 2011?
- **b** Describe the trend in the percentage of the population aged 0−14 years.
- **c** Which age groups have seen a rise in their percentage since 1911?
- **d** On the whole, is the UK population getting older or younger? Explain your answer.

Source: ONS

11 STEM / Reasoning A scientist does an experiment to measure the different pressures created by the same force. She does this by changing the area over which the force is applied. The graph shows her results.

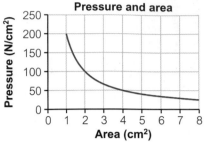

a Copy and complete: As the area increases, the pressure _____.
b What is the pressure when the same force is applied over an area of 3 cm²?
c Will the pressure ever reach zero?
d Explain why the graph will never meet the vertical axis.
e Use these results to explain why
  i people in high-heeled shoes should not walk on the gym floor
  ii a sharp knife will cut vegetables more easily than a blunt knife
  iii ballet dancers get problems with their toes.

12 Real Both graphs show how the numbers of websites have changed over time.

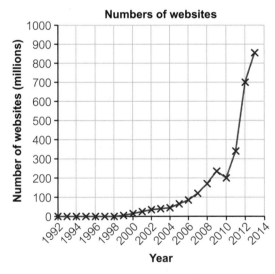

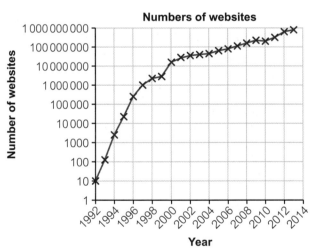

Source: www.internetlivestats.com

a In the left-hand graph, what does one square on the vertical axis represent?
b Describe how the vertical scale changes on the right-hand graph.
c When was the first website launched?
d How many websites were there in
  i 2010
  ii 2007
  iii 1996?
e Which graph was more useful for answering each question in part **d**?
f How many websites would you expect there to be in 2014?
Discussion Is this a good model for predicting the future?

13 Reasoning This table shows the speed at which some cars are travelling and their stopping distances.

Speed (km/h)	32	48	64	80	96	112
Stopping distance (m)	12	23	36	53	73	96

a Draw a graph to show this data.

b Are speed and stopping distance in direct proportion?

This table shows the speed of the cars and the thinking distances of their drivers.

Speed (km/h)	32	48	64	80	96	112
Thinking distance (m)	6	9	12	15	18	21

Total stopping distance = Thinking distance + Braking distance

c Are speed and thinking distance in direct proportion?

d Will speed and braking distance be in direct proportion?
   Explain your answer.

Q14 hint

Use a scale on the vertical axis that will give the appearance of a big increase. You could use a graph-plotting package to plot the graph.

14 The table shows the average monthly sales for a car dealership. The owner wants a loan so he can expand his business. He asks for a graph that shows 'Sales Rising Rapidly'. Draw a suitable graph for the owner.

Year	2008	2009	2010	2011	2012	2013
Average monthly sales	£65 400	£67 300	£66 900	£68 800	£68 400	£69 300

15 Oliver takes a bath. The shape of the bath is shown in the diagram.

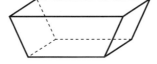

Oliver takes 5 minutes to fill the water to a depth of 50 cm. He then turns the taps off, gets in the bath and remains there for 10 minutes. He gets out, and then lets the water out. The bath takes 7 minutes to empty. Draw a depth–time graph to model this situation.

Q15 hint

What effect will the shape of the bath have on the shape of the graph?

16 STEM / Modelling / Reasoning A ball is dropped from a height of 5 m. The graph shows the height of the ball above the ground for the first 6 seconds.

a How long does it take for the ball to first hit the ground?

b During the first 2 seconds, when is the ball moving the fastest?

The point A is where the ball reaches its greatest height after the first bounce.

c At point A, what is the speed of the ball?

d If the graph continued, what would happen to the maximum height of the ball?

Discussion According to this model, would the ball ever stop bouncing?

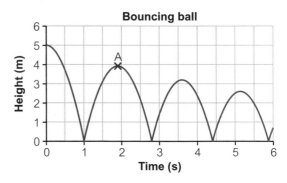

Bouncing ball

17 Reflect In these extend lessons you have used some types of graphs that you may not have used before.

a Make a list of the questions with new types of graph.

b For each graph, what did you do first to understand the graph?

c Which graph did you find the most confusing?

Compare your answers with your classmates.

4 Unit test

Log how you did on your Student Progression Chart.

1 The graph shows the number of daylight hours in London and Lerwick (Shetland Islands).

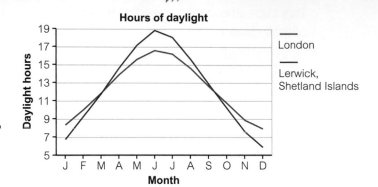

Hours of daylight

— London

— Lerwick, Shetland Islands

a Use the graph to estimate the number of daylight hours in May in
  i London   ii Lerwick.
b In which month(s) is the number of daylight hours approximately the same in both locations?
c Which place has the most daylight in the summer months?
d Which place has the least daylight in the winter months?

2 Paul drives to visit a friend. On the way there, he stops to buy petrol.
  a How long did Paul stay at his friend's house?
  b Which was the fastest part of the journey?
  c What was his average speed from his house to his friend's house?

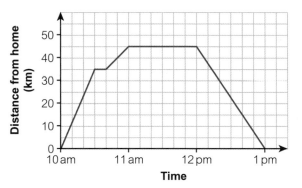

3 The graphs show the races run by 4 different athletes. Match the description to the correct graph.

i   ii   iii 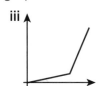   iv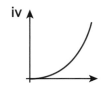

A Athlete A starts off slowly and then gradually increases speed.
B Athlete B runs at a constant speed throughout the race.
C Athlete C runs at a slow constant speed, and then a much faster constant speed.
D Athlete D starts off fast and the gradually slows down.

4 An electrician charges a call-out fee and then an hourly rate. Some of her charges are shown in the table.

Time (hours)	2	4	5
Cost (£)	70	100	115

a Draw a graph to show this information. Plot Time on the horizontal axis and Cost on the vertical axis. Use suitable scales.
b What is the electrician's callout charge?
c What is her hourly rate?
d Are time and cost in direct proportion? Explain

5 The number of new Year 7 students enrolling at 2 local secondary schools is shown on the graph.

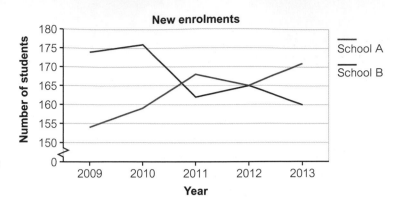

New enrolments

- **a** How many new students enrolled in school A in 2010?
- **b** Which school had the most new students in 2011?
- **c** In which year was the number of new students in school A and school B the same?
- **d** Describe the trend in the numbers of students enrolling in
  - **i** school A
  - **ii** school B.

6 The graph shows two mobile phone plans.

- **a** How much does it cost for 1 GB data on
  - **i** Plan A
  - **ii** Plan B?
- **b** For how much data do both plans cost the same?

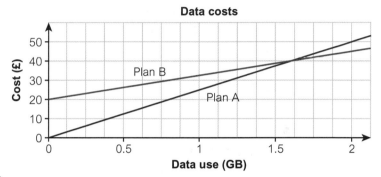

Data costs

7 Which of these graphs show direct proportion?

8 The graph shows the average weekly salary of a footballer in the top English division over the last 30 years.

- **a** Estimate the average weekly salary
  - **i** in the present
  - **ii** 10 years ago
  - **iii** 20 years ago.
- **b** Describe the trend in salaries over the last 30 years.

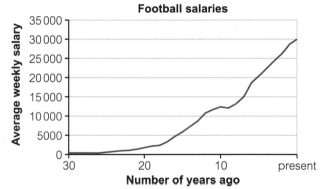

Football salaries

Challenge

9 A school says that its GCSE maths grades are rising rapidly.
Draw a line graph that will give the appearance of rapidly rising GCSE grades.

Year	2010	2011	2012	2013
Percentage of students getting grade C or better	59.3%	60.2%	60.7%	60.9%

10 Reflect Working with real-life graphs uses lots of different maths topics.
Make a list of the different maths skills you have used to answer the questions in this test.
Did you get stuck on any questions because you'd forgotten some of the maths skills? If so, ask your teacher for help.

5.1 Reflection and translation

You will learn to:
- Describe and carry out translations
- Describe and carry out reflections.

CONFIDENCE

Why learn this?
Architects use translations and reflections when designing buildings.

Fluency
Match each equation to its graph.

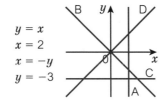

$y = x$
$x = 2$
$x = -y$
$y = -3$

Explore
How could you describe the movements of images on a screen?

Exercise 5.1

1 Copy the diagrams and **reflect** the shapes in the **mirror lines**.

a   **b**   **c**

Key point

A **reflection** is a type of transformation. You can reflect a shape in a **mirror line**. All points on the object are the same distance from the mirror line as the points in the image but on the opposite side.

2 Describe the **translation** that moves each blue shape to its **image**.

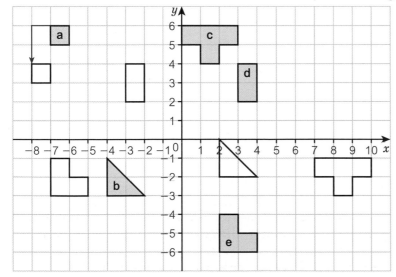

Key point

A **translation** is a type of **transformation**. A translation of a 2D shape is a slide across a flat surface. To describe a translation give the **horizontal movement** then the **vertical movement**.

Key point

The **image** is the shape after a transformation.

Q2 hint

☐ squares left, ☐ squares down

Discussion What translation takes the white square to the blue square? How could you use your answer to part **a** to answer this?

Warm up

Topic links: Coordinates, Graphs   **Subject links:** Art and design (Q3)

3 Copy the diagrams. Reflect each shape in
   i the x-axis   **ii** the y-axis.

a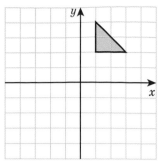

b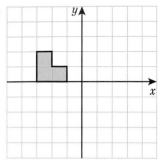

c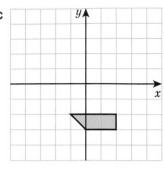

4 Draw a grid with x- and y-axes from −10 to 10.
   a Plot and join the points (2, 2), (4, 2) and (2, 4). Label the shape A.
   b Draw the line $x = 2$.
   c Reflect shape A in the line $x = 2$. Label the shape B.
   d Draw the line $y = -1$.
   e Reflect shape B in the line $y = -1$.

Q4b hint

Look at the graph $x = 2$ in the fluency question.

5 **Problem-solving** The red triangle T has been reflected in different mirror lines to give images A, B, C, D and E.

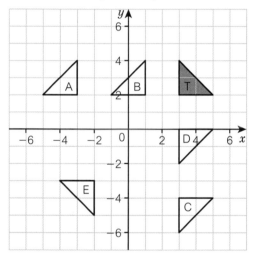

   a Copy and complete.
      A is a reflection of T in the line ____.
   b Describe the four other reflections in this way.
   Discussion Are a shape and its image **congruent** after a translation? After a reflection?

Key point

Shapes are **congruent** if they are the same shape and size.
In congruent shapes, **corresponding sides** and **corresponding angles** are equal.

Worked example

Reflect the blue shape in the mirror line.

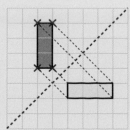

Draw a line from each vertex to cross the mirror line at right angles. Extend the line the same distance on the opposite side of the mirror line to find the vertex of the image.
It might help to turn your paper so the mirror line is vertical.

6 Copy the diagram.

  a Draw the line $y = x$.

  b Reflect the triangle in the line $y = x$.

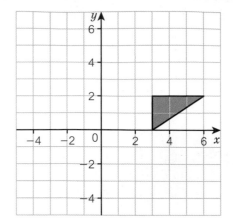

7 a Copy the coordinate axes from Q6.

  b Plot the points (1, 1), (1, 3), (2, 1), (2, 3) and join them to form a rectangle.

  c Draw the line $y = -x$

  d Reflect the rectangle in the line $y = -x$.

8 Describe these translations using **column vectors**.

  a A to B

  b B to C

  c E to B

  d E to A

  e D to E

  f E to D

  Discussion How can you use the answer to part **e** to help find the answer to part **f**?

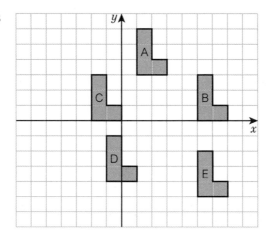

> **Key point**
>
> You can describe a translation using a **column vector**.
>
> The column vector for a translation 3 squares right, 2 squares down is $\begin{pmatrix} 3 \\ -2 \end{pmatrix}$.
>
> The top number in the column vector gives the horizontal movement. The bottom number gives the vertical movement.

9 Write the translations in Q2 using column vectors.

10 a **Problem-solving** Describe the translation that takes A to B.

  b Describe a pair of reflections that take A to B.

  c Copy the red triangle and the coordinate axes from Q6. Translate the triangle by the column vector $\begin{pmatrix} -8 \\ 0 \end{pmatrix}$. Label the image C.

  d Describe a pair of reflections that take the red triangle to C.

  e Translate the red triangle by the column vector $\begin{pmatrix} -4 \\ 1 \end{pmatrix}$. Label the image D.

  f Is there a pair of reflections that take the red triangle to D?

  Discussion Can all translations be described as two reflections?

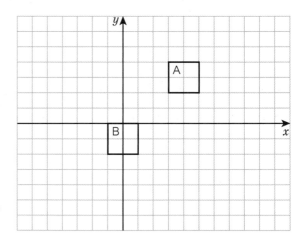

11 Explore How could you describe the movements of images on a screen?

Is it easier to explore this question now you have completed the lesson? What further information do you need to be able to answer this?

12 Reflect Jen says, 'It's easier to describe translations using column vectors – they give the same information and are easier to understand.' Do you agree with Jen? Can you think of any other advantages or any disadvantages of using column vectors?

*Active*Learn Delta 2, Section 5.1

5.2 Rotation

You will learn to:
- Describe and carry out rotations.

CONFIDENCE

Why learn this?
Engine designers need to know where parts of the engine will be after a rotation to ensure they link together.

Fluency
- How many degrees in: a complete turn, a half turn, a quarter turn, a three-quarter turn?
- Which of these arrows is clockwise and which is anticlockwise?

A   B

Explore
What is the centre of rotation of the Solar System?

Exercise 5.2

1 Which of the images show a **rotation** of 90° of the original shape?

a   b    c   d

Key point

A **rotation** is a type of transformation. You rotate a shape by rotating it around a point, called the **centre of rotation**.

2 Describe each turn by giving the **angle** of rotation and the direction (**clockwise** or **anticlockwise**).

a

b

c

d

Warm up

3 Copy the diagrams. Rotate each shape 90° clockwise about the **centre of rotation**, labelled C.

a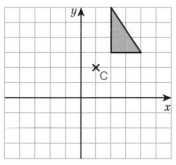

b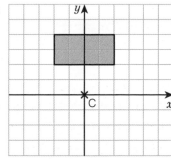

c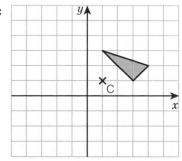

4 Copy each diagram and draw the image of the triangle after the rotation described.

a $\frac{1}{4}$ turn anticlockwise about the point $(-2, 3)$

b 90° anticlockwise about the point $(-2, 2)$

c 270° anticlockwise about the point $(-1, -1)$

d $\frac{1}{2}$ turn about the point $(1, 1)$

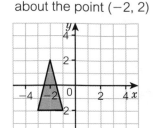

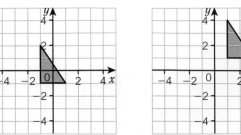

Discussion Why don't you need to give the direction for a rotation through 180°?

Q4d hint

Try rotating in both directions.

5 Copy the diagrams. Rotate each shape through the given angle about the centre of rotation marked C.

a rotate 180°

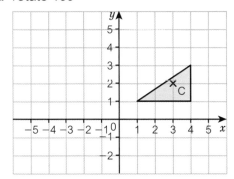

b rotate 90° clockwise

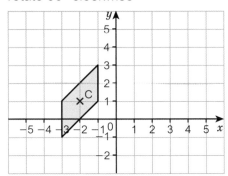

Key point

To describe a rotation you need to give the **angle** and direction (**clockwise** or **anticlockwise**) of rotation.

Discussion Are a shape and its image congruent after rotation?

Worked example

Describe the rotation that takes shape A to shape B.

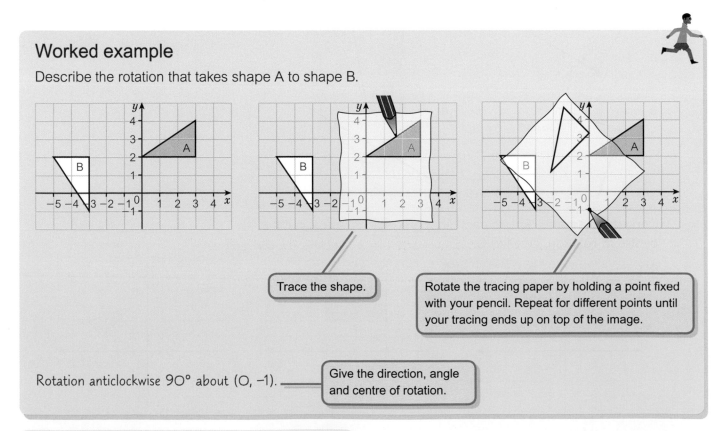

Trace the shape.

Rotate the tracing paper by holding a point fixed with your pencil. Repeat for different points until your tracing ends up on top of the image.

Rotation anticlockwise 90° about (0, −1).

Give the direction, angle and centre of rotation.

Topic links: Coordinates, Graphs

6 Describe the rotation that takes each red shape to its image.

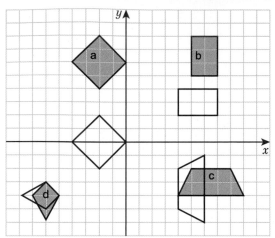

Discussion How can the answers in Q6 help you find the rotation of each white shape to its red shape?

7 **Problem-solving / Reasoning** Find pairs of shapes on this grid that rotate on to each other.
Describe each rotation fully.

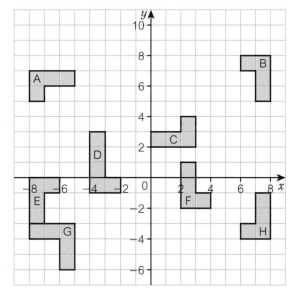

8 **Explore** What is the centre of rotation of the Solar System? Is it easier to explore this question now you have completed the lesson? What further information do you need to be able to answer this?

9 **Reflect** Najid says, 'A shape and its image are always congruent, so you can always rotate a shape onto a congruent shape.'
Kunal doesn't agree. Give a counter example to show when Najid is wrong.

5.3 Enlargement

You will learn to:
- Enlarge a shape
- Describe an enlargement.

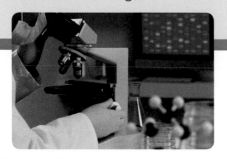

Why learn this
A microscope enlarges the image so scientists can study bacteria.

Fluency
Work out
- 2 × 8
- 3 × 0
- 5 × 3

Explore
What does the zoom function do on a camera?

Exercise 5.3

1 Shape A has been **enlarged** to make shape B. What number have the side lengths been multiplied by?

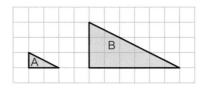

Key point
An **enlargement** is a type of transformation where all the side lengths of a shape are multiplied by the same amount called the **scale factor**.

2 Copy each shape on to squared paper. Enlarge it by the **scale factor** given.

a Scale factor 2

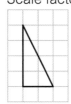

b Scale factor 3

c Scale factor 4

Key point
When you enlarge a shape about a **centre of enlargement**, multiply the distance from the centre to each point on the shape by the scale factor.

Worked example

Enlarge this rectangle using a scale factor 2 and the marked **centre of enlargement**.

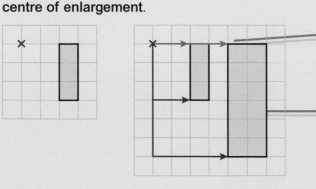

Multiply all the distances from the centre by the scale factor. Count the squares from the centre of enlargement.

The top left vertex of the rectangle changes from 2 right to 4 right.
The bottom left vertex changes from 3 down and 2 right to 6 down and 4 right.

Topic links: Coordinates, Congruency

3 Copy these shapes and the centres of enlargement onto squared paper. Enlarge them by the scale factors given about the centres.

a Scale factor 2   **b** Scale factor 3   **c** Scale factor 2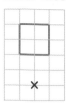

4 Copy these shapes and the centres of enlargement onto squared paper. Enlarge them by scale factor 2.

a   **b**   **c**   **d**

Q4 hint

When the centre of enlargement is on one of the vertices of the shape, the distance from the centre to the vertex is 0.

5 Draw a grid with x- and y-axes from −10 to 10.
Copy triangle A on to your grid.

a Enlarge triangle A by scale factor 2, centre of enlargement (0, 0).

Key point

Two shapes are **similar** when one is an enlargement of the other.

b Enlarge triangle A by scale factor 2, centre of enlargement (8, 1).

c Enlarge triangle A by scale factor 2, centre of enlargement (1, 3).

Discussion Are the angles of a shape the same after an enlargement? What can you say about the angles and lengths of two **similar** shapes? What scale factor would you use to make two congruent shapes?

Key point

To describe an enlargement you need to give the scale factor and the centre of enlargement.

6 Shape A has been enlarged to give shape B.

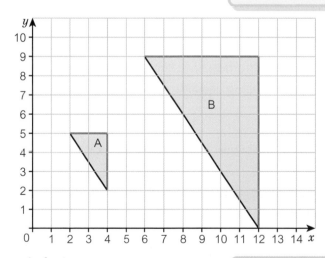

a What is the scale factor of the enlargement?

b Copy the diagram. Use straight lines to join equivalent vertices on the object and image.

c What are the coordinates of the centre of the enlargement? Use the lines you drew in part **b**.

d Copy and complete to describe the enlargement from A to B.
Centre of enlargement at ___ with scale factor ___

Key point

To find the scale factor of enlargement compare the lengths of corresponding sides.

7 **Explore** What does the zoom function do on a camera?
Look back at the maths you have learned in this lesson.
How can you use it to answer this question?

8 **Reflect** Multiplication, ratios and enlargement are all linked mathematically. Do you find it helpful to 'link up' areas of maths when solving problems? Explain why or why not.

5.4 More enlargement

You will learn to:
- Enlarge a shape using a negative scale factor
- Enlarge a shape using a fractional scale factor.

CONFIDENCE

Why learn this
Enlargement is used in arts and crafts all over the world.

Fluency
Work out
- 3×0.5
- $\frac{1}{2} \times 14$
- $\frac{1}{3} \times 15$

Explore
How does 25% enlargement change the size of a photo?

Exercise 5.4

Warm up

1 Draw a grid with x- and y-axes from -10 to 10.
   a Plot the points $(-1, 2)$, $(-2, 2)$, $(-2, 5)$ and $(-1, 5)$.
      Join the points to form a rectangle and label it A.
   b Enlarge shape A by scale factor 2, centre of enlargement $(-2, 4)$.
      Label it B
   c Enlarge shape A by scale factor 3, centre of enlargement $(-4, 3)$.
      Label it C.

Worked example

Enlarge this triangle using **negative scale factor** -2 and centre of enlargement $(3, 2)$.

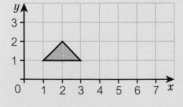

Count the squares from the centre of enlargement.

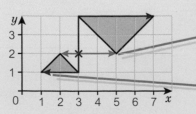

The top vertex of the small triangle changes to the bottom vertex of the enlarged triangle, from 1 left to 2 right.

The bottom left vertex of the triangle changes to the top right vertex of the enlarged triangle, from 1 down and 2 left to 2 up and 4 right.

Key point

A **negative scale factor** has the same effect as a positive scale factor except it takes the image to the opposite side of the centre of enlargement.

Topic links: Coordinates, Congruency

2 Copy these diagrams. Enlarge the shapes using the marked centres of enlargement and negative scale factors.

a scale factor −3

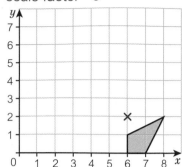

b scale factor −2

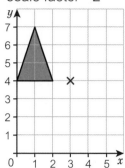

c scale factor −6

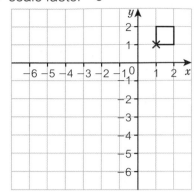

Discussion Which enlargements give a congruent image?

3 Copy each diagram. Enlarge each shape by the scale factor given.

a scale factor $\frac{1}{2}$

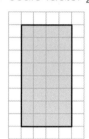

b scale factor $\frac{1}{3}$

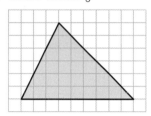

> **Q3a hint**
>
> Multiply all the lengths by $\frac{1}{2}$.

> **Q3b hint**
>
> Divide the base and the vertical height by 3.

4 Enlarge each shape by scale factor $\frac{1}{2}$ about the centre of enlargement shown. The first one has been started for you.

a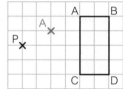

b

c

> **Key point**
>
> To enlarge a shape by a fractional scale factor:
> • multiply all the lengths by the scale factor
> • multiply the distance from the centre to each point on the shape by the scale factor.

Discussion Are an object and its image similar after a fractional enlargement?

5 Reasoning
   a i Draw a shape on squared paper. Choose a centre of enlargement and enlarge the shape by scale factor $\frac{1}{3}$.
   ii Enlarge the image by scale factor 3 using the same centre of enlargement.
   iii What can you say about the original shape and the final image?
   b Shape A is enlarged by scale factor 4 about centre (0, 1) to give shape B. Describe the enlargement that takes shape B to shape A.

6 Explore How does 25% enlargement change the size of a photo?
Look back at the maths you have learned in this lesson.
How can you use it to answer this question?

7 Reflect Rajeev says, 'When you enlarge a shape it gets bigger.'
Julia says, 'When you enlarge a shape it changes size.'
Amrita says, 'When you enlarge a shape it changes size and sometimes position.'
Who do you agree with the most?
Give an example to show what each person means.
Compare your examples with your classmates.

5.5 STEM: Combining transformations

You will learn to:

- Transform 2D shapes using a combination of reflection, rotation, enlargement and translation.

Why learn this?
In video games, character movements are programmed using transformations.

Fluency
Work out the area and perimeter of this rectangle.

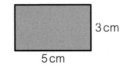

3 cm

5 cm

Explore
Is there always more than one way of describing a transformation?

Exercise 5.5: Computer graphics

1 For each diagram:

a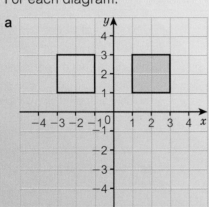

b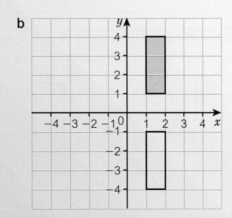

c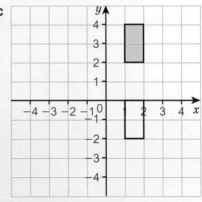

i describe the reflection that takes the orange shape to its image

ii describe the translation that takes the orange shape to its image.

2 Copy the diagram.

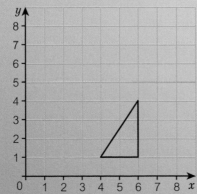

Reflect the shape in the line $y = x$.

> **Q1 hint**
>
> Reflection in the line _____
>
> Translation by $\begin{pmatrix} \square \\ \square \end{pmatrix}$

> **Key point**
>
> You can use dynamic software to carry out the transformations in this lesson.

Topic links: Lines of symmetry, Coordinates   **Subject links:** Design and technology (Q4, 5, 6), Science (Q10)

3 Copy the diagram on the right.

  a Translate the green shape by the column vector $\begin{pmatrix} -3 \\ -5 \end{pmatrix}$.

  b Reflect the new shape in the y-axis.

4 **STEM / Problem-solving** Here is a Christmas tree company logo.

  a Draw a coordinate grid with x- and y-axes from −10 to 10.

  b Plot the points (0, 2), (0, 3) (2, 0), (2, 1) and join them to make a parallelogram.

  c Translate the parallelogram up twice, to make the right hand side of the logo. Write down the column vectors for your translations.

  d Use a reflection to complete the logo. Describe the reflection you used.

  e A graphics designer starts by reflecting the parallelogram and then translating it to create this logo. Write down the instructions to create the logo this way.

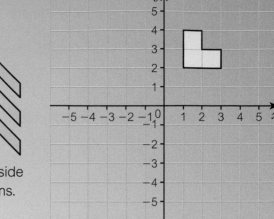

5 **STEM / Problem-solving** This logo design is based on a parallelogram. Draw a coordinate grid with x- and y-axes from −10 to 10.

  a Plot the points (0, 0) (2, 0) (2, 2) and (4, 2) to make a parallelogram.

  b Reflect your parallelogram in the line $y = x$.

  c Use more reflections to complete the logo. Write down the reflections you use.

  Discussion Could you use rotation to create this logo?

6 **STEM** A video game character travels along this path from A to B to avoid different objects in the game.

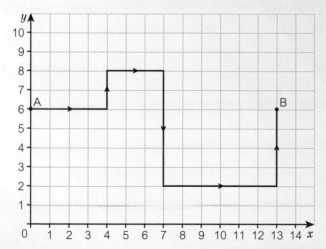

  a Write down the column vectors to describe the movements.

  The character jumps straight from point B back to point A.

  b Describe the reflection that makes this jump.

7 **a** Copy the diagram.

  Reflect triangle A in the line $y = x$. Label the image B.

  b Translate triangle B $\begin{pmatrix} -6 \\ -3 \end{pmatrix}$. Label the image C.

  c Rotate triangle C through 180° about the point (−3, 0). Label the image D.

  d Can you describe a reflection that takes triangle A directly to triangle D?

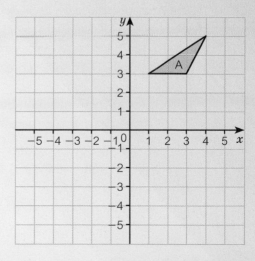

8 **Reasoning** The rectangle shown has a perimeter of 14 cm.
Work out the perimeter of the image after each transformation.
a Reflection in the line $y - 2$
b Rotation through 90° about the point (1, 2)
c Enlargement by scale factor 2, centre of enlargement (5, 5)
d Translation of $\begin{pmatrix} -4 \\ -2 \end{pmatrix}$
e Do you need to carry out the transformations to answer these questions?

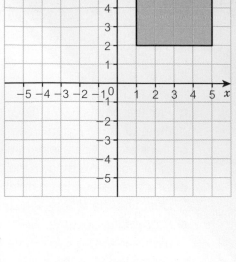

9 **Reasoning** A company uses this logo.
To generate the logo a computer programmer
plots the smallest square and enlarges it.

a Plot the points (1, 1), (2, 1), (2, 2) and (1, 2)
on a coordinate grid. Join them to make a square.
b Enlarge the square by scale factor 2, centre of enlargement (1, 1).
c What enlargement of the smallest square will give the largest
square? Draw it to check.

10 **STEM / Modelling** A biologist uses computer graphics to model
bacteria growth.
A bacteria sample enlarges by scale factor 2 every day.
The biologist draws a 16 by 16 coordinate grid and plots a 2 by 2
square in the centre. The square represents the bacteria sample at
the start of day 1.

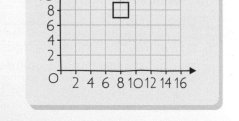

a Copy her diagram and enlarge the square by scale factor 2,
about the midpoint of the square.
This models the sample at the start of day 2.
b Enlarge the image to model the sample at the start of day 3.
c On what day will the sample completely cover the grid?

Investigation Problem-solving

Draw a coordinate grid with the x- and y-axis from −8 to 8.
1 Plot and join the points (2, 2), (3, 2) and (2, 5) to form a triangle. Label the triangle A.
2 Reflect the triangle in the line y-axis. Label the triangle B.
3 Reflect triangle B in the x-axis. Label the triangle C.
4 Describe the single transformation that takes triangle A to triangle C.
5 On the same grid repeat steps **2** to **4** for reflection in the line $x = -1$ followed by reflection in the line $y = 1$.
  Label the images D and E.
6 Describe the single transformation that is equivalent to reflection in the line $x = 1$ followed by reflection in the line $y = -1$.
  Draw the transformations to check your answer.

Discussion Does it matter what order you do the reflections in? Explain your answer.

---

11 **Explore** Is there always more than one way of describing a
transformation?
Look back at the maths you have learnt in this lesson.
How can you use it to answer this question?

12 **Reflect** Q8 asked you to carry out four types of transformations.
Which did you find hardest?
Which did you find easiest?
Write a hint for the one you found hardest.

ActiveLearn Delta 2, Section 5.5

5.6 2D shapes and 3D solids

You will learn to:

- Identify planes of reflection symmetry in 3D solids
- Find the perimeter and area of 2D shapes after enlargements
- Find the volume of 3D solids after enlargements.

CONFIDENCE

Why learn this?
3D models are built to scale from 2D plans.

Fluency
Which of these shapes are 3D solids?
- square
- cube
- cuboid
- rectangle
- circle
- sphere

Explore
What is the area of a tennis court in a model village?

Exercise 5.6

1 Work out the perimeter and area of each shape.

a 3 cm, 3 cm

b 2 m, 4 m

c 4 mm, 6.4 mm, 5 mm

2 Work out the volume of each solid.

a 3 cm, 2 cm, 5 cm

b 2 mm, 2 mm, 2 mm

3 Copy each shape and draw on all the lines of symmetry.

a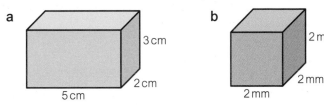

b

c

Q4 hint

Sketch a new copy for each plane you show.

4 Sketch a copy of each solid and draw in a **plane of symmetry**.
How many planes of symmetry does each solid have?

a 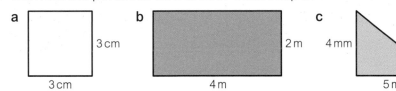   **b**   **c**   **d**

Key point

A 2D shape can have lines of symmetry. A 3D solid can have **planes of symmetry**. On either side of the plane of symmetry the solid is identical.

Discussion Which solids have an infinite number of planes of symmetry?

Warm up

5 A rectangle has two sides of length 3 cm and 5 cm.
 a Work out the perimeter.
 b The rectangle is enlarged by scale factor 2.
   i What are the lengths of the sides of the enlargement?
   ii What is the perimeter of the enlarged shape?
 c What are the lengths of the sides and the perimeter when the rectangle is enlarged by scale factor 3?
 Discussion When a shape is enlarged by scale factor 4, what happens to its perimeter?

6 A shape has perimeter 10 cm.
 Work out the perimeter if it is enlarged by scale factor
 a 2   **b** 3   **c** 4   **d** $\frac{1}{2}$

7 For each pair of shapes:

a

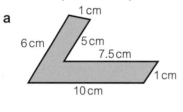 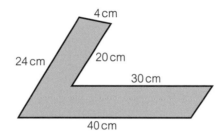

Q7a hint
6 cm × ☐ = 24 cm

b

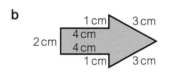 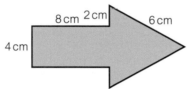

 i work out the scale factor of the enlargement
 ii work out the perimeter of the smaller shape
 iii use your answers to parts **i** and **ii** to work out the perimeter of the enlargement.

Investigation   **Reasoning**

1 Draw a square with sides of length 1 cm on squared paper.
2 Enlarge the square by
 a scale factor 2   **b** scale factor 3   **c** scale factor 4.
3 Copy and complete the table.

Scale factor of enlargement	Side of enlarged square (cm)	Area of square (cm²)
1 (original square)		
2		
3		
4		

4 Predict the area when the square is enlarged by scale factor 10.
5 Now complete this table for enlarging a cube of side 1 cm.

Scale factor of enlargement	Side of enlarged cube (cm)	Volume of cube (cm³)
1 (original cube)		
2		
3		
4		

6 Predict the volume when the cube is enlarged by scale factor 10.

Topic links: Lines of symmetry, Perimeter, area and volume

8 The sides of a rectangle are 3 cm and 5 cm.

  a Work out the area of the rectangle.

  The rectangle is enlarged by scale factor 3.

  b Work out the area of the enlarged rectangle.

  Discussion How did you find the area of the enlarged rectangle?
  Is there more than one way?

9 **Real** A photograph is enlarged by scale factor 2.

5 cm

7 cm

  What is the area of the enlarged photograph?

10 **Problem-solving** In a set of three trays, the smallest tray has area
  180 cm².

  The middle tray is an enlargement scale factor 2 of the smallest tray.

  a What is the area of the middle tray?

  The largest tray is an enlargement scale factor 3 of the smallest tray.

  b What is the area of the largest tray?

11 **Problem-solving** A cuboid measuring 3 cm by 4 cm by 5 cm is
  enlarged by scale factor 2.

  What is the volume of the new cuboid?

12 **Problem-solving** A cone with a volume of 1250 cm³ is enlarged by
  scale factor 4.

  What is the volume of the new cone?

13 **Explore** What is the area of a tennis court in a model village?
  Is it easier to explore this question now you have completed
  the lesson? What further information do you need to be able to
  answer this?

14 **Reflect** Look again at Q10 and Q11.
  How were the methods you used the same?
  How were they different?
  Did you have to visualise or draw a sketch for one question and
  not the other?

5 Check up

Log how you did on your Student Progression Chart.

Reflection, rotation and translation

1 Describe each translation.
   a Shape A to shape B
   b Shape B to shape C

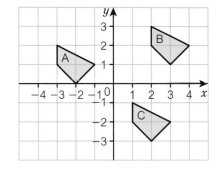

2 Describe the rotation that takes shape A to shape B.

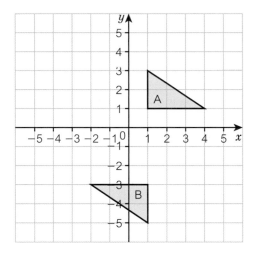

3 Describe the reflection that takes
   a shape A to shape B
   b shape B to shape C.

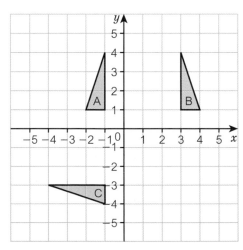

4 A triangle has perimeter 12.5 cm. Write down the perimeter of the image after each transformation.
   a Reflection in the x-axis
   b Translation 5 squares left and 4 squares down
   c Rotation through 90°

5 Copy the diagram.

  a Rotate triangle A 90° anticlockwise about the point (2, 0).
Label the image B.

  b Reflect A in the line $y = -x$.
Label the image C.

  c Translate A by $\begin{pmatrix} -3 \\ 1 \end{pmatrix}$.
Label the image D.

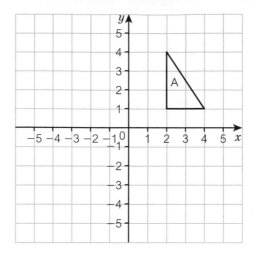

Enlargement

6 Copy the diagrams. Enlarge each shape by the scale factor given using the centre of enlargement marked.

  a scale factor 2

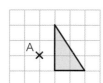

  b scale factor 3

7 Copy the diagram in Q5. Enlarge triangle A by scale factor −2 with centre of enlargement (0, 0).

8 A cylinder with volume $10\,cm^3$ is enlarged by scale factor 2.
What is the volume of the enlargement?

Planes of symmetry

9 How many planes of symmetry does this cuboid have?

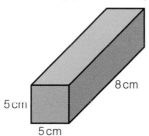

5 cm

8 cm

5 cm

10 **How sure are you of your answers? Were you mostly**
  😟 **Just guessing** 😐 **Feeling doubtful** 🙂 **Confident**
What next? Use your results to decide whether to strengthen or extend your learning.

Reflect

Challenge

11 A cuboid is enlarged by scale factor 3.
How many of the original cuboids will fit inside the enlargement?

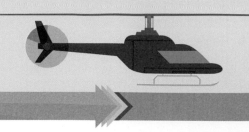

5 Strengthen

You will:
- Strengthen your understanding with practice.

Reflection, rotation and translation

1 Copy this shape on to squared paper.
Draw the image of the shape after these translations.
a 2 squares right, 3 squares up. Label this shape B.
b 4 squares left, 1 square down. Label this shape C.

Q1 hint

Translate one vertex of the shape at a time.

2 Describe the translation that takes:
a A to B
b A to C
c A to D
d A to E.

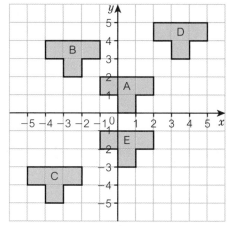

Q2 hint

Draw in lines from matching vertices on A to B, and count the squares up and across.

Q3 hint

Join corresponding vertices of A and B. Mark the midpoint on the line. The mirror line goes through the midpoint.

3 In each diagram the red shape has been reflected in a mirror line.

a 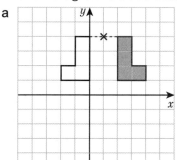 **b** 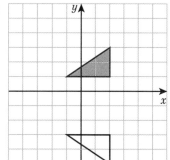 **c**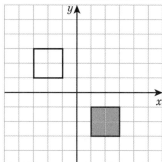

  i Copy each diagram and draw the mirror line.
 ii Write down the equation of the mirror line.

4 Which of these diagrams shows an accurate reflection of the red rectangle in the line $y = x$?

Q4 hint

Turn the book so the mirror line is vertical. Are the object and image the same distance from the mirror line?

A 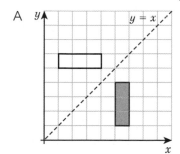 B 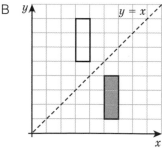 C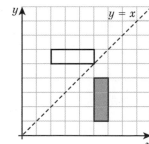

5 Margareta has started to reflect the rectangle in the mirror line $y = x$.
   a Copy the diagram.
   b Turn the page so the mirror line is vertical and continue the reflection.
   c Trace your completed diagram. Fold your diagram along the line $y = x$. What happens to the image and the object?

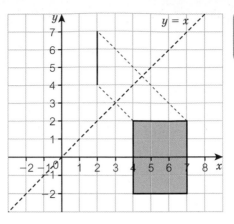

Q5 hint

Reflect each vertex in the mirror line.

6 Draw a coordinate grid with x- and y-axes from −8 to 8.
   a Plot and join the points (−2, 3), (−2, 6), (0, 3), (0, 6).
   b Draw the line $y = -x$.
   c Reflect the shape from part **a** in the line $y = -x$.

Q6 hint

Use the method from Q5.

7 Copy the diagram. Trace the shape.
   a To rotate the shape 90° clockwise about (0, 0) hold your pencil on the centre of rotation (0, 0).
     Rotate the tracing paper clockwise 90°, so the vertical line of the triangle is now horizontal on your tracing.
     Lift the tracing paper to mark the shape on your grid.
   b Rotate the shape 90° anticlockwise about (0, 0).
   c Rotate the shape 180° about (1, 2).
   d Rotate the shape 90° clockwise about (3, 2).

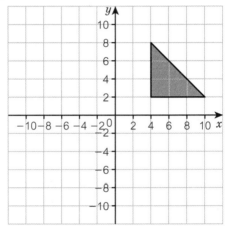

Q7b hint

Use the method from part **a**.

8 The red triangle has been rotated through 90° clockwise.
   Which of the points A, B or C is the centre of rotation?

9 Describe the rotation that takes shape A to
   a shape B   b shape C.

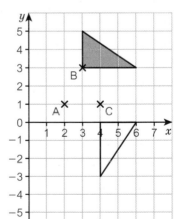

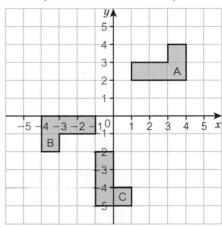

Q8 hint

Trace the shape and put your pencil on one of the points. Rotate the tracing paper through 90° clockwise. Is the triangle over its image?

Q9 hint

Rotation, centre (□,□),
□° anticlockwise/clockwise.

10 Copy the diagram on the right.
Transform the shape using these transformations.
The first one is partly done for you.

a A translation 3 squares right and 2 squares up followed by a
reflection in the line $y = 3$.

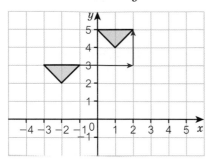 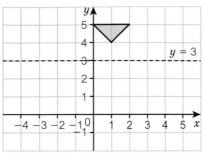

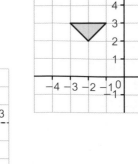

b A rotation 90° anticlockwise about (−3, 2) followed by a translation
2 squares right and 2 squares down.

c An enlargement of scale factor 2 at (−1, 2) followed by a reflection in
the x-axis.

d A reflection in the line $x = 2$ followed by a rotation 180° about (2, 2).

Enlargement

1 Eric has started to enlarge the rectangle by scale factor 2 about the
centre of enlargement Y.

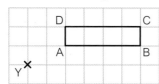

Y to A   2 right, 1 up $\overset{\times 2}{\curvearrowright}$ 4 right, ☐ up

Y to B   6 right, 1 up

a Copy the diagram. Work out the distances from Y to points C and D.
Multiply the distances by 2.

b Plot the new points and join them up.

> **Q1b hint**
>
> Check that the lengths on the
> enlargement are twice as long as on
> the original.

2 Copy and complete to enlarge the shape by scale factor 3.

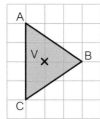

Point A: $\overset{\times 3}{\curvearrowleft}$ 1 left, 2 up $\overset{\times 3}{\curvearrowright}$ ☐ left, ☐ up

> **Q3 hint**
>
> When the centre of enlargement is
> on the shape, imagine the shape
> is pinned to the page at that point.
> Each side needs to be 3 times as
> long but the 'pinned' point doesn't
> move.

3 Enlarge the rectangle by scale factor 3.

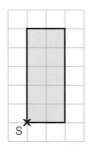

> **Q4a hint**
>
> 3 × ☐ = 15
> 1 × ☐ = 5
> Check that both missing numbers
> are the same.

4 Work out the scale factor of enlargement for each pair of rectangles.

a 3 cm / 1 cm   15 cm / 5 cm   **b** 6 cm / 2 cm   60 cm / 20 cm

 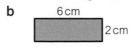

5 A rectangle is 4 cm long and 3 cm wide.
   It is enlarged by scale factor 3.
   a Work out
      i the perimeter of the original rectangle
      ii the perimeter of the enlarged rectangle.
   b Find the missing number.
      Enlarged perimeter = original perimeter × ☐

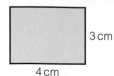

3 cm

4 cm

Q5 Strategy hint

Sketch the rectangle. Mark on the lengths after the enlargement.

6 a For the rectangle in Q5 work out
      i the area of the original rectangle
      ii the area of the enlarged rectangle.
   b Find the missing number.
      Enlarged area = original area × ☐

Q6 hint

Use your sketch and measurements from Q5a.

7 A cuboid is enlarged by scale factor 2.
   a Work out
      i the volume of the original cuboid
      ii the volume of the enlarged cuboid.
   b Find the missing number.
      Enlarged volume = original volume × ☐

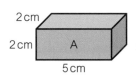

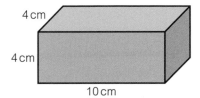

Planes of symmetry

Q1 hint

The two pieces must be reflections of each other about the plane of symmetry.

1 The diagrams show a cuboid divided by four planes.
   Which diagram does *not* show a plane of symmetry?

   A   B   C   D

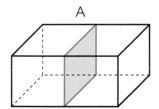
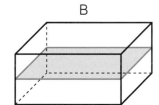
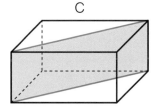
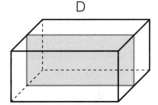

2 In this triangular prism the cross-section is an isosceles
   triangle. How many planes of symmetry does the
   prism have?

Q2 hint

How many ways could you cut it in half? Would each half be a reflection of the other?

Enrichment

1 Draw a grid with x- and y-axes from −10 to 10.
   a Plot the point (3, 4).
   b Reflect the point in the x-axis.
   c What are the coordinates of the new point?
   d Copy and complete the table.

Point	(3, 4)	(2, 7)	(1, 5)	(9, 2)	(−1, 3)	(2, −4)	(−2, −7)	(−8, −1)	(0, 3)
Reflection in the x-axis									

   e Is there a way of working out the reflection without plotting the points?
   f Repeat for reflecting points in the y-axis.

2 **Reflect** In these lessons you have answered questions about
      reflection   rotation   translation   enlargement
   Write a definition for each of them, using one of these descriptions:
      flips over   changes size   changes position   turns around
   For each definition, draw a sketch to show what the definition means.
   How did your definition help you choose the shapes?

Reflect

5 Extend

You will:
• Extend your understanding with problem-solving.

1 Copy the diagram.

  a Reflect shape A in the line $y = x$.
    Label the image B.

  b Rotate shape B through 90° anticlockwise about the origin. Label the image C.

  c Describe the reflection that will take shape C to shape A.

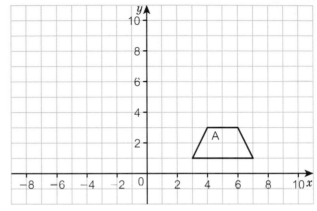

2 **a** Draw a grid with x- and y-axes from −8 to 8.

  b Plot and join the points
    (5, 1), (7, 1), (8, 1.5), (7, 2), (5, 2).

  c Reflect the shape in the line $y = x$.

  d Reflect the image in the y-axis.

  e Reflect the image in the line $y = -x$.

  f Reflect the image in the x-axis.

  g Reflect the image in the line $y = x$.

  h Reflect the image in the y-axis.

  i Reflect the image in the line $y = -x$.

  j How many lines of symmetry does your final diagram have?

> **Q1b hint**
> The origin is the point (0, 0).

3 **STEM** Greenhouse gases slow down or prevent the loss of heat from the Earth. These are models of two different greenhouse gases. How many planes of symmetry does each molecule have?

  a Ozone (O_3)
                         b Nitrogen trifluoride (NF_3)

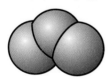
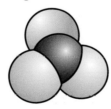

4 **a** Draw a grid with x- and y-axes from −7 to 7.

  b Plot and join the points (−2, 1), (−7, 1), (−5, 3) and (−3, 3).

  c Work out the area of the shape.

  d Translate the shape by $\begin{pmatrix} 4 \\ -6 \end{pmatrix}$.

  e **Reasoning** Write down the area of the new shape.

5 Reasoning Copy this diagram.

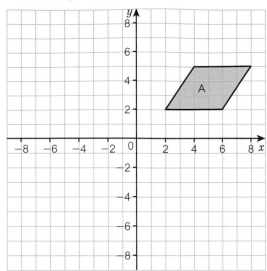

a Translate shape A by $\begin{pmatrix} -5 \\ -4 \end{pmatrix}$. Label the image B.

b Translate B by $\begin{pmatrix} 4 \\ 2 \end{pmatrix}$. Label the image C.

c Write the column vector for the translation that takes shape A to shape C.

Discussion Could you have worked out the answer to part **c** without drawing the diagram?

6 Problem-solving On a grid a translation of $\begin{pmatrix} -2 \\ 5 \end{pmatrix}$ takes shape A to shape B and $\begin{pmatrix} 4 \\ -1 \end{pmatrix}$ takes shape B to shape C.

Write down the column vector that takes

a shape A directly to shape C   **b** shape C directly to shape A

Q6 hint

Look at your answer to Q5.

7 Problem-solving This triangle is enlarged by scale factor 5. Work out the length of the perimeter of the enlarged triangle.

4 cm

3 cm

8 Copy this diagram.

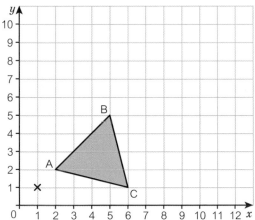

a Enlarge the triangle by scale factor 2, centre of enlargement (1, 1).

b Work out the length of the line BC in the enlargement.

9 Decide if each statement is true (T) or false (F).

a A shape and its reflection are congruent.

b A shape and its translation are congruent.

c A shape and its enlargement are always congruent.

d A shape and its rotation are congruent.

10 Enlarge each shape by the given scale factor using the centre of enlargement marked.

  a scale factor $\frac{1}{4}$

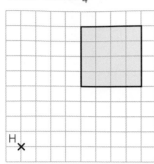

  b scale factor $\frac{1}{3}$

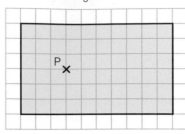

  c scale factor $\frac{1}{5}$

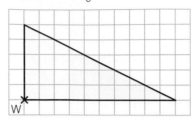

11 Work out the scale factor of enlargement for each pair of shapes or solids.

  a

> **Q11a hint**
>
> Compare the lengths of two corresponding sides.

  b

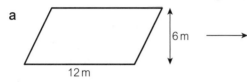

  c

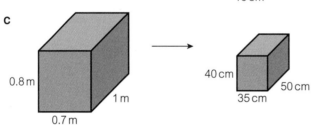

12 Reasoning Copy this diagram.

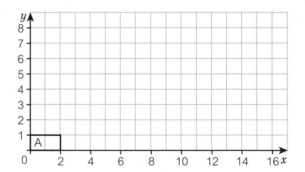

  a Enlarge shape A by scale factor 4 and centre of enlargement (0, 0). Label the image B.

  b Enlarge shape B by scale factor 2 with centre of enlargement (0, 0). Label the image C.

  c What is the scale factor that takes shape A to shape C?

  d Could you have worked out the answer to part **c** without drawing the diagram?

  e Does it matter what order you do the enlargements in?

13 Cardboard boxes come in three standard sizes.

The smallest measures 30 cm by 60 cm by 80 cm.

The medium size measures 90 cm by 180 cm by 240 cm.

The large size measures 120 cm by 240 cm by 320 cm.

What is the scale factor of enlargement from

  a a small to medium box   **b** a medium to large box

  c a small to large box   **d** a medium to small box

  e a large to small box?

Discussion How could you work out the answer to part **c** from parts **a** and **b**?

Topic links: Area of trapezium, Area of circles, Volume, Converting between units of area, Pythagoras

Subject links: Science (Q3, Q15), Design and technology (Q17)

14 Problem-solving A circle with radius 5 cm is enlarged by scale factor 3. What is the area of the enlarged circle?

15 STEM / Modelling A group of cells in a Petri dish doubles in area every day. One day the cells cover a roughly circular area of radius 3 mm.
 a What will the radius of the circular area of cells be the next day?
 b What will the area of the cells be the next day?

16 Draw a grid with x- and y-axes from −8 to 8.
 a Plot and join the points (1, 1), (5, 1) and (5, 5) to make a triangle.
 b Enlarge the triangle by scale factor $-\frac{1}{4}$ with centre of enlargement (−3, −7).

17 Real / Problem-solving A gardener plants a flower bed measuring 3 m by 4 m.
 For each square metre he needs 30 bulbs.
 Bulbs come in bags of 50 and cost £6.99 per bag.
 a What is the cost of bulbs for this flower bed?

 Another flower bed is 3 times as long and 3 times as wide.
 b How many bulbs will he need for this flowerbed?
 c What is the cost of bulbs for this flowerbed?

 It takes him 4 hours to plant the bulbs in the flowerbed measuring 3 m by 4 m.
 d How long will it take him to plant the bulbs in the larger flowerbed?

18 A cuboid has surface area 77.5 m² and volume 43.75 m³.
 The cuboid is enlarged by scale factor 2.5. Work out
 a the surface area of the new cuboid
 b the volume of the new cuboid.
 Give your answers to 3 significant figures.

19 Problem-solving Sian needs 15 ml of paint for a model of a ship.
 She makes another model enlarged by scale factor 4.
 How much paint does she need for the new model?

Q20 hint

You need to give the scale factor and the centre of enlargement.

20 Problem-solving Describe the enlargement of each red object to its blue image.

a 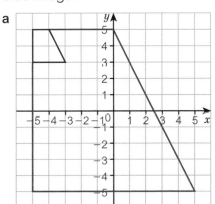   b 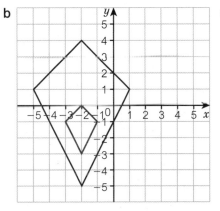   c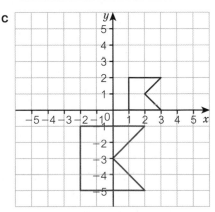

21 Reflect Look back at the questions you answered in these extend lessons.
 They were all about transformations.
 List all the other mathematics topics you used to answer these questions.
 Beside each one, write the type of transformation you used it for.

Master
P101

Check
P117

Strengthen
p119

Extend
p123

TEST

5 Unit test

Log how you did on your Student Progression Chart.

1 Describe fully the rotation that takes shape A to shape B.

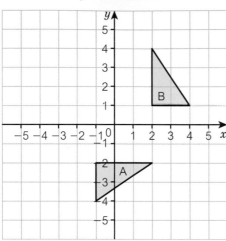

2 Copy the diagram.

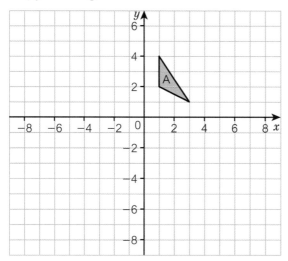

a Reflect shape A in the *y*-axis. Label the image B.

b Rotate shape B 180° about the origin. Label the image C.

c Translate shape C by $\binom{3}{2}$. Label the image D.

d Describe the transformation that takes shape C to shape A.

3 How many planes of symmetry does this regular hexagonal prism have?

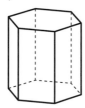

4 Copy the diagram from Q2. Enlarge shape A by

   a centre of enlargement (2, 2), scale factor 2

   b centre of enlargement (0, 1) scale factor −1

   c centre of enlargement (4, −3) scale factor $\frac{1}{2}$

5 Work out the scale factor used to enlarge each shape.

   a
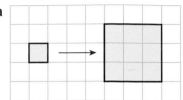
   b
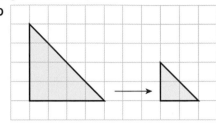

6 A triangle with perimeter 17 cm is enlarged by scale factor 3.
What is the perimeter of the enlarged triangle?

7 A ball with volume 60 cm³ is enlarged by scale factor 2.
What is the volume of the enlarged sphere?

Challenge

8 In the game of Tetris there are seven different tiles you can translate
and rotate to fill a grid with no gaps.

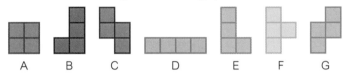

   A   B   C   D   E   F   G

   a Are any of these tiles congruent?

   b Are any tiles rotations of each other?

   Copy this grid. Use the tiles to fill the grid.

   c How many lines can you fill completely?

   d Start with an empty grid then choose
the order of the tiles and see if you
can complete the grid without leaving
any gaps.

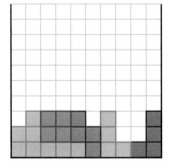

9 **Reflect** List the four transformations you have learned about in this
unit.

Draw a sketch for each of them, to remind you what each
transformation does.

Now read this sentence carefully:

   After _____ the shape and its image are congruent.

Complete this sentence with one or more transformation.

Explain your choice of word(s).

6.1 Recurring decimals

You will learn to:
- Recognise fractional equivalents to some recurring decimals
- Change a recurring decimal into a fraction.

Why learn this?
Some fractions have simple decimal equivalents, but some have recurring digits that go on indefinitely. You need to be able to deal with these decimals when they occur.

Fluency
Round these decimals to 2 decimal places:
3.456, 12.607, 30.0067

Explore
Can you prove that 0.999 999… = 1?

Exercise 6.1

Warm up

1 Convert these fractions to decimals.

   a $\frac{1}{8}$ **b** $\frac{7}{8}$ **c** $\frac{1}{12}$

2 Write each **recurring decimal** using dot notation

   a 0.666 66…   **b** 0.171 717 171…   **c** 0.548 548 548….

> **Q2 Literacy hint**
> In a **recurring decimal** the digits repeat in a pattern forever.

3 Simplify

   a $10x - x$ **b** $100x - x$

4 Solve

   a $7x = 42$ **b** $8x = 72$

5 Solve

   a $2x = 1$ **b** $4x = 3$ **c** $9x = 54$

   d $9x = 12$ **e** $99x = 17$ **f** $99x = 30$

> **Q5 hint**
> Give your answers as fractions in their simplest form.

Investigation   **Problem-solving**

1 Change the fraction $\frac{1}{3}$ into a decimal.
What do you notice?
2 Change $\frac{1}{9}$ into a decimal.
What do you notice?
3 Try changing any proper fraction with 9 as the denominator into a decimal.
What always happens?

---

6 a Write $\frac{1}{6}$ as a decimal.

   b What would be the decimal value of $\frac{10}{6}$? Use your answer to part **a** to help you.

Topic links: Solving equations, Ratio and proportion, Fractions

7 a Reasoning Convert $\frac{1}{11}$ and $\frac{2}{11}$ into decimals.

b Use your answers to part **a** to write the values of $\frac{3}{11}, \frac{4}{11}, \frac{5}{11}, \frac{6}{11}, \frac{7}{11}, \frac{8}{11}, \frac{9}{11}, \frac{10}{11}$.

8 Finance On one day £11 is worth €12.
How much is €1 worth?

9 This cake recipe is for 12 people.
Work out how much of each
ingredient is needed for a
recipe for 7 people.

flour	200 g
butter	150 g
sugar	180 g
eggs	4
vanilla	50 ml

$\frac{7}{12} \times 150$

$\times 1$

> **Q8 Strategy hint**
> Give your answer to the nearest penny.

Worked example

Write $0.\dot{7}$ as a fraction.

$0.\dot{7} = 0.7777777... = n$ — Call the recurring decimal n.

$10n = 7.7777777...$ — Multiply the recurring decimal by 10.

$10n - n = 7.7777777... - 0.7777777...$

$\qquad = 7.000000...$ — Subtract the value of n from the value of $10n$ so you get all the decimal places to zero.

$9n = 7$

$n = \frac{7}{9}$ — Solve the equation.

10 Write these recurring decimals as fractions.

a $0.\dot{1}$ **b** $0.\dot{6}$

> **Q11 Strategy hint**
> Multiply by 100 or 1000.

11 Write each two-figure recurring decimal as a fraction.

a $0.\dot{1}\dot{7}$ **b** $0.8\dot{3}\dot{1}$ **c** $0.\dot{2}3\dot{4}$

12 Write these recurring decimals as fractions.

a $0.1\dot{6}$ **b** $0.2\dot{3}$ **c** $0.4\dot{5}$

> **Q12 Strategy hint**
> Find $100n$ and $10n$, then subtract when you only have the recurring digit after the decimal point.

13 Change these recurring decimals into mixed numbers.

a $3.\dot{4}$ **b** $6.\dot{1}\dot{4}$ **c** $12.\dot{3}\dot{5}$

14 Finance On a particular day the exchange rate is £1 = $0.737373....
Give the exchange rate as £ to $ using whole numbers of £ and $.

> **Q13 Strategy hint**
> Use the same method as Q12 but take care with your equations.

15 Finance On a different day the exchange rate is £1 = $0.787878...
Give the exchange rate as £ to $ using whole numbers of £ and $.

16 Explore Can you prove that 0.999999... = 1?
Is it easier to explore this question now you have completed the lesson?
What further information do you need to be able to answer this?

17 Reflect In this lesson you have been doing lots of work with decimals.
Imagine someone had never seen a decimal point before. How would you
define it? How would you describe what it does? Write a description in your
own words. Compare your description with others in your class.

Explore

Reflect

6.2 Using percentages

You will learn to:
• Calculate percentages
• Work out an original quantity before a percentage increase or decrease.

Why learn this?
You can use percentages to work out an original amount before an increase or decrease.

Fluency
10% is £5. What is 100%?
20% is £20. What is 100%?
25% is £16. What is 100%?

Explore
Employment has risen by 2% to 6.8 million people. How many people were employed before the increase?

Exercise 6.2

1 Write the multiplier for each percentage increase or decrease.
  a 10% increase   **b** 15% increase   **c** 23% decrease
  d 5% decrease   **e** 2.5% increase   **f** 9% decrease

2 In a '20% off' sale there was £60 off a laptop.
  What was the original price?

3 The height of a sunflower seedling increases by 25% from 8.4 cm.
  What is the new height?

Q2 hint

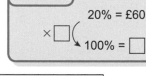

$$20\% = £60$$
$$\times \square \left(\begin{array}{c} \\ 100\% = \square \end{array} \right) \times \square$$

4 **Finance** In an electrical wholesalers, VAT (20%) is added to the selling price of goods at the till. The company provides a table for customers that shows examples of the total price after VAT is added.
Copy and complete the table.

Without VAT	Including VAT
£10	
£15	
£25	
£40	
£60	
£100	
£150	

5 A company emails an offer to 255 customers.
This is 5% of all their customers.
How many customers do they have?

6 A shop owner offers discounts on some items in a sale.
Work out the new price after the discount for each item.
Round your answers to the nearest penny.

Item	Original price	Discount
scented candles	£12.50	25%
house signs	£14.99	20%
desk tidies	£10.50	15%
sealed jars (small)	£7.99	12%
sealed jars (large)	£9.99	14%
coasters	£6.00	22%

7 The value of a car depreciates by 30%.
It originally cost £8000.
What is its value now?

Q7 Literacy hint
Depreciates means goes down in value.

Topic links: Decimals   **Subject links:** Science (Q14)

Worked example

The price of a car is reduced by 15% in a sale to £3825.
What was the original price of the car?

100% − 15% = 85% = 0.85

Original number → ×0.85 → 3825 —— Draw a function machine.

4500 ← ÷0.85 ← 3825

The car's original price was £4500.

Hint

x is the original price:
$x \times 0.85 = 3825$
$0.85x = 3825$
$x = \dfrac{3825}{0.85}$

8 In a sale there is 30% off a pair of jeans.
The sale price is £56. What was the price before the sale?

9 The price of a house increased by 10% to £275 000.
What was the price before the increase?

Q9 hint

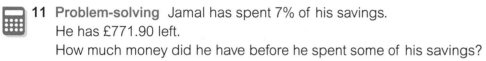

□ → ×1.1 → 275 000

10 **Problem-solving** Michael has been awarded a pay rise of 4%.
His new salary is £24 492.
What was his salary before the pay rise?

11 **Problem-solving** Jamal has spent 7% of his savings.
He has £771.90 left.
How much money did he have before he spent some of his savings?

12 A businesswoman has paid the following expenses including VAT (20%).
She needs to know the costs before VAT was added.
a Taxi fare £8.50 including VAT
b Stationery equipment £45.75 including VAT

13 **Modelling** Fuel prices have increased by 9% this year.
The Smith family's fuel bill for this year is now £1956.
a How much was the bill likely to have been last year?
b Why can't you work out exactly how much the bill was last year?

14 The house sparrow population has decreased by 41% since 1977.
The population is now approximately 6.5 million pairs of birds.
What was the estimated sparrow population in 1977?

15 A TV programme is edited for broadcasting and 17% of the original
programme is cut.
The programme is now $1\frac{1}{2}$ hours long. How long was the original
programme?

16 Holiday prices are 14% higher than last year.
A holiday this year costs £940.50. How much would it have cost last year?

17 **Explore** Employment has risen by 2% to 6.8 million people. How many
people were employed before the increase?
Is it easier to explore this question now you have completed the lesson?
What further information do you need to be able to answer this?

18 **Reflect** Look back at the worked example.
Did the function machine help you to work with percentages?
What other methods have you used in this lesson to help you?

Explore

Reflect

6.3 Percentage change

You will learn to:
- Calculate percentage change.

Why learn this?
Businesses use percentage change to compare profits in different years.

Fluency
What is £20 as a percentage of
- £40
- £80
- £200?

Explore
How can you work out who has made the biggest improvement in maths tests over the year?

Exercise 6.3

1 Rewrite these statements using percentages. Write one number as a percentage of the other. Round your answer to 1 d.p. where necessary.
  a 8 out of 10 cats
  b 15 out of 70 in a test
  c 42 out of 350 computers
  d £2.75 out of £5

2 The number of students in a sixth form centre has increased from 350 to 385.
  a What is the change in the number of students?
  b Write your answer to part **a** as a percentage of the original number, 350.
  Discussion What percentage have student numbers increased by?

3 **Reasoning** 4 people spent 2 weeks training for a weightlifting competition.
  a Calculate the percentage increase in weights lifted by each person.
  b Who made the biggest percentage improvement?

Person	Original weight (kg)	Final weight (kg)
A	74	78
B	68	70
C	90	93
D	107	112

Key point

You can calculate the **percentage change** using the formula
$$\text{percentage change} = \frac{\text{actual change}}{\text{original amount}} \times 100$$

Q3a hint

A $\frac{4}{74} = \square$%

4 **Problem-solving** A new manufacturer claims that you get at least 15% more copies by using their printer ink.
  An office tests this by recording how many copies each printer can make with the old ink and the new ink.
  Is the manufacturer's claim true?
  Discussion How did you work this out? Is there another way?

Printer	Old ink	New ink
printer A	1254	1456
printer B	4152	4786
printer C	4563	5554
printer D	2759	3173

5 **Finance** Neville's salary has risen from £24 558 to £25 540.
  What is the percentage change in his salary? Give your answer to the nearest 0.1%.

Topic links: Using formulae, Rounding

Subject links: Science (Q7), History (Q10)

6 Problem-solving Following a successful series, the producers of a TV programme have been told that the programme will be increased from a $1\frac{1}{2}$ hour programme to a 1 hour 40 minute programme.
The main presenter is claiming that she should get a 7% increase in her salary, because that is the increase in length of the show.
   a Is she right?
   b What do you think her percentage rise should be?

7 Reasoning A fuel company has developed a new fuel that will increase fuel efficiency for cars.
They research the impact of their fuel by testing several different cars and comparing the average distances they can travel on a gallon of the standard fuel and a gallon of the new fuel.

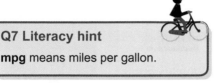

Q7 Literacy hint

mpg means miles per gallon.

Car	mpg (standard fuel)	mpg (new fuel)
A	46.5	51.2
B	42.3	46.7
C	47.6	52.5
D	49.5	55.5

   a On which car does the fuel make the most impact?
   b The new fuel is 10% more expensive than the old fuel. Would it be worth buying it?

8 Finance / Real The Davis family try shopping in a different supermarket to save money.
They used their old supermarket one week, then bought the same items the next week in the new supermarket.
In the first week their bill was £105.20. In the second week it was £98.50.
   a What was the change in their bill?
   b Use the first bill and your answer to part **a** to work out the percentage decrease.

9 Finance Max bought a TV for £3200. He sold it for £800.
What percentage loss did he make on the TV?

10 Real England's population in 1347 was estimated at 4 million.
During the Black Death plague of 1348–50 it fell to 2.5 million.
What was the percentage change in the population after the Black Death?

11 A school changes its lesson times.
Lessons now start at 8.55 am instead of 9.00 am, and finish at 3.05 pm instead of 3.20 pm.
What is the percentage change in the length of the school day?

12 Real / Problem-solving The table shows the estimated population of various pets in the UK between 1965 and 2000.
Which pet population has increased by the greatest percentage?

Pet	1965 population	2000 population
dog	4.7 million	6.5 million
cat	4.1 million	8.0 million
budgerigars	3.3 million	1.0 million

13 Explore How can you work out who has made the biggest improvement in maths tests over the year?
Is it easier to explore this question now you have completed the lesson?
What further information do you need to be able to answer this?

14 Reflect
   a Write a percentage change question where the answer is a 100% profit.
   b Write a percentage change question where the answer is a 100% loss.
   How did you know what kinds of numbers you would need?

6.4 FINANCE: Repeated percentage change

You will learn to:
• Calculate the effect of repeated percentage changes.

CONFIDENCE

Why learn this?
When you save or borrow money the interest is calculated using repeated percentage changes.

Fluency
What is the multiplier for a percentage increase of
• 8%
• 12%
• 0.6%
• 200%?

Explore
How much will your savings be worth in 3 years' time if interest rates stay the same?

Exercise 6.4: Investment and loans

Warm up

1 A bank pays interest on savings at 0.5% per year. Work out the amount in the account at the end of the year when you start with
  a £450   **b** £395

2 Work out
  a 1.15^2 **b** 1.02^4 **c** 2750×1.04^3 (to 2 d.p.)

Investigation

Denise starts with £700 in a bank account that pays 0.8% interest per year. The interest is paid into her account.

1 How much money does she have in her account at the end of year 1?

Your answer to Q1 is the starting amount for year 2.

2 How much money does she have in her account at the end of year 2?

Copy and complete this table to find how much money she has in her account at the end of Year 4..

	Start	Working	End
Year 1	£700	£700 × ☐ _1.08_	756
Year 2	756	×1.08	
Year 3			
Year 4			

---

3 **Problem-solving** Manoj inherits £5400.
A savings account pays him 2.5% **compound interest** per year.
How many years will it be before he has £6000?

Key point

In **compound interest**, the interest earned each year is added to money in the account and earns interest the next year. Most interest rates are compound interest rates.

4 Two competing banks have very similar interest rates.
Work out the difference in the final balances if you invest £5000 in both banks for 4 years.

Bank	Interest rate	Start balance	End of year 1 balance	End of year 2 balance	End of year 3 balance	End of year 4 balance
Bank A	1.2%	£5000	5060	5120.72		
Bank B	1.3%	£5000				

Topic links: Rounding, Using formulae, Index laws, Decimals

Subject links: Science (Q8, Q11), Geography (Q10)

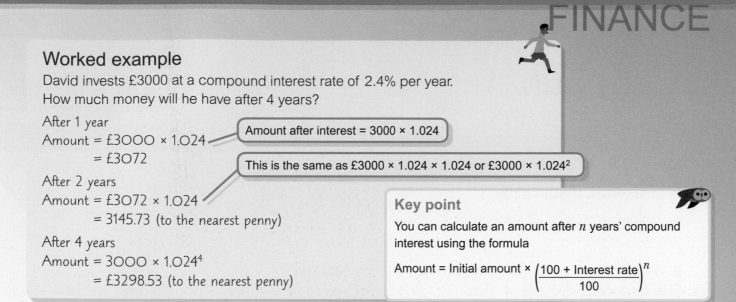

Worked example

David invests £3000 at a compound interest rate of 2.4% per year.
How much money will he have after 4 years?

After 1 year
Amount = £3000 × 1.024
= £3072

> Amount after interest = 3000 × 1.024

> This is the same as £3000 × 1.024 × 1.024 or £3000 × 1.024²

After 2 years
Amount = £3072 × 1.024
= 3145.73 (to the nearest penny)

After 4 years
Amount = 3000 × 1.024⁴
= £3298.53 (to the nearest penny)

> **Key point**
>
> You can calculate an amount after n years' compound interest using the formula
>
> $$\text{Amount} = \text{Initial amount} \times \left(\frac{100 + \text{Interest rate}}{100}\right)^n$$

5 **Finance** Nikita's salary will rise by 3.2% every year for the next 5 years.
Her starting salary is £24 500. What will she earn in 5 years' time?

6 **Finance** A credit card company charges interest at 2% per month on any outstanding balance.
A balance of £1500 is left unpaid. What is the balance after
  a 1 month   b 6 months   c 1 year?

> **Q6 hint**
>
> 1500 × ☐   1 month
> 1500 × ☐² 2 months

7 **Reasoning / Modelling** A colony of rabbits without predators can grow at a rate of 40% per year.
A colony has 20 rabbits. After how long will there be more than 100 rabbits?

8 The value of a car depreciates by 10% every year.
A car cost £26 500. How much is it worth after 5 years?

9 **Real / Modelling** The world population at the end of 2013 was approximately 7.2 billion people. The current growth rate is 1.1% per year.
  a If this growth rate continues, what will the population be in 2100?
  b If the growth rate slows to 0.7% per year, what will the population be in 2100?

10 **Problem-solving** There are 10 bacteria in a Petri dish at the start of the day.
The number doubles every hour.
  a What is the percentage increase from 10 to 20 bacteria?
  b How many bacteria will there be after 24 hours?
  Discussion Why is it not sensible to work out the number at the end of the first week?

11 **Real / Finance** When people have an overdraft at a bank they are charged interest.
Sonny is £45 overdrawn. His bank charges interest at a rate of 2.2% per month.
Sonny doesn't pay off any of his debt for a year but he doesn't spend any more.
How much will he owe at the end of the year?

12 **Explore** How much are my savings going to be worth in 3 years' time if interest rates stay the same?
Is it easier to explore this question now you have completed the lesson?
What further information do you need to be able to answer this?

13 **Reflect** Look back at Q10. Was your answer bigger than you expected?
How did you check whether your answer was sensible?

Explore

Reflect

Master
P129

CHECK

Strengthen
P139

Extend
P143

Test
P147

6 Check up

Log how you did on your
Student Progression Chart.

Recurring decimals

1 Write each fraction as a decimal.

a $\frac{2}{9}$ **b** $\frac{5}{6}$

2 Write the first 12 decimal digits of these recurring decimals.

a $0.\dot{1}4285\dot{7}$

b $0.06\dot{8}\dot{1}$

3 Write these recurring decimals as fractions.

a $0.\dot{7}$

b $0.72\dot{3}\dot{5}$

Using percentages

4 Find the new prices after the given percentage increases.

a £35 increased by 10%

b £105.99 increased by 12%

5 Match each percentage change to a multiplier.

A	increase of 20%	1	0.8
B	decrease of 20%	2	1.02
C	increase of 2%	3	1.8
D	decrease of 98%	4	1.2
E	increase of 0.2%	5	1.002
F	increase of 80%	6	0.02

6 In a supermarket the amount of shelf space for food is being reduced.
Work out the new area for each food type.

a Tea and coffee: $56\,m^2$ reduced by 15%

b Fresh vegetables: $76.5\,m^2$ reduced by 7.5%

7 A television has increased in price by 5%.
The new price is £194.25. What was the original price?

8 A tree surgeon reduces the height of a beech tree by 32%.
The tree is now 4.42 m tall.
How tall was it before it was reduced?

9 The number of bees in a hive has increased from 550 to 649.
Express this change as a percentage.

 10 The average attendance at two football clubs is given for two
seasons below.

Club	2012 attendance	2013 attendance
Denes Dynamos	34 500	30 705
Edgefield Eagles	24 100	21 208

Work out the percentage change in attendance for each club.

Repeated percentage change

 11 Bonita invests £450 in a building society with compound interest rate
of 5% per annum.
How much will she have at the end of 3 years?

 12 Phil is overdrawn by £80 and is charged 2.1% interest per month on
his debt.
At the end of a year he hasn't paid back any money but hasn't spent
any more. How much does Phil owe?

 13 Kimberley buys a car for £7800.
The car depreciates in value by 8% every year.
What is it worth after 4 years?

14 How sure are you of your answers? Were you mostly
😞 **Just guessing**   😐 **Feeling doubtful**   🙂 **Confident**
**What next? Use your results to decide whether to strengthen or
extend your learning.**

Challenge

15 Stephen's grandmother wants to give him some money.
She says he can choose between:
- £500 increasing by 5% every year for 5 years
- £10 per month for 5 years
- £550 increasing by 3% every year for 5 years
- £20 doubling at the end of each year for 5 years
Which should Stephen choose?

6 Strengthen

You will:
- Strengthen your understanding with practice.

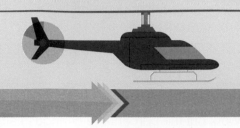

Recurring decimals

1 Which of these are recurring decimals?
  a 0.582 472...
  b 0.666 666...
  c 0.382 382...

Q1 hint

Is there a repeating pattern?

2 Write the first 12 decimal digits of these recurring decimals.
  a 0.$\dot{7}$
  b 0.1$\dot{3}$
  c 0.$\dot{1}\dot{3}$
  d 0.12$\dot{3}$
  e 0.2$\dot{3}\dot{1}$
  f 0.$\dot{3}$1$\dot{7}$

Q2 hint

The digits with dots show the repeating pattern.
So 0.$\dot{2}\dot{4}$ means 0.242 424...
   0.2$\dot{4}$ means 0.244 444...
   0.$\dot{4}$3$\dot{6}$ means 0.436 436...

3 Write as a decimal, using dot notation:
  a $\frac{1}{15}$
  b $\frac{1}{7}$

4 a Write $\frac{1}{6}$ as a decimal using dot notation.
  b Write $\frac{4}{6}$ as a decimal using dot notation.
  c Write another fraction that has the same decimal equivalent as $\frac{4}{6}$.
  d Do all fractions with a denominator of 6 recur? Explain your answer.

Q3a hint

$15\overline{)1.000}$

5 Copy and complete the working to convert 0.$\dot{4}$ into a fraction.

$$n = 0.444...$$
$$10n = 4.444...$$
$$10n - n = \quad 4.444...$$
$$\underline{\quad\quad - 0.444...}$$
$$9n = \square$$
$$n = \square$$

Q4d hint

Try other fractions with a denominator of 6.

6 Write these recurring decimals as fractions.
  a 0.$\dot{6}$
  b 0.$\dot{3}$
  c 0.$\dot{5}$

Q6 hint

Use the same method as in Q5.

7 Write these recurring decimals as fractions.
The first part has been started for you.
  a 0.$\dot{2}\dot{3}$

$$n = 0.2323...$$
$$100n = 23.2323...$$
$$100n - n = \quad 23.2323...$$
$$\underline{\quad\quad\quad - 0.2323...}$$
$$99n = \square$$
$$n = \square$$

  b 0.$\dot{7}\dot{4}$
  c 0.$\dot{8}\dot{1}$

8 Write these recurring decimals as fractions. The first part has been started for you.

a 0.1$\dot{6}$

$$n = 0.1666...$$
$$10n = 1.666...$$
$$100n = 16.666...$$
$$100n - 10n = \square$$
$$90n = \square$$
$$n = \square$$

b 0.6$\dot{7}$　　　　　　**c** 0.4$\dot{6}$

Using percentages

1 Convert these percentages to decimals.
　a 120%　　　　**b** 115%　　　　**c** 90%

 2 Find the new quantities after these percentage increases.
　a Increase 65 by 20%　　**b** Increase 80 by 15%
　c Increase 140 by 7.5%

 3 Find the new quantities after these percentage decreases.
　a Decrease 85 by 10%　　**b** Decrease 120 by 20%
　c Decrease 96 by 24%

 4 Car prices have risen by 5.6%.
　Work out the new price of each car.

Car	Original price
A	£10 500
B	£12 300
C	£5600
D	£22 400

 5 During a recession house prices decrease by 15%.
　Find the new prices of these houses.
　a £185 000　　**b** £225 450　　**c** £375 900

 6 In a shop all prices have been increased by 8%.
　What was the original price of a jacket that now costs £60.48?
　Copy and complete the working.

$$÷108 \Big(\begin{array}{c} 108\% = £60.48 \\ 1\% = £0.56 \\ 100\% = \square \end{array} \Big) ÷108$$
$$×100 \qquad\qquad\qquad ×100$$

 7 Work out the original prices.
　a Riding lessons have increased by 5%.
　　A riding lesson now costs £31.50.
　b Swimwear prices have increased by 12%.
　　A swimsuit now costs £20.16.
　c A phone contract has increased by 11% to £19.98 per month.

Q1 hint

120% = $\frac{120}{100}$

Q2a hint

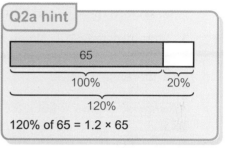

120% of 65 = 1.2 × 65

Q3a hint

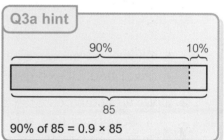

90% of 85 = 0.9 × 85

Q4 hint

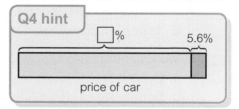

price of car

Q5 hint

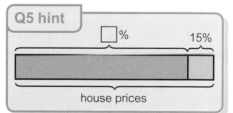

house prices

Q6 hint

100% + 8% = 108%

£60.48

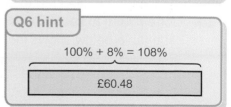

Q7 Strategy hint

Follow the same method as in Q6.

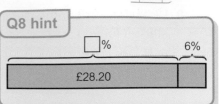

8 In a sale the price of jeans has been reduced by 6% to £28.20.
Copy and complete the working to find the original price before the sale.

$$
\begin{array}{l}
\div 94 \left(\begin{array}{l} 94\% = £28.20 \\ 1\% = £0.30 \\ 100\% = \square \end{array} \right) \div 94 \\
\times 100 \qquad\qquad\qquad \times 100
\end{array}
$$

Q8 hint

$\square$%   6%

£28.20

9 In a sale, television prices have been reduced.
Work out the original prices.
   a Reduced by 4% to £600
   b Reduced by 16% to £630
   c Reduced by 7.5% to £693.75

Q9 hint

Follow the same method as in Q8.

Percentage change

1 Jane invests £6000. When her investment **matures** she receives £6240.
   a Copy and complete the workings to calculate the percentage increase.

   Original amount = £6000

   Actual change = £6240 − £6000 = £240

   Percentage change = $\dfrac{\text{actual change}}{\text{original amount}} \times 100 = \dfrac{£240}{£6000} \times 100 = \square$

   b Check your answer by increasing £6000 by the percentage you calculated. Do you get £6240?

Q1 Literacy hint

Matures means the investment period has finished and the money, plus any interest, is returned to the investor.

Q1a hint

Draw the information given as a bar model.

£6000   £$\square$

£6240

2 a Work out the percentage profit made on each item.
      i Bought for £12, sold for £15
     ii Bought for £15, sold for £19.50
    iii Bought for £240, sold for £444
   b Check your answers.

Q2 hint

Follow the same workings as in Q1.

3 Work out the percentage loss made on each of these items.
   a Bought for £12, sold for £9
   b Bought for £120, sold for £102
   c Bought for £21, sold for £13.23

Q3a hint

Actual change = £3.

4 Marta notices that items have become more expensive at her local supermarket.
She records the old and new prices.
Calculate the percentage change for each item

Item	Old price	New price
multipack crisps	£1.25	£1.30
baked beans (tin)	64p	68p
milk (litre)	£1.50	£1.56
washing powder (1 kg)	£4.80	£5.10

5 Some friends decided to start an exercise regime
for a month to keep fit and healthy.
The table below shows their original mass and their mass after the programme.

Person	Original mass	New mass
Shemar	94 kg	89.3 kg
Daniel	82.5 kg	85.8 kg
Jennifer	76 kg	74.1 kg

   a Calculate the percentage change for each person.
   b Who has lost the greatest proportion of their original mass?
   c Who has gained the greatest proportion of their original mass?

6 Marika invests £800 in the bank at 3% compound interest per year. She leaves all the money in the bank. Copy and complete to work out the amount at the end of 1 year, 2 years and 3 years.

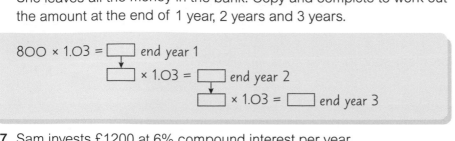

$800 \times 1.03 = \boxed{}$ end year 1

$\boxed{} \times 1.03 = \boxed{}$ end year 2

$\boxed{} \times 1.03 = \boxed{}$ end year 3

7 Sam invests £1200 at 6% compound interest per year. He leaves all the money in the bank. How much will he have at the end of the third year?

8 Three members of the same family invest money in different savings accounts.
Who has the most money after 4 years?

Name	Investment	Interest rate
Anya	£1000	2%
Birgitte	£800	3%
Carlos	£1200	1.9%

9 Samos has stopped using his credit card but he can't pay his credit card bill.
He owes £285 and is charged 2.4% interest per month.
Use the formula

$$\text{amount} = \text{initial amount} \times \left(\frac{100 + \text{interest rate}}{100}\right)^n$$

to work out his debt after 1 year.

10 The value of office equipment depreciates at approximately 20% per year.
Sean says this means his £1000 photocopier will be worth nothing in 5 years' time.
a Explain why Sean is wrong.
b How much will it be worth in 5 years' time?

11 Zunera buys a car for £18500.
It depreciates by 12% per year.
How much will it be worth in 4 years' time?

Enrichment

1 £100 is invested at 1% compound interest for 5 years.
Another £100 is invested at 2% compound interest for 5 years.
Does investing at 2% give you double the increase of 1%?

2 **Reflect** These strengthen lessons suggested using bars to help you answer questions.
Look back at the questions where you used bar models.
Did they help you?
If the bars did help, did you draw your own bar model for other questions?
If they didn't help, what strategies did you use to answer the questions?

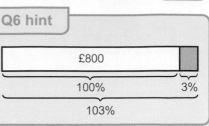

£800

100% 3%

103%

Q7 hint

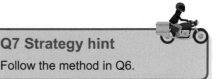

£1200

100% 6%

106%

Q7 Strategy hint
Follow the method in Q6.

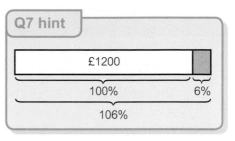

Q8 hint
Work out the amount for each person, then compare.

Q9 hint
Use the compound interest formula with $n = 12$, as interest is charged monthly.

Q10b hint
Follow the same workings as Q8.

Q11 hint
Use the same method in Q10.

Reflect

6 Extend

You will:

- Extend your understanding with problem-solving.

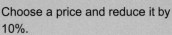

1 A DIY store advertises a '10% off' day.
  The next day prices return to normal.
  A competitor says that the prices have gone up 10% in a day.
  a Is the competitor right?
  b Explain your answer with an example.

Q1 Strategy hint
Choose a price and reduce it by 10%.

2 Find the decimal equivalent of all the fractions with the denominator 14.
  Discussion What is strange about this set of decimals?

Q2 hint
Look at the recurring digits in the answers.

3 Write these recurring decimals as fractions.
  a $0.2\dot{2}\dot{5}$ **b** $0.6\dot{7}\dot{4}$ **c** $0.4\dot{9}\dot{8}$ **d** $0.24\dot{3}$

Q3 hint
You might need to form equations for 10, 100 or 1000 × the decimal.

4 Write $0.\dot{7}14\,28\dot{5}$ as a fraction.

 5 In a large department store all workers have been given a pay rise.
  Find the original salary of each worker given their new salaries and
  these percentage increases:

Staff	Pay rise	New salary
shop floor staff	2.4%	£18 022.40
shop floor manager	2.8%	£24 106.60

Q4 Strategy hint
Choose which multiple of 10 to use when forming your equation.

 6 A large business had to cut back its staff due to falling orders.
  a Calculate the number of staff that used to work in each department.

Q5 Strategy hint
Remember the inverse of multiplication is division.

Department	Percentage reduction	New staff number
telemarketing	7.1%	236
sales	20.6%	448
administration	12.9%	216
accounts	9.8%	462

  b What is the overall reduction in staff as a percentage?

 7 A TV channel has changed the length of various shows to fit into a new
  schedule.
  The new times are given in the table, along with the percentage change.
  Work out how long the shows used to be.

Show	Percentage change	New length
Breakfast show	12.5% reduction	35 minutes
Buy that house!	8.3% increase	1 hour 5 minutes
Rip-off busters	6.7% increase	1 hour 20 minutes
Helicopter rescues	21.4% decrease	55 minutes
Lunchtime news	44.4% decrease	45 minutes

Original value	Percentage decrease	New value	Percentage increase	Original value
100	10%	90	11.1%	100

In the table a quantity has been reduced by a percentage, then increased by a different percentage to return to the original value.
Investigate other percentage decreases. Is there a pattern in the increase required to return the quantity to its original value?

Hint

It might help to think of the percentage decrease and increase as fractions.

 8 Problem-solving The perimeter of the blue square is 20% greater than the perimeter of the green square.
Work out the side length of the green square.

perimeter = 32.8 cm

☐ cm

 9 Reasoning Between the ages of 3 and 5 years old a tree grows at a rate of approximately 10% per year.
At 5 years old it is 2.5 m tall.

  a Work out the height of the tree when it is
    i 4 years old   **ii** 3 years old.
    Write each answer correct to the nearest cm.

  b Andy says, 'The tree has grown 10% each year for 2 years, which makes 20% in total. This means if I divide 2.5 m by 1.2 I will find the height of the tree when it is 3 years old.'
    Is Andy correct? Explain your answer.

 10 Problem-solving Between 2011 and 2012 visitor numbers to a museum increased by 25%.
Between 2012 and 2013 visitor numbers to the museum decreased by 10%.
In 2013 there were 71 856 visitors.
How many visitors were there in 2011?

Q10 Strategy hint

Work out how many visitors there were in 2012 first.

11 Problem-solving There are 10 singers in a church choir.
One singer leaves and another singer arrives.
The mean age of the choir increases by 5% to 63 years old.

  a What is the mean age of the singers before the first singer leaves?
The singer who leaves is 32 years old.

  b What is the age of the singer who arrives?

Q11 hint

Work out the total age of the singers before the first singer leaves and after the second singer arrives.

 12 Jonah has been observing wild birds in his garden since he put in a new bird table.
This table shows how many birds visited on 2 different days.

Bird	Day 1	Day 2
sparrow	56	95
chaffinch	45	84
gold crest	25	37
blue tit	98	135
blackbird	17	24

Which type of bird has had the greatest percentage increase?

13 **a** Copy and complete the table.

Fraction	$\frac{1}{2}$	$\frac{1}{3}$	$\frac{1}{4}$	$\frac{1}{5}$	$\frac{1}{6}$	$\frac{1}{7}$	$\frac{1}{8}$	$\frac{1}{9}$	$\frac{1}{10}$	$\frac{1}{12}$	$\frac{1}{20}$
Decimal	0.5	0.$\dot{3}$	0.25	0.2							

b Which denominators give recurring decimals?

c Which denominators give **finite** decimals?

d Write each denominator as a product of prime factors.

e Dan says, 'If the denominator only has prime factors of 2 and 5, the fraction is finite'.

Is Dan correct? Test his idea on these fractions.

$\frac{3}{5}$ $\frac{3}{17}$ $\frac{9}{25}$ $\frac{12}{40}$ $\frac{11}{100}$ $\frac{157}{160}$

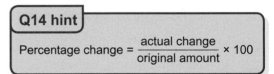

Key point

Finite decimals stop after a number of decimal places.

14 **Real / Reasoning** The line graph shows the mean household mortgage and rent payments from 2011 to 2013.

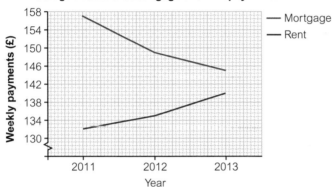

Average household mortgage and rent payments

— Mortgage
— Rent

Weekly payments (£)

Year

a Work out the percentage increase, to the nearest 1%, in rent payments for the average household between
   i 2011 and 2012   **ii** 2012 and 2013   **iii** 2011 and 2013.

b Explain why the sum of your answers to parts **i** and **ii** is not the same as your answer to part **iii**.

c Work out the percentage decrease, to the nearest 1%, in mortgage payments for the average household between
   i 2011 and 2012   **ii** 2012 and 2013.

Q14 hint

$$\text{Percentage change} = \frac{\text{actual change}}{\text{original amount}} \times 100$$

15 **Real / Reasoning** The pie charts show the proportion of oil used for energy in the UK in 1980 and 2012.

In 1980 the total amount of oil used for energy in the UK was 150 million tonnes.

In 2012 the total amount of oil used for energy in the UK was 140 million tonnes.

a How many tonnes of oil was used by transport in 1980?

b How many tonnes of oil was used by transport in 2012?

c Work out the percentage increase in the amount of oil used by transport from 1980 to 2012.

d Work out the percentage decrease in the amount of oil used by industry from 1980 to 2012.

e 'Other' accounted for 13% in 1980 and 2012. Does this mean that the same amount of oil was used by 'Other' activities in 1980 and 2012?

Explain your answer.

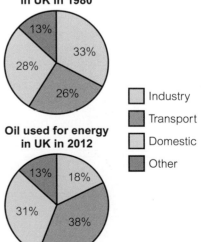

Oil used for energy in UK in 1980

13%
33%
28%
26%

Oil used for energy in UK in 2012

13%
18%
31%
38%

☐ Industry
☐ Transport
☐ Domestic
☐ Other

Source: DECC

Topic links: Ratio

16 £8000 is invested in a savings account at a compound interest rate of 3% per year.

$$\text{Amount} = \text{initial amount} \times \left(\frac{100 + \text{interest rate}}{100}\right)^n$$

a How much is the investment worth after 5 years?

b How many years will it be before the investment is worth more than £10000?

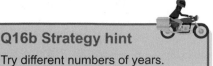
Q16b Strategy hint
Try different numbers of years.

 17 Some mortgages charge interest on a daily basis.
Boris has a £178000 mortgage that charges interest at 0.02% per day.
How much does he owe in total at the end of a 31-day month when he does not make any payments?

 18 In 2012 the population of the UK was 63.23 million.
What will the population be in 2020 if the population increases at a rate of 0.9% per year?

19 Reasoning / Modelling On a small island there is a population of 500 rabbits and 60 foxes.
The rabbit population increases at a rate of 24% per year.
The fox population increases at a rate of 85% per year.

a How many rabbits and foxes will there be after 10 years?

b When does the population of foxes first become greater than the population of rabbits?

 20 Some mortgages charge interest annually. Frank has a mortgage like this.
He has borrowed £120000 to buy a house and is charged 3.5% interest on the outstanding debt at the start of each year.

a He pays £800 per month in mortgage repayments.
How much does he owe at the start of the second year?

b The interest rate stays the same and so do his repayments.
How much does he owe at the start of the third year?

c How many years will it take Frank to pay off his mortgage?

21 Reflect Look back at Q20. How did you decide what to do first?
Did your strategy work the first time?
For what other questions did you need to make a plan first?
Did it help you?

6 Unit test

1 Write each fraction as a decimal.

   a $\frac{5}{9}$

   b $\frac{5}{12}$

   c $\frac{7}{15}$

   d $\frac{8}{11}$

2 Write each recurring decimal using the correct notation.

   a 0.166666…

   b 0.232323…

   c 0.136136…

3 Find the new value after each quantity has been increased by the given percentage.

   a 56 kg increased by 15%

   b 436 g increased by 12.5%

4 Find the new value after each quantity has been decreased by the given percentage.

   a 43 cm decreased by 20%

   b £550 decreased by 8.5%

5 The price of an MP3 player is increased by 8% to £52.92.
   What was the original price?

6 The population of blackbirds in a park is counted every year.
   The population decreases by 24% to 323.
   What was the original population?

7 Write each recurring decimal as a fraction.

   a $0.\dot{8}$

   b $0.\dot{2}\dot{7}$

   c $0.3\dot{9}$

   d $0.\dot{3}4\dot{5}$

8 Which of these fractions can be written as recurring decimals?

   a $\frac{3}{5}$

   b $\frac{3}{20}$

   c $\frac{4}{25}$

9 Marcia bought a car for £34 500 and sold it for £29 700.
   What was her percentage loss?

10 A sunflower has increased in height from 72.4 cm to 86.2 cm. What is the percentage increase?

11 Lyndal invests £4650 in a savings account paying compound interest of 3%. How much money will she have in her account after 3 years?

12 The number of foxes on an island is reducing at the rate of 23% per year. There are 96 foxes to start with. How many will there be after 5 years?

13 The value of a car depreciates by 12% per year. If the car was £24 500 when it was new, find the predicted value after 3 years.

14 Josh has an overdraft of £80 at the bank. He is charged interest at 1.9% per month. He doesn't pay any money back but nor does he spend any more. How much will he owe by the end of a year?

15 The population of Scotland in 2012 was 5.3 million. Calculate the population of Scotland in 2020 if the growth rate is 1.1% per year.

Challenge

16 A 10 volt battery loses 1% of its capacity every time it is recharged. How many times can it be recharged before its capacity falls to below 1 volt?

17 **Reflect** Make a list of all the different ways you have used multiplication in this unit. Compare your list with your classmates.

Reflect

7.1 Accurate drawings

You will learn to:
- Draw triangles accurately using a ruler and protractor
- Draw diagrams to scale.

CONFIDENCE

Why learn this?
Mapmakers and surveyors use accurate scale drawings to work out positions of objects.

Fluency
$10 \times \square = 130$
$100 \times \square = 240$

Explore
How is triangulation used to make maps?

Exercise 7.1

Warm up

1 Draw an accurate line 8.2 cm long.

2 Draw these angles accurately.

a

27°

b
138°

3 Sketch a triangle ABC with a right angle at B.
Mark the right angle.
Label side AB 5 cm. Label CÂB 40°.

4 For each triangle
   i use a ruler and protractor to draw each triangle accurately
   ii measure the length of side BC and write it on your diagram
   iii measure angles ABC and BCA and write them on your diagram.

a
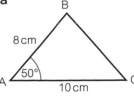
B
8 cm
A 50°
10 cm
C

b
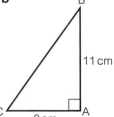
B
11 cm
C
8 cm
A

c
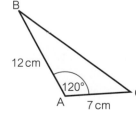
B
12 cm
120°
A 7 cm
C

Q4a Strategy hint

Draw one side accurately.
10 cm

Draw the angle accurately.
50°
10 cm

Make the other side the correct length.
8 cm
50°
10 cm

Draw the third side.
8 cm
50°
10 cm

Topic links: Properties of triangles and quadrilaterals, Compound measures

Subject links: Geography (Q14)

5 a Draw accurately an isosceles triangle DEF with DE = DF = 12 cm and angle EDF = 32°.

b Measure and write the length of EF.

Q5a hint

Sketch the triangle first.

6 Use a ruler and protractor to draw each triangle accurately.

a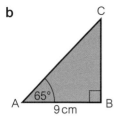

b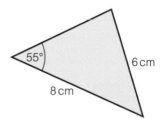

Q6a hint

Draw lines at 40° and 70° to AC.
Point B is where the two lines cross.

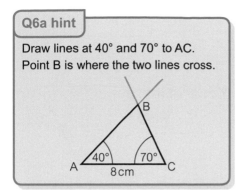

7 Use a ruler and protractor to accurately draw each triangle PQR.

a PQ = 7.5 cm, QP̂R = 45°, PQ̂R = 55°

b PQ = 8.2 cm, QR = 10.3 cm, PQ̂R = 90°

c PQ = 6.5 cm, PQ̂R = 130°, QR = 8.5 cm

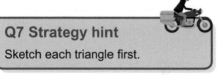

Q7 Strategy hint

Sketch each triangle first.

8 Reasoning Is it possible to draw this triangle accurately? Explain your answer.

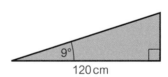

Q8 hint

Start by drawing the 8 cm side and the line at angle 55°.

9 Real The diagram shows a wheelchair ramp.

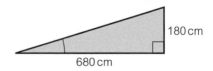

Key point

A **scale** of 1 cm to 10 cm means that 1 cm on the **scale drawing** represents 10 cm in real life.

a Make an accurate **scale drawing** of the ramp.
Use a **scale** of 1 cm to 10 cm.

b Measure the sloping length of the scale drawing.

c Work out the sloping length of the actual ramp.

Q9a hint

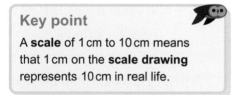

10 Reasoning The diagram shows a water ski jump.

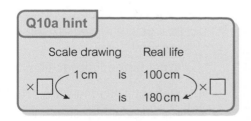

a Make an accurate scale drawing of the water ski jump.
Use a scale of 1 cm to 100 cm.

b Measure the marked angle the jump makes with the horizontal.

c i Measure the sloping length of the scale drawing.
ii Work out the sloping length of the actual jump.

Q10a hint

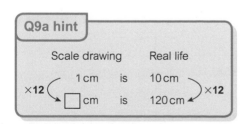

11 Problem-solving Use a ruler and protractor to draw each quadrilateral accurately.

a
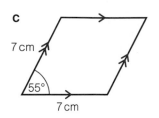
4.3 cm
8.5 cm

b
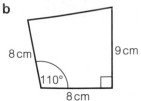
8 cm   9 cm
110°
8 cm

c
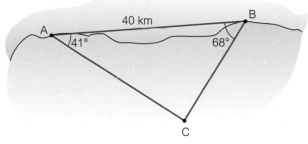
7 cm
55°
7 cm

d
12 cm   5 cm
140°
12 cm   5 cm

Q11c, d Strategy hint

Sketch the quadrilateral first. Use your knowledge of quadrilaterals to label the angles and sides on your sketch.

12 Real The diagram shows two radar stations A and B detecting a yacht C in trouble.
The radar stations are 40 km apart.

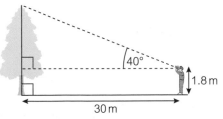

A   40 km   B
41°   68°
C

a Make an accurate scale drawing using a scale of 1 cm to 5 km.
b Work out the real distances AC and BC.
c A lifeboat travels from each radar station at a speed of 25 km/h.
Use the formula time = $\frac{\text{distance}}{\text{speed}}$ to work out how long it takes each lifeboat to reach the yacht at C.

Q12b hint

Start by using your scale drawing to measure the distance of the yacht from each radar station.

13 STEM / Real Gareth uses a **clinometer** to work out the height of a tree by measuring the angle between the top of the tree and his eye level. He is 1.8 m tall.

40°
1.8 m
30 m

Make a scale drawing of the right-angled triangle and work out the height of the tree.

Q13 Literacy hint

A **clinometer** is a tool used to measure the angle from the horizontal in a right-angled triangle.

Q13 hint

Don't forget to add Gareth's height to the height of the triangle.

14 Explore How is triangulation used to make maps?
Is it easier to explore this question now you have completed the lesson?
What further information do you need to be able to answer this?

15 Reflect Rhianne says, 'You can draw a triangle with any length sides, as long as they aren't negative.'
Give an example to show that Rhianne is wrong.

7.2 Constructing shapes

You will learn to:

* Draw accurate nets of 3D solids
* Construct triangles using a ruler and compasses
* Construct nets of 3D solids using a ruler and compasses.

CONFIDENCE

Why learn this?
Packaging designers need to construct accurate nets for boxes.

Fluency
How many faces does each 3D solid have?
* cuboid
* triangular prism
* square-based pyramid

Explore
What area of cardboard is needed to make a box for a rolled-up poster?

Exercise 7.2

1 Here are the nets of some 3D solids.
Name the 3D solid made by each net.

a

b

c

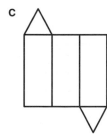

d

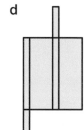

Warm up

2 Use a ruler and protractor to accurately draw a net of each triangular prism.

Q2 Strategy hint
Sketch the net first. Write all the lengths you know on your sketch. Mark the right angles.

a

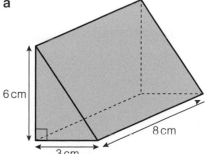

6 cm
8 cm
3 cm

b

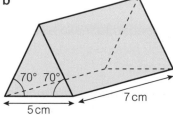

70° 70°
5 cm
7 cm

Worked example

Construct a triangle with sides 10 cm, 11 cm and 7 cm.

1	2	3	4	5
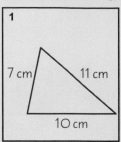	10 cm	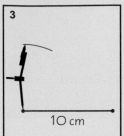 10 cm	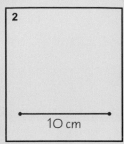 10 cm	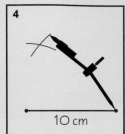

1 Sketch the triangle first.
2 Draw a 10 cm line.
3 Open your compasses to 7 cm. Place the point at one end of the 10 cm line. Draw an arc.
4 Open your compasses to 11 cm. Draw an arc from the other end of the 10 cm line.
 Make sure your arcs are long enough to intersect.
5 Join the intersection of the arcs to each end of the 10 cm line.
 Don't rub out your construction marks.

Key point

To **construct** means to draw accurately using a ruler and compasses.

3 Construct each triangle ABC.
  a AB = 9 cm, BC = 6 cm and CA = 6 cm
  b AB = 7 cm, BC = 3 cm and CA = 8.5 cm
  c AB = 12.8 cm, BC = 11.9 cm and CA = 3.2 cm

Q3 Strategy hint

Sketch the triangles first.
Remember not to rub out your construction marks.

4 Draw an equilateral triangle with sides 7.5 cm.
 Check the angles using a protractor.
 Discussion How could you construct an angle of 60° without using a protractor?

5 **Real** The diagram shows a 900 cm ladder leaning against a wall.
 The foot of the ladder is 270 cm from the wall.
 The ladder reaches a height of 830 cm up the wall.
  a Use a ruler and compasses to make an accurate scale drawing.
     Use a scale of 1 cm to 100 cm.
  b Safety guidelines say that a ladder should make a maximum angle of 75° to the ground. Use your protractor to check if this ladder is safe.

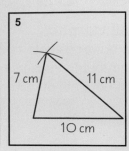
900 cm · 830 cm · 270 cm

6 Each face of a four-sided dice is an equilateral triangle.
 Use a ruler and compasses to construct a net of the dice.

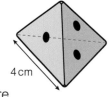
4 cm

7 The Great Pyramid of Khafre has a square base of side 220 m and a sloping edge of length 210 m.
 Construct a net of the pyramid on squared paper.
 Use a scale of 1 cm to 50 m.

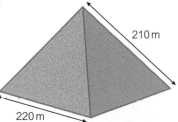
210 m · 220 m

8 **Explore** What area of cardboard is needed to make a box for a rolled-up poster? Look back at the maths you have learned in this lesson. How can you use it to answer this question?

9 **Reflect** In this lesson and the last one you drew constructions and accurate diagrams. What were you good at? What were you not so good at? Write yourself a hint to help you with the constructions or diagrams you are not so good at.

Q7 hint

Start by drawing two sides of the square base.
Then draw two arcs to find the other corner of the square.

7.3 Constructions 1

You will learn to:

* Bisect a line using a ruler and compasses
* Construct perpendicular lines using a ruler and compasses.

Why learn this?
Constructions reduce measurement error.

Fluency
What do these words mean?
* perpendicular
* intersect
* arc

Explore
What is the shortest distance from a point in a field to the edge?

Exercise 7.3

1 Use a ruler and compasses to construct this triangle.

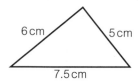

6 cm   5 cm
7.5 cm

2 a What is the name of this quadrilateral?
  b How many lines of symmetry does it have?
  c Sketch the quadrilateral and draw the diagonals.
  d Write on the diagram any information you know about its angles, lengths, parallel sides and right angles.

3 a Draw two intersecting circles with radius 5 cm.

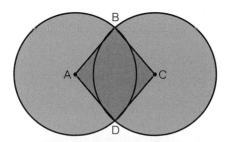

  b Join the centres to the points of intersection, B and D.
  c What is the name of the quadrilateral ABCD?
    Explain your answer.
  d Join the centres A and C using a straight line.
    Join the points of intersection B and D using a straight line.
  e What can you say about the point of intersection of AC and BD?

Q3e hint

Measure the lines and angles.

Worked example

Draw a line 7 cm long.
Construct its **perpendicular bisector**.

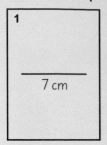
1

2

3

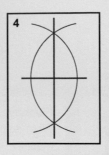
4

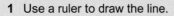
7 cm

1 Use a ruler to draw the line.
2 Open your compasses to more than half the length of the line.
   Place the point on one end of the line and draw an arc above and below.
3 Keeping the compasses open to the same distance, move the point to the
   other end of the line and draw a similar arc.
4 Join the points where the arcs intersect.
   Don't rub out your construction marks.
   This vertical line is the perpendicular bisector.

Key point

A **perpendicular bisector** cuts a
line in half at right angles.

Literacy hint

To **bisect** means to cut in half.

4 a Draw a straight line AB 8 cm long.
   Construct its perpendicular bisector.
   b Use a ruler and protractor to check that it bisects your line at a right angle.
   c Mark any point P on your perpendicular bisector.
   Measure its distance from A and from B.
   Discussion What do you notice about point P?

5 In triangle ABC, AB = 5 cm, AC = 7 cm and BC = 7 cm.
   a Use a ruler and compasses to construct the triangle.
   b What kind of triangle is ABC?
   c Construct the perpendicular bisector of AB.
   d Describe the shapes you have made.

Q5d hint

Use mathematical words.

6 a Draw a straight line AB 12 cm long.
   Mark the point P on AB 7 cm from A.
   b Follow these steps to construct a line through P that is
   perpendicular to AB.
   i Open your compasses to less than the distance PB.
   ii Put the point of the compasses at point P.
   iii Draw the two red arcs centred on P. Label them Q and R.
   iv Open your compasses a little more.
   v Construct the perpendicular bisector of QR.

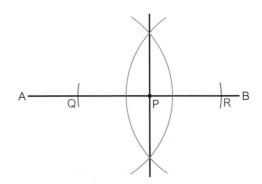

7 Use the method in Q6 to construct each pair of perpendicular lines.

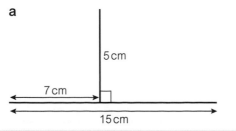
a

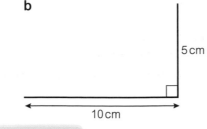
b

Q7a hint

Label your diagram with letters as
in Q6.

Q7b hint

Draw your starting line much longer
than 10 cm, so that you can construct
the arcs.

Topic links: Area of a triangle

8 Use a ruler and compasses to construct

  a a rectangle with length 9 cm and width 6 cm

  b a right-angled triangle ABC where angle ABC = 90°,
    AB = 7.5 cm and BC = 4 cm

  c a square of side 6.2 cm.

Q8 hint

Sketch each shape first. Label it with the information you know. Think through the steps you need to carry out.

9 **Reasoning** Daniel is drawing the perpendicular from point P to line AB.
He has drawn an arc centred on P.

  a Draw the line AB and point P.
    Draw your own arc.
    Label the points Q and R.

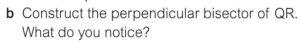

Q9a hint

Choose a large arc to make Q and R far apart. This makes it easier to bisect QR.

  b Construct the perpendicular bisector of QR.
    What do you notice?

  Discussion What is the shortest distance from P to the line AB?

10 The diagram shows the plan of part of a prison.
The scale is 1 cm to 10 m.

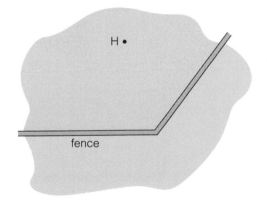

fence

The prisoners want to dig two tunnels from their hut H to each section of fence.
The tunnels must be as short as possible.

  a Trace the diagram.

  b Use a ruler and compasses to construct the route of each tunnel.

  c Work out the difference in the lengths of the tunnels.

Investigation   **Problem-solving**

How many different triangles ABC can you construct with
AB = 8 cm, BC = 4 cm and angle CAB = 30°?
Use a ruler and compasses to construct your triangles.

Hint

There is more than one.

---

11 **Explore** What is the shortest distance from a point in a field to the edge?
Look back at the maths you have learned in this lesson.
How can you use it to answer this question?

12 **Reflect** Look back at the investigation.
What was the first step you took in solving the problem?
Is it possible to write a similar problem where there are more possible triangles?
Explain your answer.

Explore

Reflect

7.4 Constructions 2

You will learn to:
- Bisect angles using a ruler and compasses
- Draw accurate diagrams to solve problems.

Why learn this?
A ruler and compasses can be used to draw angles and solve problems without using a protractor.

Fluency
Describe a trapezium.
How can you work out the area of a trapezium?

Explore
Which regular polygons can you draw using only a ruler and compasses?

Exercise 7.4

1 Construct a 60° angle.

2 Use only a ruler and compasses to construct each diagram.

a
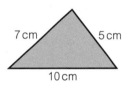
7 cm 5 cm
10 cm

b
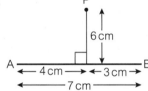
P
6 cm
A 4 cm 3 cm B
7 cm

Q2 hint

Remember to show all your construction marks.
Don't rub them out.

3 In a scale drawing 1 cm represents 4 m.
 a What does a 3 cm line on the scale drawing represent in real life?
 b How long is 10 m in real life on the scale drawing?

Worked example

Draw an angle of 70°.
Construct the **angle bisector**.

Key point

An **angle bisector** cuts an angle exactly in half.

1	2	3
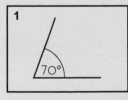 70°	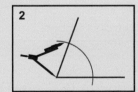	

4	5
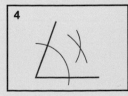	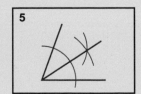

1 Draw the 70° angle using a protractor.
2 Open your compasses and place the point at the vertex of the angle. Draw an arc that cuts both arms of the angle.
3 Keep the compasses open to the same distance.
 Move them to one of the points where the arc crosses the arms. Make an arc in the middle of the angle.
4 Do the same from the point where the arc crosses the other arm.
5 Join the vertex of the angle to the point where the two small arcs intersect. Don't rub out your construction marks.
 This line is the angle bisector.

4 For each angle
  i draw the angle using a protractor
  ii bisect the angle using a ruler and compasses
  iii check your two smaller angles using a protractor.

Q4 hint

Measure each angle first, using a protractor.

a 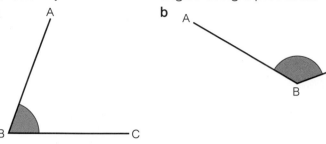   **b**

5 Problem-solving Use a ruler and compasses to construct each angle. Check your angles using a protractor.
  a 30°   **b** 45°
  Discussion What is the same about constructing a perpendicular to a line and bisecting a 180° angle?

Q5 Strategy hint

Start by constructing a larger angle, then bisect it.

6 STEM / Problem-solving The diagram shows a rectangular room with a burglar alarm sensor in one corner. Any movement in the shaded area triggers an alarm.
  a Make a scale drawing of the rectangle on squared paper.
  b Use a ruler and compasses to construct the angle.
  c Calculate the shaded area.

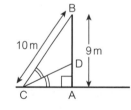

Q6a hint

Choose a suitable scale.

7 Problem-solving Two wires connect the mast AB to the deck of a yacht. The wire CD bisects angle ACB.
  a Use a ruler and compasses to construct a scale drawing. Use a scale of 1 cm to 2 m.
  b Work out the length of the wire CD.

Q7 hint

Start by constructing the perpendicular AB.

8 Problem-solving Use a ruler and compasses to construct this kite.

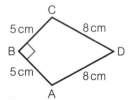

9 Problem-solving / Reasoning Sketch a quadrilateral for a classmate to construct. Make sure you can construct it yourself first.

Q9 hint

Think of the different quadrilaterals you've learned to construct, and the facts you know about them.

10 Explore Which regular polygons can you draw using only a ruler and compasses? Look back at the maths you have learned in this lesson. How can you use it to answer this question?

12 Reflect Look back at the constructions you did in this and the previous lesson.
  Which do you find easier:
  • using a straight edge and compasses to construct, or
  • using a ruler and protractor to measure lengths and angles accurately?
  Explain your answer.

Explore

Reflect

7.5 Loci

You will learn to:
- Draw a locus
- Use loci to solve problems.

Why learn this?
GPS pinpoints your location using the intersection of spheres around satellites.

Fluency
How can you check that two lines are parallel?
What is an angle bisector?

Explore
How much of a car's windscreen can you wipe with two wipers?

CONFIDENCE

Exercise 7.5

1 Draw a circle with radius 7 cm.
   Measure the distance from the centre of the circle to the outside edge in any direction. What do you notice?

2 Draw a line of length 6.8 cm.
   Construct the perpendicular bisector.

3 Draw an angle of 80°.
   Construct the angle bisector.

4 A 5 m dog lead is attached to a spike on a beach. At the other end of the lead is a dog. The dog runs with the lead pulled tight.
   Sketch the dog's path (or **locus**).

> **Key point**
> A **locus** is the set of all points that obey a certain rule. Often the locus is a path.

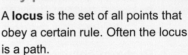

> **Q4 Literacy hint**
> The plural of locus is **loci**.

Investigation — Reasoning

Mark two points 12 cm apart. Label them A and B.
1 Mark a point that is
   a 6 cm from point A and from point B
   b 7 cm from point A and from point B
   c 8 cm from point A and from point B
2 Join the points you have drawn with a line. What does this line show?
3 How could you draw a line showing all the points **equidistant** from A and B?

> **Key point**
> Points that are **equidistant** from points A and B are the same distance away from points A and B.

5 **STEM** Two identical magnets are fixed 12 cm apart, with the north poles facing each other.
   a Draw a diagram to show this.
   A metal ball moves so it is always equidistant from both north poles.
   b Construct the locus of the moving ball.

> **Key point**
> Points equidistant from points A and B lie on the perpendicular bisector of line AB.

6 a Draw an angle of 60°.
   b Construct the angle bisector.
   c Measure a distance of 3 cm from the vertex along each arm of the 60° angle and mark each point.

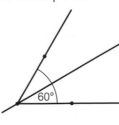

Subject links: Science (Q5)

d Measure the shortest distance from each point to the angle bisector.

e Repeat with two new points 5 cm from the vertex.

Discussion What do you notice? What could you say about any point on the angle bisector?

7 **Real** Two houses share a garden as shown. The owners agree to divide the garden between them with a new fence equidistant from the existing two fences.

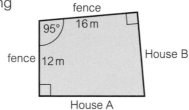

fence
95° 16 m
fence 12 m
House B
House A

a Draw an accurate diagram showing where the new fence will be. Use a scale of 2 cm to 1 m.

b How long will the new fence be?

Key point

Points equidistant from two lines lie on the angle bisector.

8 **a** Draw a 9 cm line on cm squared paper. A point moves so it is always exactly 3 cm away from the line.

b Draw points 3 cm from the line.

c Use compasses to draw points 3 cm from the ends.

Discussion Describe the locus of a point that moves at a fixed distance from a line.

9 Draw a 7 cm by 9 cm rectangle on cm squared paper. Draw the locus of a point that is 4 cm away from this rectangle.

10 **Problem-solving** Two mobile phone masts are 11 km apart. Each mast transmits 6 km in any direction.

a Draw a scale diagram to show clearly the range of each mast. Use a scale of 1 cm to 2 km.

b Is there anywhere on the straight line between the masts where there is no phone signal? Explain your answer.

Q10a hint

What shape do the points that are 6 km away in any direction make?

11 **STEM** A radio transmitter on a space station transmits in every direction. The signal strength is strong up to a distance of 100 km from the transmitter. What shape is the region with a strong signal?

12 **Explore** How much of a car's windscreen can you wipe with two wipers? Is it easier to explore this question now you have completed the lesson? What further information do you need to be able to answer this?

13 **Reflect** Isabel says, 'This lesson is about loci, but I've used lots of other mathematics knowledge and skills.' Look back at all the questions in this lesson and make lists of all the knowledge and skills you have used. Read your lists. Put a star beside any of the knowledge or skills you do not feel confident about. Ask a friend or your teacher to explain them to you.

Explore

Reflect

7 Check up

Log how you did on your Student Progression Chart.

Accurate drawings

1 Use a ruler and protractor to draw each triangle.

a

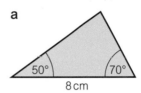

50°   70°
8 cm

b

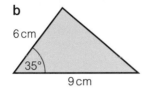

6 cm
35°
9 cm

2 Make a scale drawing of this park. Use a scale of 1 cm to 100 m.

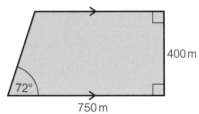

400 m

72°

750 m

Constructions

3 a Draw an angle of 120° using a protractor.

120°

b Construct the angle bisector.

4 a Draw a line AB 10 cm long.
b Construct the perpendicular bisector of AB.

5 Construct a net of this triangular prism on centimetre squared paper.

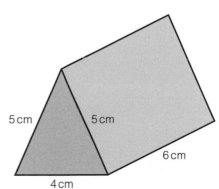

5 cm   5 cm

6 cm

4 cm

Loci

6 A 12 m rope is attached to a metal spike into the ground.
At the other end of the rope is a paintbrush.
The rope is pulled tight and the end moved clockwise.

a Sketch the shape the paintbrush draws on the ground.

b Draw a scale diagram of this.
Use a scale of 1 cm to 3 m.

paintbrush

12 m rope

spike

7 Draw two points that are exactly 5 cm apart.
Construct the locus of the points that are equidistant from these two points.

8 Draw two lines meeting at an angle of 70°.
Construct the locus of the points that are equidistant from the two lines.

9 a Draw a line 8 cm long.

b Construct the locus of points exactly 4 cm from the line.

10 **How sure are you of your answers? Were you mostly**

😟 **Just guessing**   😐 **Feeling doubtful**   🙂 **Confident**

What next? Use your results to decide whether to strengthen or extend your learning.

Reflect

Challenge

11 The scale drawing shows two pyramids A and B and a watering hole W. The scale of the diagram is 1 cm to 10 km.

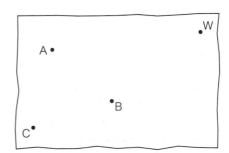

A camel train sets off from C.
It follows a path equidistant from both pyramids.

a Trace the diagram.

b Construct the camel train's path.

c Work out its shortest distance from the watering hole.

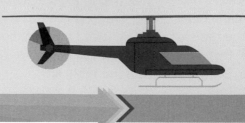

7 Strengthen

You will:
- Strengthen your understanding with practice.

Accurate drawings

1 a Use a ruler and protractor to draw this angle.

   b Join points B and C to make a triangle.

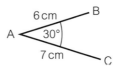

2 Use a ruler and protractor to draw each triangle accurately.

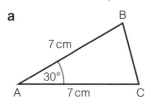   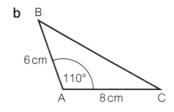   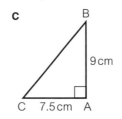

Q2 Strategy hint

Draw the angle first.

3 Use a ruler and protractor to draw each triangle accurately.

   a DE = 6 cm, DF = 7 cm, $E\hat{D}F$ = 40°

   b PQ = 8.5 cm, PR = 8.5 cm, $Q\hat{P}R$ = 90°

   c XY = 7.3 cm, XZ = 8 cm, $Y\hat{X}Z$ = 120°

Q3 Strategy hint

Sketch each triangle first.
Label lengths and angles.

4 Use a ruler and protractor to draw each triangle accurately.

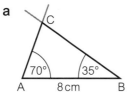   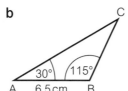   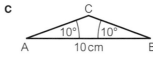

Q4 Strategy hint

Draw the line.

Draw one angle.

Draw the other angle.

5 Use a ruler and protractor to draw these triangles accurately.

   a DE = 7 cm, $D\hat{E}F$ = 15°, $E\hat{D}F$ = 85°

   b PQ = 8.5 cm, $P\hat{Q}R$ = 130°, $Q\hat{P}R$ = 20°

   c XY = 6.2 cm, $X\hat{Y}Z$ = 90°, $Y\hat{X}Z$ = 25°

6 Here is a sketch of a field.

   a On a scale drawing of the field,
   where 1 cm represents 100 m,
   how long is

     i 700 m

     ii 500 m

     iii 650 m?

   b Make an accurate scale drawing of the field using a
   ruler and protractor.

   c Measure the diagonal BD.

   d Work out the real distance BD.

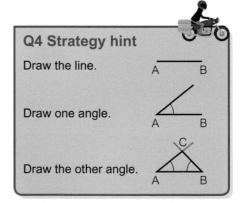

Q5 Strategy hint

Sketch each triangle first. Label
lengths and angles.

Q6a hint

Use a double number line.

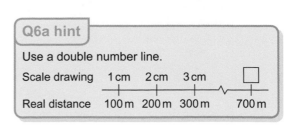

Constructions

1 Follow these instructions to accurately construct a triangle with sides 7 cm, 8 cm and 9 cm.

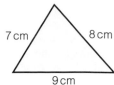

7 cm 8 cm

9 cm

a Use a ruler to draw the 9 cm side accurately.

b The 7 cm side starts at the left-hand end of this line. Open your compasses to exactly 7 cm and draw an arc from the left-hand end of the line.

c Open your compasses to exactly 8 cm and draw an arc from the other end.

d Use the point where the arcs cross to create the finished triangle.

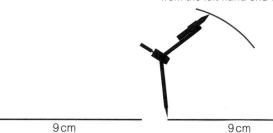

9 cm

9 cm

9 cm

7 cm 8 cm

9 cm

2 Construct this triangle.

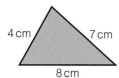

4 cm 7 cm

8 cm

3 Construct a scale diagram of this triangle. Use the scale 1 cm to 1 m.

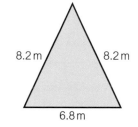

8.2 m 8.2 m

6.8 m

Q4 Strategy hint

Sketch the net and write the measurements on it.
Make an accurate drawing of the rectangles using a ruler and protractor.
Construct the triangles using compasses.

4 Draw and construct an accurate net of this triangular prism.

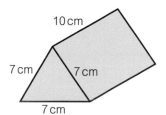

10 cm

7 cm 7 cm

7 cm

5 Draw a line 14 cm long.
Follow these instructions to construct the perpendicular bisector of this line.

Q5 Strategy hint

Remember this diagram.

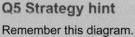

a Draw the line. Open your compasses to more than half the length of the line.

b Draw the first arc.

c Draw the second arc.

d Draw the perpendicular bisector.

14 cm

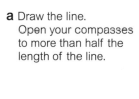

Q5 hint

Check by measuring that the angle is 90° and the line is cut in half.

6 Use a ruler to draw a line 11.5 cm long.
Construct the perpendicular bisector of this line.

7 Use a protractor to draw an angle of 60°.
Follow these instructions to construct the bisector
of this angle.

a Draw the angle.   **b** Draw an arc from   **c** Draw another arc between   **d** Draw a second arc.   **e** Draw the angle bisector.
                         the vertex of the angle.   the two sides of the angle.

   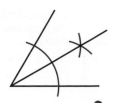

8 Use a protractor to draw an angle of 120°.
Construct the bisector of this angle.

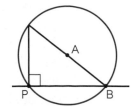

> **Q7 Strategy hint**
>
> Remember this diagram.

9 Draw a line and point A above the line.
Follow these instructions to construct a perpendicular line from the
point A to the line.

a Draw an arc from point A   **b** Keep compasses open the same   **c** Join the points where
that intersects the line twice.   distance. Draw an arc from each   these two arcs intersect.
                                   of the two points where the first
                                   arc crosses the line.

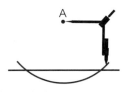 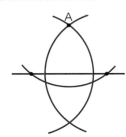 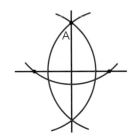

10 The diagram shows a sketch plan of
a garden with a washing line pole.
Construct an accurate plan
showing the washing line meeting
the house at right angles.

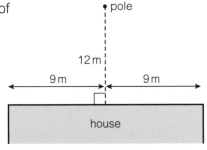

> **Q10 hint**
>
> Use the perpendicular construction
> you used in Q9. Start by drawing an
> arc from the pole.

11 Point P is close to the end of a line.
Follow the instructions to construct a perpendicular to the
line at point P.

a Mark point A to the right of point P.   **b** Mark point B where your   **c** Draw a line across the   **d** Join point P to the
Point A should be near to, but not on   circle crosses the   circle through point A   circle.
the line. Put your compasses on point   line again.   and point B.
A and draw a circle through point P.

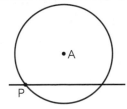 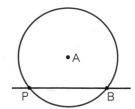 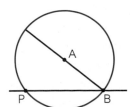 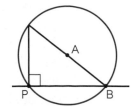

Loci

1 a Put a dot somewhere near the middle of a blank sheet of paper.
Draw as many points as you can exactly 5 cm from your dot.
b What shape have you created?
c Write the missing word in this sentence.
'Points that are all the same distance from a dot make a _____.'

2 a Mark an X on a piece of paper.
b Draw an accurate diagram to show all the points 4 cm away from the
centre of the X.

3 a Draw the perpendicular bisector of a line AB 9 cm long.
b i Choose a point on the perpendicular bisector.
ii Measure its distance from A and from B.
iii Do this again for another point on the perpendicular bisector.
What do you notice?
c Write the missing words in this sentence.
'Points that are all the same distance from two dots make the
_____ of the line joining them.'

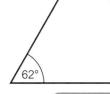
9 cm
A   B

4 Hamish and Jasmine are standing 2 m apart. Manjeet walks between
them, the same distance away from each of them.
Sketch the path that Manjeet takes. Construct a scale diagram of this
path accurately.

5 a Draw the angle bisector of a 62° angle.
b i Choose a point on the angle bisector.
ii Measure its shortest distance from each of the two lines.
iii Do this again for another point on the angle
bisector. What do you notice?
c Write the missing words in this sentence.
'Points that are all the same distance from two lines meeting at an
angle make the _____ of the angle.'

62°

6 a Draw a line 10 cm long.
b Mark some crosses exactly 3 cm from your line.
c What shape do your crosses make at the ends of the line?

> **Q6c hint**
>
>
>
> Draw enough crosses to show you
> the shape.

Enrichment

1 Match each sketch on the right to
its locus description.

2 Reflect Look back at the steps for
one of the questions in the
Constructions section.
For each step, answer these questions:
- Do I need compasses?
- If no, what tool(s) do I need?
- If yes, where do I put the point of
the compasses? Where do I draw?
Repeat this process for a different construction.
Do you think you could do one of the constructions
without the hints? Have a go!

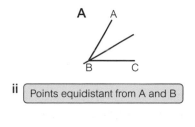

ii | Points equidistant from A and B |

iii | Points 5 cm from A |

D A——B

v | Points 5 cm from ABC |

i | Points equidistant from AB and BC |

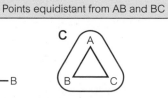

iv | Points 5 cm from AB |

E •A

Unit 7 Constructions and loci   166

Master
P149

Check
P161

Strengthen
P163

EXTEND

Test
P171

7 Extend

You will:
• Extend your understanding with problem-solving.

1 The diagram shows a person walking a tightrope.
   The two poles are 16 m apart.
   The two halves of the tightrope make an angle of
   10° to the horizontal.
   a Make a scale drawing of the triangle ABC using
     a ruler and protractor. Use a scale of 1 cm to 2 m.
   b How long is the tightrope ABC?

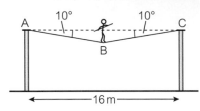

2 **Reasoning**
   a Construct triangle ABC where AB = 8 cm, BC = 6 cm and
     AC = 7.5 cm.
   b Construct the perpendicular bisectors of AB and BC.
     Mark the point P where they cross.
   c Construct the perpendicular bisector of AC.
     What do you notice?
   d Draw accurately a circle with centre P and radius PC.
     What do you notice?
   e Draw another triangle ABC, this time with an obtuse angle.
     Repeat the steps in parts **b** to **d**.

3 **Problem-solving** Use a ruler and compasses to construct
   these angles.
   Check your angles using a protractor.
   a 15°   b 105°

Q3 hint

How do these relate to angles you
know such as 60° and 90°?

4 a Use a ruler and compasses to construct triangle ABC.

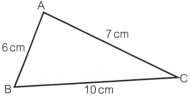

   b Construct the perpendicular
     from A to the base BC.
   c Work out the area of the triangle.

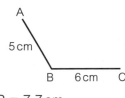

5 **Problem-solving**
   a Construct these two sides of triangle ABC.
     Join AC.
   b Use your triangle to construct the quadrilateral
     ABCD where CD = 4 cm and AD = 7 cm.
   c Construct another quadrilateral ABCD where AB = 7.7 cm,
     BC = 5.2 cm, CD = 6.4 cm, AD = 7.7 cm.

Q5b hint

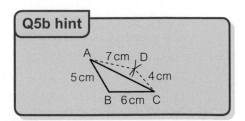

Topic links: Polygons, 3D solids, Pythagoras' theorem, Quadratic graphs   **Subject links:** Science (Q16)

6 a Sketch this kite ABCD.

b Split it into two congruent triangles.

c Construct the kite using the method in Q5.

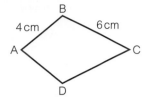

7 Problem-solving The diagram shows the penalty area of a football pitch.

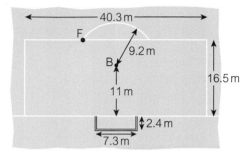

a Make a scale drawing of the penalty area.
Use a scale of 1 cm to 4 m.

b A footballer at F runs straight to the ball B on the penalty spot and kicks it towards the goal at an angle of 120° to FB.
Could she score a goal?

Q7b hint

Draw the line and angle on your diagram.

8 Problem-solving

a Draw the right-angled triangle ABC on squared paper where AB = 8 cm, BC = 6 cm and angle ABC = 90°.

b Construct the perpendicular bisector of the hypotenuse AC.
Mark the point P where the bisector intersects AC.

c Draw the circle with centre at point P with radius PA.
What do you notice?

d Draw around a circular object.
Use your discovery in part **c** to find the centre of the circle.

Q8d Strategy hint

Mark any point Q on the circumference.
Construct a right-angled triangle with the right angle at P.

9 The diagram shows three sides of a regular octagon.
ABP is a straight line. The length of each side is 5 cm.

a Work out the marked exterior angle.

b Draw accurately the sides AB and BC.

c Continue in the same way to complete the octagon.

10 Problem-solving The diagram shows a rolled-up poster inside a cardboard box. The box is a triangular prism.

a Construct the triangular cross-section.

b Bisect two of its angles.
Mark the point P where the angle bisectors cross.

c Bisect the third angle of the triangle.
What do you notice?

d Construct a perpendicular from P onto one of the sides.
Mark the point Q where it meets the side.

e Draw a circle with centre P and radius PQ.

f Another poster is rolled up with a diameter of 8 cm.
Construct the triangular cross-section of a box for it.

11 Problem-solving / Reasoning The diagram shows a hexagonal pyramid. The base is a regular hexagon.

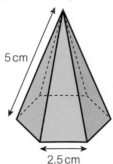

5 cm

2.5 cm

Q11 hint

Hexagonal base:

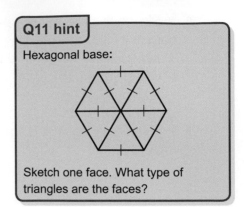

Sketch one face. What type of triangles are the faces?

Construct the net of a hexagonal pyramid using a ruler and compasses.

12 Real The diagram shows the loci of two water sprinklers on a football pitch.

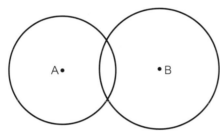

A•   •B

a Copy the diagram and shade the intersection.

b Describe what happens in the shaded area.

13 Real The diagrams show the watering systems for four flower beds. Each flowerbed has sprinklers that can move along rails. From any point on its rail, each sprinkler can reach plants up to 4 m away.

a 1 m

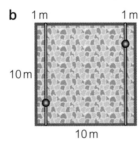

10 m

10 m

b 1 m   1 m

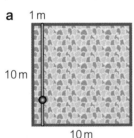

10 m

10 m

c

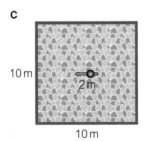

10 m

2 m

10 m

For each flower bed

i copy the diagram

ii construct and shade the locus of points the sprinklers can reach. Use centimetre squared paper and a scale of 1 cm to 1 m.

iii Which system waters the largest area of the flowerbed?

14 a Construct this triangle.
   b Measure the hypotenuse.
   c Use Pythagoras' theorem to check your answer.

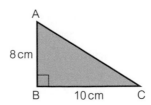

A

8 cm

B   10 cm   C

15 Problem-solving / Real Damian has a square garden of side 12 m.

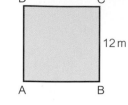

D   C

12 m

A   B

  a Make a scale drawing of the garden.
     Use a scale of 1 cm to 2 m.

He wants to prevent cats from crossing his garden from the wall AB to the opposite wall CD.

A sensor S detects when a cat has entered a sector of a circle of radius 9 m and angle 90°.

  b Choose a position for the sensor.
     Shade the area where the sensor will detect the cat.

He puts a hosepipe spray at the sensor. When the sensor detects the cat, the hosepipe sprays water over a sector of a circle of radius 8 m and angle 150°.

  c For the position in part **b**, shade the area where the cat will get wet.

  Discussion Is there a position that will prevent cats crossing Damian's garden at all?

16 STEM A GPS satellite is always 18 000 km above the surface of the Earth. The diameter of the Earth is approximately 12 750 km.
Describe the locus of the satellite's possible positions.

Investigation   **Problem-solving**

A field is 20 m square.
Four goats are tethered to the four corners of the field.
The ropes are all the same length, and the goats must not be able to reach each other.
1 Draw a plan of the field using a scale of 1 cm to 2 m.
2 a Draw the maximum area that the goats can graze.
  b Work out this area.
Now the goats are tethered to the midpoint of each side of the field.
Again, all the ropes are the same length and the goats cannot reach each other.
3 a Draw the maximum area that the goats can graze now.
  b Work out this area.
4 Which area is larger?

A   B

D   C

---

17 Reflect Look back at the questions in these extend lessons.
  a Write down the question that was the easiest to answer.
     What made it easy?
  b Write down the question that was the most difficult to answer.
     What made it difficult?
  c Look again at the question that you wrote down for part **b**.
     What could you do to make this type of question easier to answer?

> **Q17 hint**
> Ask your classmates how they answered this question. Do they have some hints for you?

Reflect

Master
P149

Check
P161

Strengthen
P163

Extend
P167

TEST

7 Unit test

Log how you did on your
Student Progression Chart.

1 Use a ruler and protractor to draw these triangles.

a

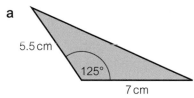

5.5 cm

125°

7 cm

b

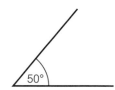

70°

4.5 cm

75°

2 Use a ruler and protractor to draw a plan of this garden.
Use a scale of 1 cm to 10 m.

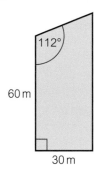

112°

60 m

30 m

3 a Draw this angle accurately using a protractor.
b Construct the angle bisector.

50°

4 a Construct this parallelogram.

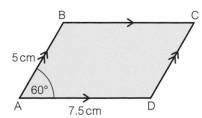

B   C

5 cm

60°

A   7.5 cm   D

b Construct the perpendicular from B to AD.

5 Draw a line 9.5 cm long and construct the perpendicular bisector.

6 A treasure hunt takes place in this field.

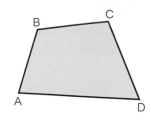

   a Trace the plan of the field.
The first clue says that the treasure is buried at a point equidistant from A and D.

   b Draw the locus of possible positions for the treasure using this clue.

The second clue says that the treasure is buried at a point that is equidistant from AB and BC.

   c Draw the locus of possible positions for the treasure using this clue.

   d Write X on your plan to show where the treasure is buried.

7 Construct the locus of a point that moves so it is always 5 cm from point A.

8 A guard dog is connected to a 10 m rail with a rope 6 m long. The end of the rope can slide along the rail.

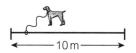

Draw accurately the locus of the points that the dog can reach. Use a scale of 1 cm to 2 m.

9 Draw and construct an accurate net of this triangular prism on squared paper.

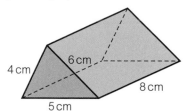

Challenge

10 Draw a map for a treasure hunt.
Mark some features on your map, for example a hill, a cave, trees, a lookout point.
Without using compass directions, describe the locus of buried treasure to a partner.
How many different types of locus can you use?

11 **Reflect** For this unit, copy and complete these sentences.
I showed I am good at _____
I found _____ hard.
I got better at _____ by _____
I was surprised by _____
I was pleased that _____
I still need help with _____

8.1 Comparing probabilities

You will learn to:
* Calculate and compare probabilities
* Decide if a game is fair.

CONFIDENCE

Why learn this?
Understanding probabilities helps you decide if a game is fair.

Fluency
Which is more likely: grey or white?

Explore
What percentage chance of rain would make you decide to take an umbrella?

Exercise 8.1

1 Which is the bigger fraction?

    a $\frac{3}{10}$ or $\frac{7}{10}$ **b** $\frac{2}{3}$ or $\frac{3}{5}$

> **Q1 hint**
> Write the fractions as equivalent fractions with the same denominator.

Warm up

2 Match the equivalent numbers.

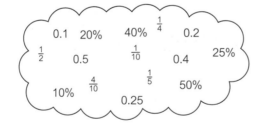

0.1   20%   40% $\frac{1}{4}$ 0.2
$\frac{1}{2}$ 0.5 $\frac{1}{10}$ 0.4   25%
10% $\frac{4}{10}$ $\frac{1}{5}$ 50%
0.25

> **Key point**
> All probabilities have a value between 0 and 1. You can use fractions, decimals and percentages to describe probabilities.

3 a Copy the probability scale.

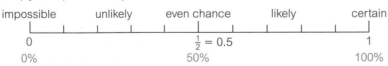

impossible   unlikely   even chance   likely   certain

0                     $\frac{1}{2} = 0.5$ 1
0%   50%   100%

   b Write the capital letter of each event in the correct place on your scale.

     A Picking a red card from a pack of cards.

     B The probability of someone born in 2012 living to 100 is about 30%.

     C If one of your parents is near-sighted, the probability that you will be near-sighted is about 0.2.

     D The probability of two left-handed parents having a right-handed child is about $\frac{3}{4}$.

     E The probability of having twins is 1%.

Topic links: Comparing and converting fractions, decimals, percentages

Active Learn   Delta 2, Section 8.1

4 Each of these **fair** spinners is spun once.

For each spinner
a write all of the possible **outcomes**
b write the total number of possible outcomes.
Discussion How many possible outcomes are there for the first ball drawn in the UK National Lottery Game?

5 A fair 6-siided dice is rolled once. What are the **successful outcomes** for each event?
a The dice lands on an even number.
b The dice lands on a number less than 5.
c The dice lands on a prime number.
d The dice lands on a prime number or an even number.

Worked example

Find the probability that
this spinner will land on red.

Probability that spinner lands on red = $\frac{2}{5}$

> There are two successful outcomes: red, red.
> The total number of possible outcomes is 5.

6 Rory spins this fair spinner once.
a What is the probability that it lands on
  i blue   **ii** white
  iii blue or green   **iv** red?

b Write your answers as decimals.
c Write your answers as percentages.
d Describe each probability using words from the probability scale in Q3.

7 You pick a card at **random** from an ordinary shuffled pack of 52 playing cards.
What is the probability of picking
a a black card
b 3 of diamonds
c a 7
d a picture card?

8 a A bag has 16 red counters and 11 blue counters. Are you more likely to pick a red or blue counter at random from the bag?
b Bag A has 8 red counters and 11 blue counters. Bag B has 8 red counters and 5 blue counters. Are you more likely to pick a red counter at random from Bag A or Bag B?

9 The table shows information about the eye colour of Year 8 students.

	Blue	Brown	Green	Hazel	Total
Girls	20	32	7	25	84
Boys	17	29	6	24	76
Total	37	61	13	49	160

A student is picked at random.
   a What is the probability that the student is
      i a girl with green eyes   **ii** a boy with blue eyes?
   b Who is more likely to be picked: a boy with hazel eyes or a girl with brown eyes?

10 Each of these fair dice is rolled once.
   a Which event is more likely?
      i The number 3 with dice B or the number 3 with dice C.
      ii An even number with dice A or an even number with dice B.

 A

 B

 C

6 sides   5 sides   10 sides

   b Which dice has the greatest probability of showing a square number?

Investigation   Problem-solving / Reasoning

Michael puts red, purple, yellow and orange counters in a bag.
He picks a counter at random.
The probability of getting each colour is:
red $\frac{1}{6}$ purple $\frac{1}{5}$ yellow $\frac{2}{15}$ orange $\frac{1}{2}$
What is the smallest number of counters that there could be in the bag?
How many counters of each colour are in the bag?

---

11 STEM When it rains, the probability of a thunderstorm is $\frac{4}{5}$ in Kampala and 66% in Singapore.
In which city is a thunderstorm more likely?

12 Problem-solving Marcus and Nora each take a card from a complete pack of 52.
Which of these rules make the game fair?
   a Marcus wins if he gets a red card. Nora wins if she gets a black card.
   b Marcus wins if he gets a picture card. Nora wins if she gets a number card.
   c Marcus wins if he gets an odd number card. Nora wins if she gets an even number card.

Key point

A game is fair if each player has the same chance of winning.

Q12 hint

If they both get a winning card, it's a draw.

13 Explore What percentage chance of rain would make you decide to take an umbrella?
Choose some sensible numbers to help you explore this situation. Use what you've learned in this lesson to help you answer the question.

14 Reflect Sophie and Will are playing a game with a fair 6-sided dice.
Sophie needs a 6 to win, but she rolls a 3.
Sophie says, 'It's not fair. It's harder to roll a 6 than a 3.'
Use what you have learned in this lesson to decide if Sophie is correct. Explain.

Explore

Reflect

8.2 Mutually exclusive events

You will learn to:

- Identify mutually exclusive outcomes and events
- Find the probabilities of mutually exclusive outcomes and events
- Find the probability of an event not happening.

Why learn this?
A roadside repair service can use probabilities to help decide on the spare parts to carry.

Fluency
A bag contains 3 red, 2 blue and 5 green sweets. One is chosen at random. What is the probability it is
- red
- blue
- green?

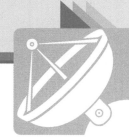

Explore
What is the probability of a car breaking down because of a flat tyre or flat battery?

Exercise 8.2

1 Work these out. Give each answer as a single fraction in its simplest form.

  a $\frac{3}{10} + \frac{1}{10}$

  b $1 - \frac{3}{10}$

  c $1 - \frac{1}{12}$

> **Q1b hint**
> $1 = \frac{10}{10}$

2 Work out

  a $1 - 0.7$

  b $100\% - 33\%$

3 Copy and complete this probability scale.

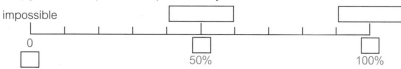

impossible | 0 | 50% | 100%

4 **Reasoning** An ordinary 6-sided dice is rolled once.

  a List all the possible outcomes.

  b What is the probability of each possible outcome?

  c What is the sum of all their probabilities?

  d Copy and complete the rule: The sum of the probabilities of all possible outcomes is ☐

  e Show that the rule works for this fair spinner.
  Discussion Why does this rule work?

5 **STEM** The computer sound cards made on a production line are either scrapped, repaired or passed. 4% are scrapped, 8% are repaired. What is the probability that a sound card is passed?

> **Q5 hint**
> The sum of the probabilities of all possible outcomes is ☐%

Warm up

6 Reasoning An ordinary 6-sided dice is rolled once.
The Venn diagram shows two events: square numbers and multiples of 3.

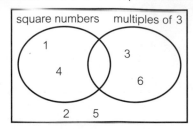

a Explain why the two events are **mutually exclusive**.
b Why are 2 and 5 outside the circles?
c What is the probability of rolling a square number?
d What is the probability of rolling a multiple of 3?
e What is the probability of rolling a square number or a multiple of 3?
f True or false: P(rolling a square number or a multiple of 3)
     = P(rolling a square number) + P(rolling a multiple of 3).
     Explain.

Key point

Two events are **mutually exclusive** if they cannot happen at the same time. For example, when you roll an ordinary dice, you cannot get a 3 and an even number at the same time.

Q6a hint

Are any numbers on a dice square numbers *and* multiples of 3?

Q6 Literacy hint

P(rolling a 4) means the probability of rolling a 4.

7 The Venn diagram shows two events when a 6-sided dice is rolled: square numbers and numbers less than 4.

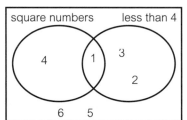

a Explain why the two events are *not* mutually exclusive.
b What is the probability of rolling a square number?
c What is the probability of rolling a number less than 4?
d What is the probability of rolling a square number or a number less than 4?
e True or false: P(rolling a square number or a number less than 4)
     = P(rolling a square number) + P(rolling a number less than 4).
     Explain.

Discussion How can you tell from a Venn diagram whether events are mutually exclusive or not?

8 These beads from Danielle's broken bracelet were put into a bag.

She took one from the bag at random. Which of these pairs of events are mutually exclusive?
a The bead is E. The bead is purple.
b The bead is red. The bead is blue.
c The bead is one of the letters D, I, N. The bead is red.
d The bead is a vowel. The bead is red.

9 A coin is taken at random from a money box containing 5p coins with different dates.
P(date is 2012) = 0.2   P(date is 2000) = 0.1   P(date is 1999) = 0.05
What is the probability the coin's date is
a 2000 or 2012   b 1999 or 2000   c 1999, 2000 or 2012?

Key point

When events are mutually exclusive you can add their probabilities.

Topic links: Venn diagrams, Adding and subtracting fractions and decimals

10 **Reasoning** An ordinary 6-sided dice is rolled once. The Venn diagram shows the three events: square number, prime number, biggest number.

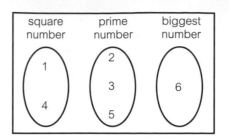

a Explain why the three events are mutually exclusive.

b What is the probability of each event?

c What is the sum of their probabilities?

d Copy and complete the rule:
The sum of the probabilities of all the mutually exclusive outcomes is ☐

11 **Problem-solving** A variety of sweetcorn plant produces 1, 2 or 3 cobs.
The probability of a plant producing 3 cobs is 0.4. 1 or 2 cobs are equally likely. Work out the probability of a plant producing 2 cobs.

Q11 hint

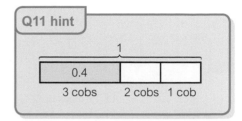

Investigation Reasoning

This fair spinner is spun once.

1 What is the probability it will land on
    a 2
    b not 2?

2 Add the probabilities together. What do you notice?

3 Draw a Venn diagram to show why you get this answer.

4 Copy and complete this rule:
    Probability of an event happening + Probability of the event *not* happening = ____

Discussion When you know the probability of an event happening, how can you find the probability of it not happening?

---

12 a The probability of a spinner landing on green is $\frac{1}{6}$.
What is the probability that it does not land on green?

b The probability of rolling an odd number with a fair dice is $\frac{3}{6}$.
What is the probability of rolling an even number?

c The probability of winning a prize in a raffle is 0.1.
What is the probability of not winning a prize?

Discussion Can the probability of an event not happening be 1?

13 The probability that a baby is born on the due date is 5%.
What is the probability that a baby is not born on the due date?

Q13 hint

How can you write a probability of 1 as a percentage?

14 **Explore** What is the probability of a car breaking down because of a flat tyre or flat battery?
Is it easier to explore this question now you have completed the lesson? What further information do you need to be able to answer this?

15 **Reflect** Sami works out that the probability of this spinner landing on an even number is $\frac{1}{2}$, and the probability of it landing on red is $\frac{2}{3}$. Use what you have learned in this lesson to explain why the probabilities don't add up to 1.

8.3 Estimating probability

You will learn to:
- Calculate the relative frequency of a value
- Use relative frequency to make estimates
- Use relative frequency to estimate the probability of an event
- Use estimated probability to calculate expected frequencies.

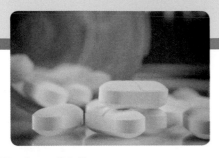

Why learn this?
A drug must be tested to estimate the probability that it will be effective.

Fluency
- What is 4 as a fraction of 10?
- What is 4 as a percentage of 20?

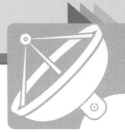

Explore
What is the probability that a drug will stop a headache?

CONFIDENCE

Exercise 8.3

Warm up

1 Work out

  a $\frac{1}{4} \times 60$ **b** $\frac{3}{5} \times 200$ **c** $\frac{7}{10} \times 150$

2 Convert these fractions to percentages.

  a $\frac{37}{100}$ **b** $\frac{18}{40}$ **c** $\frac{38}{250}$

> **Key point**
>
> For a set of data, the **relative frequency** of a value
> $$= \frac{\text{frequency of value}}{\text{total frequency}}.$$
> You can calculate the expected frequency of a value in a larger set of data.

Worked example

Some Year 8 students were asked which device they use to access the internet.

a Calculate the **relative frequencies**.

Device	Frequency	Relative frequency
Smart phone	10	$\frac{10}{50}$
Tablet	18	$\frac{18}{50}$
Computer	22	$\frac{22}{50}$
Total frequency	50	

$$\text{relative frequency} = \frac{\text{frequency}}{\text{total frequency}}$$

Add all the frequencies to find the total.

b There are 200 students in Year 8 altogether.
How many would you **expect** to use a smart phone?

$$\frac{\overset{1}{\cancel{10}}}{\underset{5}{\cancel{50}}} \times 200 = 40$$

You can expect $\frac{10}{50}$ of the 200 students to use a smart phone.

I expect 40 students to use a smart phone.

Topic links: Equivalent fractions, Percentages

3 The frequency table shows the patient outcomes in a study of a new eye treatment.

Outcome	Frequency	Relative frequency
Great improvement	75	
Slight improvement	20	
Same or worse	5	
Total frequency		

  a Copy the table.
  b Work out the total frequency.
  c Calculate the relative frequencies.
  d A further 300 people received the treatment. How many would you expect to have improved eyesight?

Discussion Is your answer to part **d** likely to be the exact number of people whose eyesight improved?

4 a In a survey of 200 households, 65 have high-speed broadband. There are 1000 households in the village. How many would you expect to have high-speed broadband?
  b 40 parents attended a school meeting. 27 said they preferred to have four school terms. 600 parents have children at the school. How many would you expect to prefer four school terms?

5 Real / Reasoning Restaurant owner Maurice recorded the number of seats reserved for each booking during a week.

Seats	Frequency	Relative frequency
2	30	
3	10	
4	25	
5	5	
6	10	
Total frequency		

  a Copy and complete the table.
  b Estimate the probability that the next booking will be for 2 seats.
  c Maurice says that it is unlikely that a booking will be for less than 4 people. Is he correct? Explain how you know.
  d The restaurant has approximately 240 bookings each month. How many of these would you expect to be for 4 seats?

> **Key point**
> Relative frequency can be used to estimate the probability of an event happening.

> **Q5b hint**
> Find the relative frequency of a booking for 2 seats.

6 Modelling An agricultural research centre counted the bananas in 1000 bunches.

Number of bananas	Frequency	Relative frequency
200–219	120	
220–239	160	
240–259	200	
260–279	230	
280–299	170	
300–319	120	

> **Key point**
> Probability can be used to **model** what happens in the future.

  a Copy the table and calculate the relative frequencies as percentages.
  b Estimate the probability that a bunch will contain
    i 300–319 bananas   **ii** at least 260 bananas.
  c A grower picks 5000 bunches one week. How many of these would you expect to contain at least 260 bananas?

Discussion Why might these estimated probabilities not be a good **model** for next year's crop?

7 Problem-solving The probability of not being connected when ringing a customer support service is 30%.
On a typical Monday, customers ring the service 400 times.
How many of these calls would you expect to be connected?

8 An optician's records show that 21 of the last 50 customers bought designer frames and 14 of them bought two pairs of glasses.
  a Estimate the probability that the next customer orders
    i designer frames
    ii two pairs of glasses.
  b Of the next 200 customers, how many would you expect to order two pairs of glasses?
  Discussion Is the probability of a customer ordering designer frames or two pairs of glasses $\frac{35}{50}$?

9 Peter tested 10 batteries and found 80% lasted more than 30 hours. Sven tested 100 of the same batteries and found 90% lasted more than 30 hours.
Whose results are more useful?

Key point

The more data you have, the more confident you can be about any conclusions based on the data.

10 Problem-solving / Reasoning
  a Edward asked 20 people which charity they donate money to. 11 said Oxfam. Estimate the probability that a person donates money to Oxfam.
  b Odval asked 80 people which charity they donate money to. 45 said Oxfam. Use his data to estimate the probability that a person donates money to Oxfam.
  c Which estimate do you think is more reliable? Give a reason for your answer.
  d Edward and Odval shared their data.
    i Use their combined data to estimate the probability that a person donates money to Oxfam.
    ii They interview another 200 people. How many would they expect to donate money to Oxfam?

11 Explore What is the probability that a drug will stop a headache? Is it easier to explore this question now you have completed the lesson? What further information do you need to be able to answer this?

12 Reflect Look back at the questions you answered in this lesson.
  a Make a list of all the different maths skills you have used.
  b Was there a question you found particularly difficult? What made it difficult?
  c Was there a question you found easy?

8.4 Experimental probability

You will learn to:
- Carry out a probability experiment
- Estimate probability using data from an experiment
- Work out the expected results when an experiment is repeated.

CONFIDENCE

Why learn this?
Scientists combine the results of repeated experiments to obtain more accurate probability estimates.

Fluency
- 3 out of 10 batteries are recycled. What is the relative frequency?
- What is the percentage probability that a battery will be recycled?
- A shop sells 60 batteries. How many do you expect will be recycled?

Explore
How many times do you have to flip a coin to be confident that it is a fair coin?

Exercise 8.4

Warm up

1 A fair 10-sided dice numbered 1 to 10 is rolled once. What is the probability of getting
   a 7
   b 2 or 7?

2 Work out
   a $\frac{3}{50} \times 100$
   b $\frac{25}{100} \times 60$

3 Omar dropped a button on the table lots of times. It landed either round side up or flat side up.
   He recorded the results in a frequency table.

Position	Frequency
Round side up	8
Flat side up	42

   a Work out the total frequency.
   b Work out the **experimental probability** of the button landing
     i rounded side up
     ii flat side up.
   c He drops the button 100 times. How many times do you expect it to land rounded side up?
   Discussion When you repeat an experiment, will you get exactly the same results?

4 From a normal pack of playing cards, what is the **theoretical probability** of picking
   a a Jack
   b a Heart?

5 **Reasoning** For which of these events can you work out the theoretical probability?
   A A scheduled aeroplane will be delayed.
   B A letter pushed through a letter box will fall stamp side up.
   C The next domino turned over will have an even number of dots.

Key point

In a **probability experiment** a **trial** is repeated many times and the outcomes recorded. For example, flipping a coin 100 times and recording heads or tails.
The relative frequency of an outcome is called the **experimental probability**.
Experimental probability of an outcome
$$= \frac{\text{frequency of outcome}}{\text{total number of trials}}$$

Key point

Theoretical probability is calculated without doing an experiment. For example, the theoretical probability of rolling a 4 with an ordinary dice is $\frac{1}{6}$.

1 What is the **theoretical probability** of flipping Heads with a fair coin?
Write your answer as a decimal.
2 a Flip a coin 20 times and record the results in a frequency table.
  b Calculate the experimental probability of Heads.
    Write your answer as a decimal.
3 a Combine your data with a classmate.
  b Calculate the experimental probability of Heads based on 40 flips.
4 Combine the data of more classmates, one at a time.
  Calculate the experimental probability of Heads based on 60, 80, 120 ... flips.
5 Plot the results on a graph like the one shown on the right.

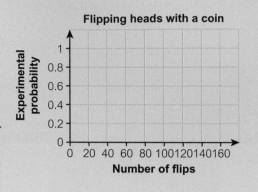

Flipping heads with a coin

6 What do you notice about the experimental probabilities as the number
of trials increases?

6 a An ordinary 6-sided dice is rolled 30 times. How many times do
you expect a 5?
  b An ordinary pack of playing cards is shuffled and the top card
turned over 100 times. How many times do you expect the top card
to be a Spade?
  c A bag contains 3 red and 2 blue counters. A counter is picked at
random and then replaced, 40 times. How many red counters do
you expect?

> **Key point**
> Theoretical probability can be used
> to calculate the frequencies you
> would expect in an experiment.

7 Reasoning In a fantasy game, players use
a spinner to see which creature they have
to fight.
  a What is the theoretical probability of
landing on Vampire if the spinner is fair?
  b How many times would you expect the
spinner to land on each creature in
100 spins?
These are the results for 100 spins.

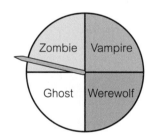

Creature	Vampire	Werewolf	Ghost	Zombie
Frequency	22	27	25	26

  c Kuni says that the spinner is fair. Do you agree?
What could she do to be more confident that the spinner is fair?

8 Explore How many times do you have to flip a coin to be confident
that it is a fair coin?
Is it easier to explore this question now you have completed the lesson?
What further information do you need to be able to answer this?

9 Reflect In this lesson you learned about experimental probability.
In lesson 8.3 you learned about relative frequency.
  a In what way are experimental probability and relative frequency the
same?
  b Describe a situation where you might use experimental probability
to describe an event. Describe a situation where you might use
relative frequency to describe an event.

8.5 Probability diagrams

You will learn to:

- List all the possible outcomes of one or two events in sample space diagrams or Venn diagrams
- Calculate probabilities of repeated events.

Why learn this?
You can use probabilities of two events, like rolling two dice, to work out strategies for games like Yahtzee or backgammon.

Fluency
- You roll an ordinary fair dice. What is
  P(5)
  P(even number)
  P(at least 3)?
- In 30 rolls, how many 2s would you expect?

Explore
How likely are you to roll a double with two dice?

Exercise 8.5

1 For this spinner, what is

   a P(red)   **b** P(blue)

   c P(red or blue)   **d** P(red and even)

   e P(blue and odd)?

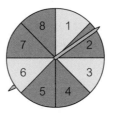

2 A 5p and 10p coin are flipped at the same time.

   a Make a list of the possible outcomes.

   b How many possible outcomes are there altogether?

   c Work out

     i P(two heads)   **ii** P(a head or a tail)

   Discussion What assumptions do you need to make to answer part **c**?

> **Q2a hint**
> Organise the outcomes so that you don't miss any. For example:
> 5p 10p
> H H

3 Maria rolls a dice and flips a coin. Copy the **sample space diagram**.

	H	T
1	H, 1	
2		T, 2
3		
4		
5		
6		

> **Key point**
> A **sample space diagram** shows all the possible outcomes of two events.

   a Write in the possible outcomes. How many possible outcomes are there altogether?

   b Work out

     i P(an even number and a tail)

     ii P(3)

     iii P(a number greater than 4 and a head)

> **Q3b ii hint**
> With head or tail.

Warm up

4 In a probability experiment, Khalid spun this fair spinner twice and added the results together.

a Copy and complete the sample space diagram.

b How many possible outcomes are there?

c Which total is most likely?

d Work out the probability that the total is

   i 2   **ii** 4   **iii** an even number   **iv** greater than 3.

e Khalid does 45 trials. How many times would he expect a total of 4?

		First spin		
		1	**2**	**3**
Second spin	**1**	2		
	2			
	3			

5 In a class of 30 students, 24 study French and 11 study German. 5 students study both French and German.

a Draw a Venn diagram to show this information.

b What is the probability that a student chosen at random is

   i studying French only

   ii studying German and French

   iii studying only one language?

   Discussion 24 study French and 11 study German. Why aren't there 35 students in the class?

> **Q5a hint**
>
> French   German
>
> French only   French   German only
>   and German

6 Julia always hits 5, 20 or 1 with a dart. She throws two darts and adds their scores.

a Draw a sample space diagram to show her possible scores.

b What is the probability that her total score will be

   i 40   **ii** 6   **iii** less than 20   **iv** at least 20?

> **Q6b hint**
>
> Make a table like the one in Q4.

7 A fair coin is flipped three times.

a List the possible outcomes.

b What is the probability of getting

   i all heads

   ii exactly two tails

   iii at least one head?

8 **Explore** How likely are you to roll a double with two dice? Is it easier to explore this question now you have completed the lesson? What further information do you need to be able to answer this?

9 **Reflect** Naringa is playing a game with a fair dice. She needs to roll two 4s to win. She rolls one 4 and says, 'Oh, I don't think I'll be able to get a 4 on *both* dice!' Use what you have learned in this lesson to decide if Naringa is less likely to roll a 4 on the second dice, given that she has already rolled a 4.

8.6 Tree diagrams

You will learn to:
- Use tree diagrams to find the probabilities of two or more events.

Why learn this?
Probability models can help to predict the characteristics of a baby.

Fluency
What is the probability of this spinner landing on:
- red
- yellow
- red or yellow
- not red?

Explore
What is the probability that a baby will be born left-handed and colour blind?

Exercise 8.6

1 Work out the probability of each event *not* happening.
  a The probability of a computer hard drive lasting 4 years is $\frac{4}{5}$.
  b There is a 42% chance that a UK marriage will end in divorce.
  c The probability of rain tomorrow is 0.7.

2 Work these out. Give each answer in its simplest form.
  a $\frac{1}{6} + \frac{2}{6}$ b $\frac{1}{12} + \frac{2}{12} + \frac{5}{12}$
  c $\frac{1}{4} \times \frac{3}{4}$ d $\frac{7}{10} \times \frac{5}{9}$

3 **Reasoning** a What is the probability of flipping heads with a coin?
  b What is the probability of picking a club from an ordinary pack?
  c The coin is flipped and a card is picked.
    i Draw a sample space diagram to show the possible outcomes.

	♣	♠	♦	♥
H	♣H			
T			♦T	

    ii What is the probability of flipping heads and picking a club?
  d Multiply your answers to parts **a** and **b** together. What do you notice?

4 **Reasoning** Are these events independent?
  a Picking a black sock from a drawer, putting it on, then picking another black sock.
  b Rolling a 6 with a dice and then rolling a 6 again.
  c Pick a Heart from a pack, put it back, shuffle, then pick another Heart.
  Discussion What if the card in part **c** is *not* put back?

5 A fair 6-sided dice is rolled twice. Work out
  a P(6 and 4)
  b P(5 and an even number)
  c P(6 and a number less than 4)

Key point
Two events are **independent** if one happening does not affect the probability of the other. For example, flipping heads with a coin has no effect on rolling an even number with a dice, so they are independent events.

Key point
To find the probability of two independent events, multiply their probabilities.
P(A and B) = P(A) × P(B)

Worked example

These YES/NO cards are shuffled and the top card turned over.

 | YES | YES | YES | NO | NO |

The cards are shuffled again and the top card turned over again.

a Draw a **tree diagram** to show the probabilities.

a

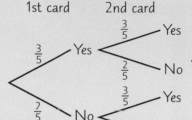

1st card   2nd card

$\frac{3}{5}$ Yes
$\frac{3}{5}$ Yes
$\frac{2}{5}$ No
$\frac{2}{5}$ No
$\frac{3}{5}$ Yes
$\frac{2}{5}$ No

> Write the probability on each branch of the diagram.

> **Key point**
>
> A **tree diagram** shows two or more events and their probabilities.

b What is the probability of two YES cards?

b $\frac{3}{5} \times \frac{3}{5} = \frac{9}{25}$

> Go along the branches for YES, YES. The 1st and 2nd cards are independent, so multiply the probabilities.

c What is the probability of one YES and one NO card?

c $\frac{3}{5} \times \frac{2}{5} = \frac{6}{25}$

> Go along the branch for YES, NO and NO, YES.

$\frac{2}{5} \times \frac{3}{5} = \frac{6}{25}$

$\frac{6}{25} + \frac{6}{25} = \frac{12}{25}$

> Add the probabilities of their outcomes.

6 At a school fete, these balls are placed in a basket. If you pick a ball with **20p** on it, you win 20p.

A player chooses a ball at random then replaces it. Then she chooses another one.

a Copy and complete the tree diagram to show the probabilities.

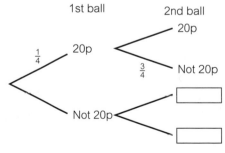

1st ball   2nd ball

$\frac{1}{4}$ 20p   20p

$\frac{3}{4}$ Not 20p

Not 20p

b What is the probability of

  i winning 40p

  ii winning nothing

  iii winning with the first ball, losing with the second ball

  iv winning 20p?

Topic links: Adding and multiplying fractions, decimals, percentages

7 Modelling The probability of being stopped at a set of traffic lights is 0.3.

   a What is the probability of not being stopped?

   b Giana goes through the traffic lights twice a day. Draw a tree diagram to show the possible outcomes.

   c What is the probability that Giana will be

   i stopped once

   ii not stopped?

Discussion Is this a good model for working out the probabilities for traffic lights?

8 In a game of SCRABBLE®, these letters are left in the bag.

  E₁   E₁   I₁   I₁   I₁

   a A player removes a letter E from the bag and doesn't replace it. What was the probability of picking an E?

   b How many letters are left in the bag?

   c The next player picks a letter from the bag. What is the probability of getting an E this time?

   d Copy and complete the tree diagram.

   e What is the probability that

   i both Es are picked

   ii one E and one I are picked

   iii a vowel is picked?

   f **Problem-solving** The second player needs an E to win the game. What is the probability that he will win?

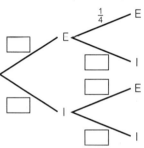

$\frac{1}{4}$ E

E

I

E

I

I

9 Problem-solving Kim's jewellery box contains 9 pairs of silver earrings and 3 pairs of gold earrings.

She always picks a pair of earrings at random. Once she's worn a pair she does not return the earrings to the box. What is the probability that the second pair of earrings she takes from the box are silver?

10 Explore What is the probability that a baby will be born left-handed and colour blind?

Is it easier to explore this question now you have completed the lesson? What further information do you need to be able to answer this?

11 Reflect In this unit you have learned vocabulary to describe different types of events.

   a Write a definition, in your own words, for mutually exclusive events and independent events.

   b Write a mutually exclusive event that involves

   i a coin   **ii** a dice.

   c Describe how mutually exclusive events and independent events are different.

   d Write a mutually exclusive event and an independent event that involves a pack of cards. Compare your events with others in your class.

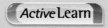
Explore

Reflect

8 Check up

Log how you did on your Student Progression Chart.

Calculating probability

1 These number cards are shuffled and turned upside down.

2   1   2   3   1   4   1   5

The top card is turned over.

a List the possible outcomes.

b What is the probability that the top card is

    i 1   **ii** odd   **iii** not 3?

2 34 students play a sport. 24 students play an instrument. 8 students play sport and an instrument.

a Draw a Venn diagram to show this information.

b What is the probability that a student picked at random plays an instrument but not a sport?

3 A bag contains some sweets with different coloured wrappers.
A sweet is taken from the bag at random.

a The probability of a toffee is $\frac{3}{8}$. What is the probability that it is not a toffee?

b The probability of a chocolate is $\frac{1}{2}$. Which is more likely: a toffee or a chocolate?

c What is the probability of choosing a toffee or a chocolate?

4 The arrow on this fair spinner is spun twice.
The results are added to get the score.

a Copy and complete the sample space diagram of possible scores.

b Work out the probability that the score is

    i 3   **ii** an even number.

c Are the two spins independent? Explain.

		1st spin		
		1	2	3
2nd spin	1			
	2			
	3			

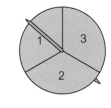

5 Doran and Mick each roll a fair dice numbered 1 to 10.
Doran scores a point if the number is even. Mick scores a point if the number is prime. Is the game fair? Show working to explain.

Estimating probability

6 Penny made this spinner and spun it 60 times.
The spinner landed on white 20 times.

a Calculate the theoretical probability of it landing on white.

b Do you think the spinner is fair? Explain.

7 The two-way table shows the membership of a tennis club.

	Under 25	25–50	Over 50	Total
Male	21	16	5	42
Female	18	13	7	38
Total	39	29	12	80

A member of the club is picked at random.

a What is the probability that this member is

  i female

  ii aged over 50

  iii a male aged under 25

  iv a female aged 25–50?

b Which type of member is more likely to be picked: a male aged 25 or over, or a females aged under 25?

c All the female members' names are put into a hat and one is picked. What is the probability that the one picked is over 50?

8 The table shows the visitors to a park on a Sunday.

a Work out the relative frequencies for Adult, Child, Dog.

b Estimate the probability that the next visitor is a child. Write your answer as a decimal.

c The park has 300 visitors one Sunday. How many dogs would you expect?

Visitor	Frequency	Relative frequency
Adult	70	
Child	90	
Dog	40	
Total frequency		

Tree diagrams

9 Lucy has a mobile phone and a landline.

The probability that the next call she receives is to her mobile phone is 0.7.

a What is the probability that the next call is to her landline?

b Lucy receives two calls. Copy and complete the tree diagram.

c Work out the probability that

  i both calls were to her mobile phone

  ii only one call was to her mobile phone.

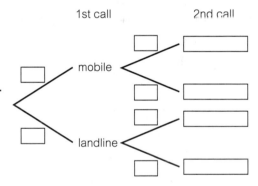

1st call   2nd call

mobile

landline

10 How sure are you of your answers? Were you mostly

😟 **Just guessing** 😐 **Feeling doubtful** 😊 **Confident**

What next? Use your results to decide whether to strengthen or extend your learning.

Reflect

Challenge

11 a Use the numbers 2 and 3 to fill in the sectors of these two spinners.

b The two spinners are spun and their results added. Make a table to show the totals.

c Work out the probability of getting a total of 4.

d Draw a tree diagram to show the results of the two spinners.

e Use your tree diagram to find the probability of spinning two 3s.

f Make up the rules of a fair game for two players using the totals of the spinner results. Each player must have their own rule for winning.

Spinner 1   Spinner 2

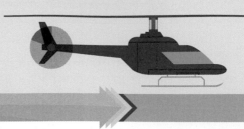

8 Strengthen

You will:
* Strengthen your understanding with practice.

Calculating probability

1 These numbered counters are placed into a bag. One is picked at random.

① ① ② ② ② ② ③ ③ ④ ⑤

  a How many possible outcomes are there?

  b How many of the possible outcomes are 2?

  c Write the probability of choosing a 2 as a fraction.

  d Work out the probability of picking

   i 1 or 2

   ii 6

   iii an even number

   iv less than 4

Q1a hint

How many counters are in the bag in total?

Q1c hint

$$\frac{\text{number of 2s}}{\text{total number of counters}}$$

2 The table shows information about the birth months of Year 8 students.

Birth month	Jan–Mar	Apr–June	Jul–Sept	Oct–Dec	Total
Girls	24	16	31	17	88
Boys	18	29	20	25	92
Total	42	45	51	42	180

  a How many girls were born in the months October to December?

  b What is the probability that a student chosen at random is

   i a girl born in the months October to December?

   ii a boy born in the months April to September?

  c A boy is chosen. What is the probability that he was born in July, August or September?

  d A girl is chosen. What is the probability that she was born in the first half of the year?

Q2b i hint

Use your answer to part **a** and the total number of students.

Q2c hint

Use only the values for boys.

3 Adam plays two racing games where he can finish 1st, 2nd or 3rd.

  a Copy and complete this sample space diagram to show all the possible outcomes for both races.

  b How many possible outcomes are there?

  c What is the probability that Adam finishes 2nd in both races?

  d Write down the outcomes that give Adam at least one win.

  e What is the probability of getting at least one win?

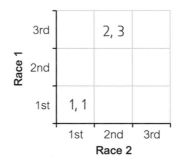

Race 1

	1st	2nd	3rd
3rd			2, 3
2nd			
1st	1, 1		

Race 2

Q3b Strategy hint

Look carefully at what each cell in the sample space tells you.

Q3d Strategy hint

'At least one win' means one win or more than one win.

Topic links: Adding, subtracting, multiplying and comparing fractions, Venn diagrams

4 Brianne spins these two spinners.

Spinner 1   Spinner 2

  a Draw a sample space diagram to show all the possible outcomes. How many are there?

  b Work out the probability of

    i a 3

    ii one number being half the other.

    iii both numbers being at least 2.

  c Which is more likely: two even numbers or two odd numbers?

  d Brianne spins the two spinners and adds the two numbers together. Draw a new sample space diagram to show the scores.

  e Which score is most likely?

  f What is the probability of scoring at least 4?

Q4a hint

Put spinner 1 on the horizontal axis and spinner 2 on the vertical axis.

Q4d hint

Use the same axes. For the result 1, 2, the score is 1 + 2 = 3

5 Each of these spinners is spun once.

Spinner A   Spinner B

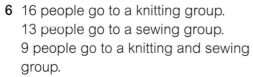

  a Which spinner is more likely to land on blue?

  b Which spinner is more likely to land on red?

  c Work out P(grey) for each spinner. What do you notice?

Q5a hint

Compare the probabilities.

For spinner A, P(blue) = $\frac{\Box}{4}$ = $\frac{\Box}{8}$

For spinner B, P(blue) = $\frac{\Box}{4}$

6 16 people go to a knitting group.
13 people go to a sewing group.
9 people go to a knitting and sewing group.

  a Copy the Venn diagram.

    i Write the number for knitting and sewing in the section where the circles overlap.

    ii How many people need to go in the rest of the knitting circle?

    iii How many people need to go in the rest of the sewing circle?

  b What is the probability that a person chosen at random goes to a

    i knitting and sewing group

    ii knitting group only?

knitting   sewing

Q6a ii hint

The total in the whole knitting circle needs to be 16.

Q7a hint

How many edges are there?

7 This fair spinner is spun once.
It is a fair spinner because it is equally likely to land on any edge.

  a How many possible outcomes are there?

  b Work out

    i P(blue)

    ii P(red)

    iii P(blue or red)

    iv P(red or yellow)

    v P(not blue)

    vi P(not yellow)

Q7b i hint

What fraction of the spinner is blue?

Q7b v hint

P(blue) = $\frac{1}{6}$

P(not blue) = $1 - \frac{1}{6}$ = $\frac{\Box}{\Box}$

8 **Problem-solving**

For this spinner P(red) = $\frac{3}{8}$ and P(blue) = $\frac{1}{8}$.

What is the probability of the spinner not landing on blue or red?

Q8 hint

Copy the spinner and colour the blue and red sectors.

9 Tom and Jen flip 2 coins.
Tom wins if he flips 2 heads. Jen wins if she flips a head and a tail.
Work out P(H, H) and P(H and T)?
Is the game fair?

Q9 hint

Do they both have the same probability of winning?

Estimating probability

1 A potter made 100 plates. 10 of them cracked.

a Estimate the probability that the next plate the potter makes cracks.

b The potter makes 200 plates. How many would you expect to crack?

Q1a i hint

'Estimate' means 'do a calculation' not just guess.

2 Anton's aquarium has three types of fish: catfish, rainbowfish and sunfish.
He recorded the first 20 fish to swim to the surface.

Fish	Frequency	Relative frequency
catfish	6	$\frac{6}{20}$
rainbowfish	10	$\frac{\square}{20}$
sunfish	4	$\frac{\square}{20}$
Total frequency	20	

a Estimate the probability that the next fish to swim to the surface is a catfish.

b Estimate the probabilities for rainbowfish and sunfish.

c Anton recorded the next 60 fish to swim to the surface.
How many would you expect to be
i catfish   **ii** rainbowfish   **iii** sunfish?

Q2a hint

Use the relative frequency as the estimate of probability.

Q2c i hint

$\frac{6}{20}$ of 60 = $\frac{6}{20} \square$ 60 = $\square$

3 Penny makes a dice.
She rolls it 240 times and gets 24 sixes.

a How many sixes would you expect in 240 rolls of a fair dice?

b Do you think Penny's dice is fair? Explain.

Q3 hint

Is the expected number close to the actual number?

Tree diagrams

1 **Reasoning** The probability of picking a red card from a pack is $\frac{1}{2}$.
The probability of picking a Queen is $\frac{4}{52}$.

a Which calculation gives the probability of picking a card that is red and a Queen?

A $\frac{1}{2} + \frac{4}{52}$ **B** $\frac{1}{2} \times \frac{4}{52}$

b Work out the probability of picking a card that is red and a Queen.

Q1 hint

Is a red Queen more or less likely than any red card?

2 The tree diagram shows probabilities of picking red and yellow counters from a bag.

a Work out the probability of picking two yellows.

b Work out the probability of picking
i yellow then red (Y, R)
ii red then yellow (R, Y)
iii red or yellow in any order.

1st pick   2nd pick

Q2a hint

Move your finger along the branches for yellow, then yellow. Do you add or multiply?

Q2b iii hint

This means (R, Y) or (Y, R). Is the probability of these two outcomes greater than the probability of just one of them? Do you add or multiply?

3 Jan and Flavia play draughts.
They play two games. The result of the
first game does not affect the result of
the second game.
   a Copy and complete the tree diagram.
   b Work out the probability that
   i Jan wins both games
   ii Flavia wins both games
   iii Jan and Flavia win one game each.

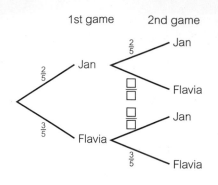

> **Q3a hint**
>
> The second game results are
> independent of the first game
> results.
> So each pair of branches for the
> second game is the same as for the
> first game.

4 4 red and 2 blue counters are placed inside a bag.
One of the counters is removed from the bag.

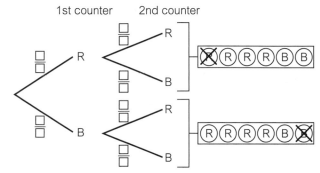

   a What is the probability that the counter is
   i red   **ii** blue?
   b The first counter is not replaced.
   How many counters are left in the bag?
   c Copy and complete the tree diagram.
   d Work out the probability that
   i both counters are red
   ii both counters are blue
   iii the counters are different colours.

Enrichment

1 a Sketch five 8-sided fair spinners like this.
   b Fill in the sectors with any numbers between 1 and 8, so that:

Spinner 1 $P(5) = \frac{1}{2}$

Spinner 2 $P(\text{less than } 3) = \frac{1}{4}$

Spinner 3 $P(\text{not a } 6) = \frac{3}{8}$

Spinner 4 $P(2 \text{ or } 7) = \frac{5}{8}$

Spinner 5 $P(\text{at least } 4) = \frac{3}{4}$

2 Reflect In these strengthen lessons you have answered probability questions
that use
   • Venn diagrams
   • sample space diagrams
   • two-way tables
   • tree diagrams.
Which types of question were easiest? Why?
Which types of question were hardest? Why?
Write down one thing about probability you think you need more practice on.

8 Extend

You will:
• Extend your understanding with problem-solving.

1 **Reasoning a** When you drop a matchbox, is it equally likely to land face up or end up?

   b Marvin says, 'A matchbox has six faces. The probability of it landing on one face is $\frac{1}{6}$.' Explain why he is wrong.

2 Order these events from least likely to most likely.

Event		Probability
A	A person will make a New Year's resolution.	$\frac{9}{20}$
B	A New Year's resolution is related to money.	0.34
C	A person will keep their resolution for more than a month.	$\frac{2}{3}$
D	A New Year's resolution is related to self improvement.	47%

3 Moira recorded the darts thrown by two of her favourite players.

   a Estimate the probability of each player hitting a treble.

   b Which player is more likely to hit a treble? Explain your answer.

   c Modelling Whose estimated probability is a more reliable model for their future dart throws? Explain why.

   d Arrows Alan throws 200 darts.
     Estimate the number of trebles he hits.

	Captain Cole	Arrows Alan
Single	38	8
Double	31	4
Treble	24	8
25 ring	6	2
Bull	1	3

> **Q3b hint**
>
> Write the probabilities as percentages.

4 Design a set of counters so that P(yellow) = P(red) = $\frac{1}{4}$ and P(blue) = $\frac{1}{8}$. There are 3 times more green counters than blue ones.

5 **Real** The frequency table shows the weights of organic Savoy cabbages grown without pesticide or artificial fertiliser.

   a Estimate the probability that an organic Savoy cabbage weighs 1.3 kg or more.

   b A supermarket only buys Savoy cabbages that weigh between 0.9 kg and 1.3 kg. A farmer produces 20 000 organic Savoy cabbages each year. How many of these can the farmer expect to sell to the supermarket?

   c Reasoning A Savoy cabbage on a market stall weighs 1450 g. The stallholder says it is organic. Do you believe him? Explain.

Weight, w (kg)	Frequency
$0.6 \leqslant w < 0.7$	20
$0.7 \leqslant w < 0.8$	60
$0.8 \leqslant w < 0.9$	90
$0.9 \leqslant w < 1.0$	130
$1.0 \leqslant w < 1.1$	220
$1.1 \leqslant w < 1.2$	150
$1.2 \leqslant w < 1.3$	80
$1.3 \leqslant w < 1.4$	40
$1.4 \leqslant w < 1.5$	10

6 **Problem-solving / Reasoning** The probability of a red raffle ticket winning is 0.3.
The probability of a 3-digit raffle number winning is 0.8.
Are there any red 3-digit raffle tickets? Explain your answer.

Topic links: Converting and comparing fractions, decimals, percentages, Adding, subtracting and multiplying fractions, Venn diagrams

7 STEM The table shows the percentage of computer failures caused by each component.

Computer part	Percentage of failures
Motherboard	8
RAM	24
CPU	3
Hard disk	22
PSU	34
Disk drive	6
Other	3

a A computer breaks down. What is the probability that

   i it has a faulty motherboard or hard disk

   ii it does not have a faulty PSU or CPU?

b 80 computers break down. How many do you expect to

   i have a faulty hard disk

   ii have a faulty RAM, disk drive or CPU?

Discussion A shop finds that on average 2 out of 5 computers of a certain brand have faulty RAM. Is this brand worse than average?

8 Annabel rolls an ordinary 4-sided dice and Ben spins the fair spinner. The player with the higher number wins a point. Neither player wins if the numbers are the same.

  a List the possible outcomes.

  b Is the game fair? Explain your answer.

  c Annabel and Ben win 60 points between them. How many points would you expect each player to have won?

Annabel   Ben

> **Q8a hint**
>
> Draw a table.

9 Reasoning Some students built this game to raise money for charity.
A ball falls at random into one of the holes.
Red wins a prize of 50p, blue wins 20p, yellow wins nothing.

  a Copy the table and complete the first three columns.

Colour	Probability	Prize	Expected number of wins in 200 games	Expected prizes in 200 games

b In 200 games

   i how many times would you expect the ball to fall into each colour? Fill in the fourth column.

   ii how much money would be won on each colour? Fill in the last column.

   iii how much are the expected prizes in total?

c How much should the students charge to play the game to make a profit? Explain your answer.

10 The Venn diagram shows people's choice of pepperoni (P), ham (H) and mushrooms (M) as pizza toppings in a restaurant.

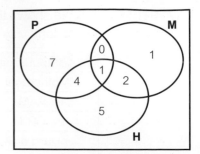

   a How many people had

      i three toppings

      ii only one topping?

   b How many people had pizza?

   c What is the probability that one of these people, picked at random, had two toppings?

Investigation　　　　　　　　　　　　　　　　　　　　　　　　　　**Reasoning**

1 Roll two ordinary dice numbered from 1 to 6 and record their total. Record 100 totals in a frequency table.

2 Draw a bar chart for the results.

3 Which is the most likely total?

4 Work out the theoretical probability of getting a total of 7. (Draw a sample space diagram for the possible outcomes.)

5 Compare the experimental probability of a 7 with the theoretical probability.

6 Do you think the dice is fair? Explain.

---

11 Problem-solving Two players are playing a card game with these sets of cards.

Player A

Player B

Both players shuffle their cards and turn over the top card.

Make up a rule for each player to win so that the game is fair. Use probability to show that the game is fair.

12 Reasoning This table shows the probability of picking different colour counters from a bag.

Colour	Red	Blue	Green	Black
Probability	0.2		0.1	

There are twice as many blue counters as red ones in the bag.

   a Work out

      i P(Blue)　　　　**ii** P(Black)

   b There are 120 counters. How many are there of each colour?

13 Problem-solving Yasmin and Harry play table tennis together.

1st game　　2nd game

            Y < Y / H

            H < Y / H

Q13 Strategy hint

Work out the probability that Yasmin will win a game. Draw a tree diagram.

Based on previous games, Yasmin is twice as likely to win as Harry. Work out the probability that Yasmin will win only one of the next two games.

Subject links: Computing (Q7), PE (Q13)

14 Finance The number of FTSE 100 company share prices that went up from the previous day were recorded for 50 days.

Number of share prices that went up	Frequency
1–20	7
21–40	12
41–60	18
61–80	10
81–100	3

Q14 Literacy hint

The largest 100 companies on the London stock market are called the **FTSE 100**. Each day, their share prices can go up, down or stay the same.

a Estimate the probability that on the next day
  i 21 to 40 share prices will go up
  ii more than 60 share prices will go up.
b The London stock exchange trades for 357 days in a year. On how many days would you expect fewer than 21 share prices to rise?
c Estimate the probability that fewer than 21 share prices will rise on each of two consecutive days.

15 Draw a tree diagram to show the probability of picking a milk, dark or white chocolate at random from this box, eating it, then picking another chocolate at random.
Work out the probability of
a two white chocolates
b at least one milk chocolate.

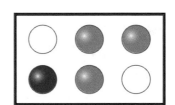

16 Reasoning Umeka placed some red and blue counters in a bag. She drew this tree diagram to show the probabilities of taking two counters from the bag at random, one at a time.

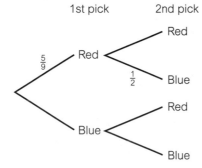

a Was the first counter replaced in the bag before the second counter was taken? Explain your answer.
b Copy and complete the tree diagram.

17 Last season, a football club won 20 games, drew 8 games and lost 10 games.
Use a tree diagram to estimate the probability that the club will
a win the next three games
b win two of the next three games.

Q17 hint

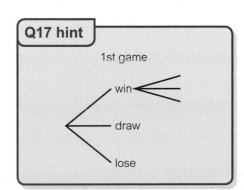

18 Reflect Write a probability question where the answer is 0.6 for each of these types of probability:
  • mutually exclusive events
  • independent events
  • experimental probability
Compare your three questions with others in your class.

Q18 hint

Look back at the lessons where you learned about these types of probability. You could use a game or a sports match as the context.

Reflect

8 Unit test

Log how you did on your Student Progression Chart

1 An ordinary dice numbered 1 to 6 is rolled once.
What is the probability of rolling

a a 6

b a number greater than 4

c not a prime number?

2 In a survey of adults who set themselves some fitness targets, 5% achieved all of them and 15% achieved some of them.
Another fitness survey questions 400 adults. How many would you expect to achieve all of their targets?

3 A farm produces eggs. The farmer discards damaged eggs and sells some for use in making food products. He classes the rest as small, medium or large and sells them in boxes.
The table shows how some eggs produced on the farm were used.

Use	Frequency	Relative frequency
Discarded	50	
Food products	250	
Small	200	
Medium	300	
Large	200	
Total frequency		

a Copy and complete the table.

b Estimate the probability that an egg is not discarded.

c The farm produces 5000 eggs in one particular week. How many would you expect to be large?

4 Antoinette puts the letters of her name inside a bag and picks one letter at random.

a What is the probability that Antoinette picks a vowel?
Erica does the same thing using her own bag with the letters of her name.

b What is the probability that Erica picks a vowel?

c Who is more likely to pick a vowel?

5 In a probability experiment, this spinner was spun twice.

a List all of the possible outcomes.

b Work out the probability of each event.

Event A: The spinner lands on red twice.

Event B: The spinner lands on the same colour twice.

c Are the events A and B mutually exclusive? Give a reason for your answer.

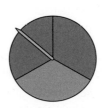

6 These dominoes are placed in a bag.

In a game, each player removes a domino and replaces it.
Player A wins a point if the sum of the dots is even.
Player B wins if there is a different number of dots in each half.
Is the game fair? Give a reason for your answer.

7 This table shows the probability of picking different colour scarves from a drawer.

Colour	White	Purple	Yellow	Pink
Probability	0.3		0.2	

There are twice as many purple scarves as yellow ones in the drawer.
a Work out
  i P(purple) **ii** P(pink)
b There are 20 scarves. How many are there of each colour?

8 A street vendor sells burgers, sausages and falafel.
Each customer gets a hot or cold drink for free. The probability that a customer buys a burger is $\frac{1}{2}$ and sausages is $\frac{1}{4}$. The probability that a customer chooses a hot drink is $\frac{1}{3}$.
a Copy and complete the tree diagram.
b Work out the probability that a customer
  i buys a burger and a cold drink
  ii buys sausages or falafel with a hot drink.

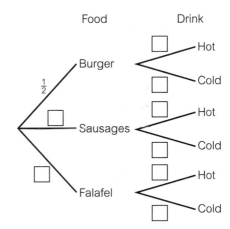

Challenge

9 a Count the letters of the first 10 words of a sentence on this page. Ignore any numbers. Record the frequencies in a table like this.

Letters	Frequency
1 or 2	
3 or 4	
5 or more	

  b Estimate the probability that a randomly chosen word has 3 or 4 letters.
  c If you chose 30 words at random, how many would you expect to have 3 or 4 letters?
  d i Choose a few more sentences at random and count the letters in the first 30 words.
  ii How close was your answer to part **b**?
  e Make a frequency table for all 40 word lengths (10 from part **a** and 30 from part **d**). Estimate the probability that a randomly chosen word has 3 or 4 letters. Compare your probability with a classmate.

10 Reflect Look back at the questions you answered in this test.
  a Which one are you most confident that you have answered correctly? What makes you feel confident?
  b Which one are you least confident that you have answered correctly? What makes you least confident?
  c Discuss the question you feel least confident about with a classmate. How does discussing it make you feel?

Q10 hint

Comment on your understanding of the question and your confidence.

Reflect

9.1 Maps and scales

You will learn to:
- Use scales in maps and plans
- Use and interpret maps.

Why learn this?
Scales on maps help you to work out the real distances between places.

Fluency
What is the scale factor of enlargement from the small rectangle to the large rectangle?

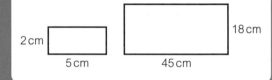

2 cm

5 cm

18 cm

45 cm

Explore
What scale would you use to fit a map of your town on a piece of paper?

Exercise 9.1

1 Copy and complete.
  a 2 m = ☐ cm
  b 620 cm = ☐ m
  c 1350 m = ☐ km

2 On a scale drawing, 1 cm represents 5 cm. What do these lengths on the drawing represent in real life?
  a 5 cm   **b** 6 cm   **c** 15 cm   **d** 4.5 cm
  e How would you represent a real-life length of 35 cm on the scale drawing?

3 This diagram shows the plan of a garden. 1 cm represents 2 m. Sketch the plan and label the real-life lengths in metres.

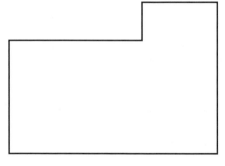

Q4a hint

Map		Real life
1 cm	=	120 m
×15 ↓		↓ ×15
15 cm	=	☐ m

4 On a map, 1 cm represents 120 m. Work out the real-life distance of
  a 15 cm   **b** 12 cm   **c** 45 cm   **d** 6 cm.

Q5a hint

Map		Real life
1 cm	=	20 m
×☐ ↓		↓ ×☐
☐	=	400 m

5 On a map, 1 cm represents 20 m. Work out the lengths on the map for these real-life distances.
  a 400 m   **b** 6000 m   **c** 900 m
  d 1 km   **e** 5 km   **f** 9 km

Subject links: Geography (Q7)

6 Real / Problem-solving Here is a map of a village.
1 cm on the map represents 50 m in real life.
   a From the map, estimate the distance as the crow flies between
      i the traffic lights and the zebra crossing
      ii the school and the playground
      iii the post office and the newsagent's.
   b Clare can walk 500 m in 5 minutes. How long will it take her to walk from her house to the school?

7 Real / Problem-solving Here is a map of Spain.

   a Copy and complete:
   ☐ cm on the map is ☐ km in real life
   b Estimate the distance in km between
      i Barcelona and Pamplona
      ii Salamanca and Valencia
      iii Granada and La Coruña.

8 Real A ladder leans against a wall. Its base is 75 cm from the bottom of the wall. It reaches 3.5 m up the wall. Make a scale drawing of the ladder. What angle does the ladder make with the ground?
Discussion Why is the angle the same on the scale drawing and in real life?

9 An artist sets up two sprinklers 12 m apart. One sprays red paint up to 10 m away from it, and the other sprays yellow paint up to 8 m. They both spray paint in all directions. Make a scale drawing, with 1 cm representing 2 m. Describe the resulting orange shape made by the two sprinklers.

10 Explore What scale would you use to fit a map of your town on a piece of paper?
Look back at the maths you have learned in this lesson.
How can you use it to answer this question?

11 Reflect Michael says, 'When working with scales on maps and diagrams, one of the most important things is multiplying by the correct scale factor'.
Do you agree with Michael? Explain.
What else is important when working with scales on maps and diagrams?

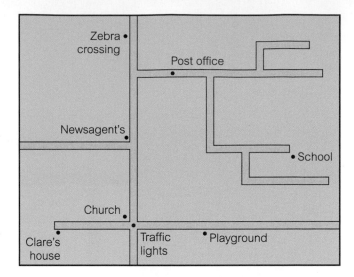

Q6 hint

Claire needs to walk along the roads.

Q11 hint

Look back at some of the things you did to answer the questions in this lesson.

9.2 Bearings

You will learn to:

* Measure and use bearings
* Draw diagrams to scale using bearings.

Why learn this?
Bearings are used in navigation. Ships and planes use them to plan their journeys.

Fluency
What is the angle when you turn
* north to south, clockwise
* north to west, clockwise
* north to south east, anticlockwise
* north to north west, anticlockwise?

Explore
How are bearings the same as angles? How are they different?

Exercise 9.2

1 Draw these angles accurately using a ruler and a protractor.
   a 75°   **b** 130°
   c 245°   **d** 192°

2 Work out the missing angles. Give reasons for your answers.

   a   **b**   **c**

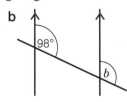
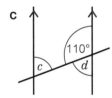

3 A map has a scale of 1 cm to 20 km.
   a What is 6 cm on the map in real life?
   b What is 120 km in real life on the map?

4 Write each compass direction as a bearing.
   a east   **b** south   **d** west
   e south east   **f** south west   **g** north west

5 a Measure the bearing of Village Green from Castle Rock.
   b Measure the bearing of Castle Rock from Village Green.

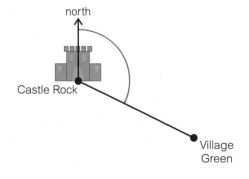

> **Key point**
>
> A **bearing** is an angle in degrees, clockwise from north.
> A bearing is always written using three digits.
>
>
>
> This bearing is 025°.

> **Q5 hint**
>
> Always measure clockwise from North.

Topic links: Angles in triangles

Worked example

Geneva Airport is 400 km from Paris Orly Airport on a bearing of 135°. Draw this bearing accurately using a scale of 1 cm to 50 km.

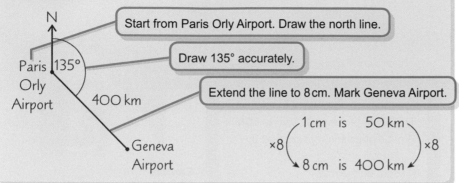

Start from Paris Orly Airport. Draw the north line.

Draw 135° accurately.

Extend the line to 8 cm. Mark Geneva Airport.

$$1\,\text{cm} \quad \text{is} \quad 50\,\text{km}$$
$$\times 8 \qquad\qquad \times 8$$
$$8\,\text{cm} \quad \text{is} \quad 400\,\text{km}$$

6 **Real** Draw these bearings accurately. Use the scale 1 cm to 50 km.
  a St Symphorien airport is 380 km from Salatos airport on a bearing of 302°.
  b Bellegarde airport is 172 km from St Symphorien airport on a bearing of 170°.

7 A ship is 120 km west of a lighthouse. The ship sails on a bearing of 060° for 18 km.
  a Make an accurate drawing with 1 cm representing 10 km.
  b What is the bearing and distance of the lighthouse from the ship?

8 A ship sails 8 km from port on a bearing of 040°. It then turns and sails for 14 km on a bearing of 200°.
  a Use a scale of 1 cm to 2 km to draw an accurate scale drawing of the journey of the ship.
  b How far away is the ship from its starting point?

9 A plane leaves the airport and flies on a bearing of 070° for 60 miles and then on a bearing of 240° for a further 100 miles.
  a Use a scale of 1 cm to 10 miles to show the plane's journey.
  b How far away is the plane from its starting point?
  c What bearing should the plane use to fly directly back to the airport?

10 **Problem-solving**
  a The bearing of B from A is 120°. Work out the bearing of A from B.
  b The bearing of C from D is 240°. Work out the bearing of D from C.
  c The bearing of E from F is 320°. Work out the bearing of F from E.

11 **Explore** How are bearings the same as angles?
  How are they different?
  Look back at the maths you have learned in this lesson.
  How can you use it to answer this question?

12 **Reflect** Sian says, 'To work out a bearing you just measure the angle between two paths.'
  Look back at the questions in this lesson.
  In what way is Sian correct?
  In what way is she incorrect?

Q8 hint

Make a sketch first. Start with:

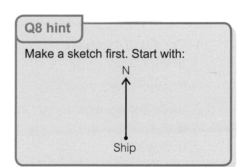

N

Ship

Q10 Strategy hint

Sketch a diagram. Use angle facts for parallel lines to work out the bearing of A from B.

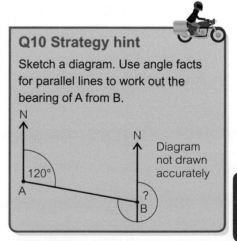

Diagram not drawn accurately

Q12 hint

Does it matter which path you place the 0 line on?

Explore

Reflect

9.3 Scales and ratio

You will learn to:
- Draw diagrams to scale
- Use and interpret scale drawings.

CONFIDENCE

Why learn this?
Architects use scale diagrams to draw plans of buildings before they are constructed.

Fluency
The scale of a map is 1 cm to 50 m.
What distance is represented by
- 2 cm
- 5 cm on the map?
How long on the map would a real-life distance of
- 350 m
- 1000 m be?

Explore
Why is it difficult to draw an accurate world map?

Exercise 9.3

Warm up

1 Copy and complete.
 a 25 000 cm = ☐ m
 b 40 000 cm = ☐ m
 c 100 000 cm = ☐ km
 d 150 000 cm = ☐ km

2 Write these ratios in the form $1:n$.
 a 2:10
 b 4:12
 c 20:300
 d 40:400

> **Q2a hint**
> 2 : 10
> ÷2 ⤵ ⤵ ÷2
> 1 : ?

3 Copy and complete these equivalent ratios.
 a 1:100 = 3:☐
 b 1:30 = 5:☐
 c 1:250 = 4:☐
 d 1:500 = 3:☐

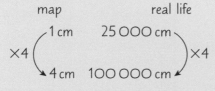

Worked example

A map has a **scale** of 1:25 000.
What is the real-life distance in metres for 4 cm on the map?

```
   map              real life
   1 cm       25 000 cm
×4 (          ) ×4
   4 cm   100 000 cm
```

1 cm represents 25 000 cm, so 4 cm represents
4 × 25 000 = 100 000 cm

100 000 cm ÷ 100 = 1000 m

> Work out how much 4 cm represents, in real life, in centimetres.

> Convert the distance to metres.

> **Key point**
> The **scale** on a map is given as a ratio $1:n$. For example, 1:25 000 means 1 cm on the map represents 25 000 cm in real life.

4 James is using a map with a scale of 1:20 000.
 He measures these distances.
 What are the distances in real life?
 Write your answers in metres.
 a 4 cm
 b 6 cm
 c 4.5 cm
 d 0.5 cm

Topic links: Area, Ratio and proportion

Subject links: Geography (Q6), Design and technology (Q7)

5 Problem-solving Match the scales **A** to **D** with **i** to **iv**.

A 1:10 000   **i** 1 cm to 2.5 km
B 1:250 000   **ii** 1 cm to 250 m
C 1:50 000   **iii** 1 cm to 500 m
D 1:25 000   **iv** 1 cm to 100 m

6 Real Here is a map of the area surrounding Liechtenstein. The scale is 1:500 000

  a **i** Measure the distance in centimetres between Ruggell and Buchs.
     ii Calculate the real-life distance in kilometres.
  b Calculate the real-life distance in kilometres between
     i Balzers and Planken
     ii Triesen and Vaduz
     iii Trübbach and Mauren.

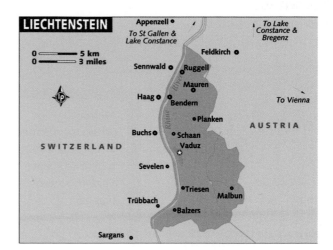

7 Problem-solving Here is a rough sketch of a house.

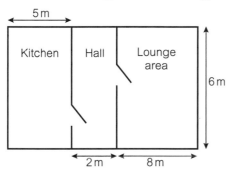

Q7 hint

Convert m on the rough sketch to cm.

  a Make an accurate scale drawing using a scale of 1:200.
  b Divide the living area into two rooms, one with an area of 30 m².
  c What is the area of the other room?

8 Problem-solving Write each scale as a map ratio.
  a 1 cm to 1 m   **b** 1 cm to 5 km
  c 5 cm to 1 km   **d** 2 cm to 1.5 km

Q8 hint

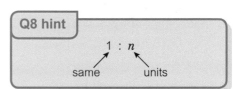

1 : n
same   units

9 a What real-life distance does 4 cm represent on maps with these scales?
    i 1:10 000   **ii** 1:50 000   **iii** 1:250 000
  b For each scale, work out the length on the map that represents a real-life distance of 10 km.
    i 1:10 000   **ii** 1:50 000   **iii** 1:250 000

10 Explore Why is it difficult to draw an accurate world map?
Look back at the maths you have learned in this lesson.
How can you use it to answer this question?

11 Reflect Jamie says, 'To write 1 cm to 50 km as a map ratio, I first multiply 1 by 100 because 1 m = 100 cm. Then I multiply that by 1000, because 1 km = 1000 m. Then I multiply by 50.'
Look back at the questions you answered in this lesson.
Did you use a method similar to Jamie's?
Compare methods with others in your class.

Explore

Reflect

9.4 Congruent and similar shapes

You will learn to:

- Identify congruent and similar shapes
- Use congruence to solve problems in triangles and quadrilaterals.

CONFIDENCE

Why learn this?
Car manufacturers produce car parts which are congruent so that they fit into all cars in the production line.

Fluency
Which transformations give
a congruent shapes
b similar shapes?
Find the missing angle in this triangle.

Explore
How do artists making special effects for film use similar shapes?

Exercise 9.4

Warm up

1 What is the scale factor of the enlargement from
a A to B
b B to A?

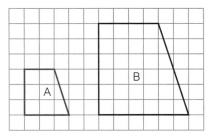

2 Which angles are equal?
Give reasons.

a

b

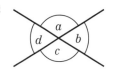

3 Which of these shapes are congruent?
Which shapes are similar?

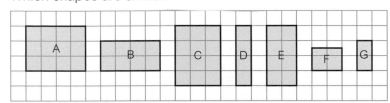

4 Reasoning Draw accurately two different triangles ABC where angle A = 30°, side AB = 6 cm, side BC = 4 cm.
Discussion If two triangles have two sides and one angle the same, are they congruent?

Q4 Strategy hint
Sketch the triangle ABC first.

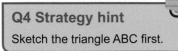

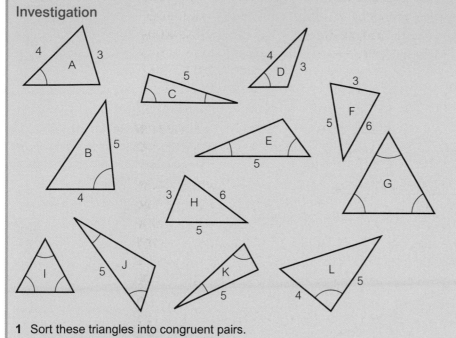

Key point

Triangles are congruent if they have equivalent
- SSS (all three sides)
- SAS (two sides and the included angle)
- ASA (two angles and the included side)
- AAS (two angles and another side).

Triangles where all the angles are the same (AAA) are similar, but might not be congruent.

1 Sort these triangles into congruent pairs.
2 Which triangles are left over? Are there any similar triangles?
3 Which of these rules define whether two triangles will be congruent or similar?
   Triangles with three sides the same (SSS)
   Triangles with two sides and the angle between them the same (SAS)
   Triangles with two angles and the included side the same (ASA)
   Triangles with all angles the same (AAA)?
4 Does having two sides and an angle the same always give congruent triangles?

5 Each pair of triangles is congruent. Explain why.

a

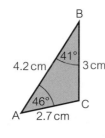

b

c

Q5 hint

Choose reasons from SSS, SAS, ASA or AAA.

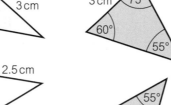

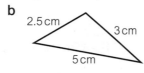

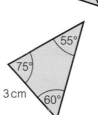

6 **Reasoning** Which of these triangles is congruent to triangle ABC?
   Give reasons.

Q6 hint

You may need to work out missing angles.

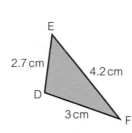

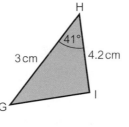

7 **Reasoning** Are all right-angled triangles with one side 6 cm and
   hypotenuse 11 cm congruent?

8 Reasoning AB and CD are parallel lines, AB = CD.

  a What can you say about angles x and y?

  b Copy the diagram. Mark pairs of equal angles.

  c Show that triangle AEB and triangle CEB are congruent.

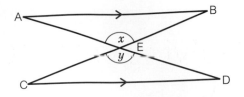

9 Reasoning Explain why triangle ABC is similar to triangle DEF.

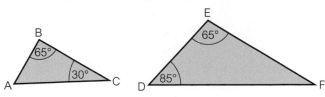

> **Key point**
>
> To show that two shapes are similar, show that corresponding angles are equal, or find the scale factor for corresponding sides.
>

  Discussion Are all squares similar? Are all regular pentagons similar?

10 Triangle A and triangle B are similar.

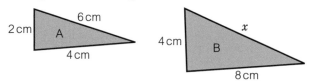

  Work out the missing length in triangle B.

> **Q10 hint**
>
> What is the scale factor of the enlargement from A to B?

11 Each set shows three similar triangles. Calculate the lengths labelled with letters.

  a

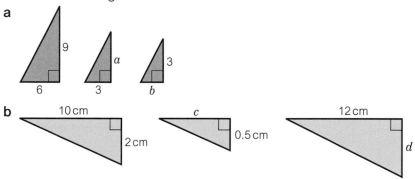

  b

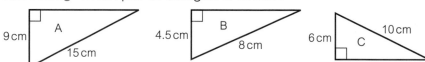

12 Reasoning Which pair of triangles is similar?

9 cm A 15 cm
4.5 cm B 8 cm
6 cm C 10 cm

13 Explore How do artists making special effects for film use similar shapes?

  Look back at the maths you have learned in this lesson.

  How can you use it to answer this question?

14 Reflect Ed says, 'Two triangles have equal length sides, so they must be congruent.'

  Rachel says, 'Two triangles have equal angles, so they must be congruent.'

  Who is right and who is wrong?

  Explain and correct the mistake that person has made.

9.5 Solving geometry problems

You will learn to:

• Use similarity to solve problems in 2D shapes.

Why learn this?
Surveyors use similar triangles to find out the heights of tall structures.

Fluency
Find the missing numbers in each equivalent ratio.

• $4:6 = 8:\square$
• $3:2 = \square:8$
• $5:7 = \square:21$
• $2:5 = 9:\square$

Explore
Can you use triangles to find the height of a tree?

Exercise 9.5

1 Are these triangles similar? Explain.

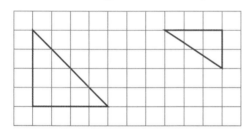

2 These shapes are similar. Find the missing side, x.

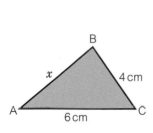 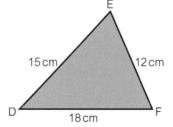

3 Reasoning

a Explain why angle a = angle e.

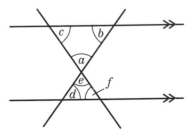

b Which angle is equal to angle b? Explain.
c Which angle is equal to angle f? Explain.

4 Reasoning a Find the angles in triangle CDE. Give reasons.

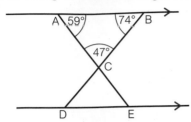

b Are triangles ABC and CDE similar? Explain.
c Sketch the triangles the same way up.
Label the vertices and angles.

5 Reasoning a Show that triangles MNP and PQR are similar.

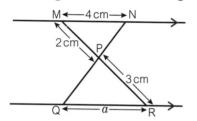

b Find the missing length, a.

Q4c hint

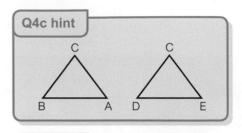

Q5a hint

Follow the method in Q4 parts **a** and **b**.

Worked example

a Explain why triangles ABD and ACE are similar.

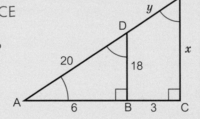

Triangle ABD	Triangle ACE
∠A	∠A
∠B = 90°	∠C = 90°

∠D = ∠E (corresponding angles)

The triangles have the same angles (AAA).

b Work out length x.

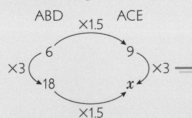

9 × 3 is easier to work out than 18 × 1.5, but they give the same answer.

$x = 9 × 3 = 27$

c Find the length of AE.

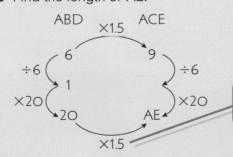

It is easier to work out 20 × 1.5 than 9 ÷ 6 × 20, but they give the same answer.

AE = 20 × 1.5 = 30 cm

d Find the length of y.

$y = 30 - 20 = 10$ cm

Topic links: Angles in triangles, Ratio and proportion

6 Reasoning

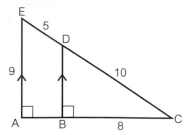

a Explain why triangle ACE and BCD are similar triangles.
b Calculate the length BD.
c Calculate the length AB.

Q6c hint

Find the length AC first.

7 Reasoning

a Explain why triangle ABC and ADE are similar triangles.

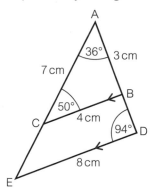

b Find the length of AE.
c Find the length of CE.
d Find the length of BD.

 8 Real / Problem-solving Calculate the height of the Eiffel Tower using similar triangles.

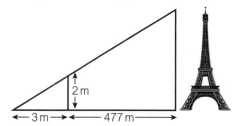

9 Explore Can you use triangles to find the height of a tree?
Look back at the maths you have learned in this lesson.
How can you use it to answer this question?

10 Reflect Look back at Q6. To answer this question you had to:
• show that triangles are similar
• identify corresponding lengths
• solve equations.
Which of these tasks was easiest? Explain.
Which of these tasks was hardest? Explain.

9 Check up

Log how you did on your Student Progression Chart.

Maps and scales

1 A diagram uses a scale of 1 cm to 12 cm.
Calculate the real-life length represented by 4 cm.

2 A map uses this scale: 1 cm to 30 m.
What distance on the map represents 15 m?

3 This map of a town has a scale of 1 cm to 50 m.

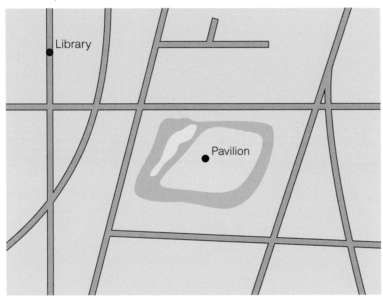

a Find the distance in metres between the Library and the Pavilion as the crow flies.
b The distance between the Library and the Town Hall is 400 m.
What is the distance on the map?

4 A map has a scale of 1 : 25 000.
What distance in metres does 4 cm on the map represent?

Bearings

5 The diagram shows the location of two airports in London.
Measure the bearing of Stansted airport from London City airport.

6 A ship sails 12 km from port on a bearing of 080°.
It then turns and sails for 9 km on a bearing of 140°.
a Use a scale of 1 cm to 3 km to draw an accurate scale drawing of the journey of the ship.
b How far away is the ship from its starting point?
c What bearing should the ship sail to return to port?

Congruence and similarity

7 Which two of these triangles are congruent? Give a reason.

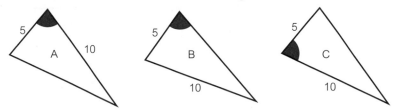

8 All three triangles are similar. Find the missing lengths.

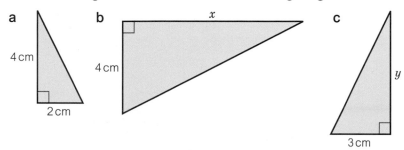

9 Explain why triangles ABC and ADE are similar.

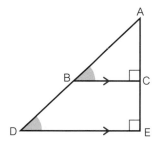

10 a Show that triangles ABC and ADE are similar.
   b Work out the lengths marked with letters.

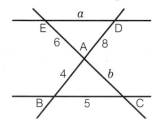

11 How sure are you of your answers? Were you mostly
   ☹ **Just guessing**   😐 **Feeling doubtful**   🙂 **Confident**
   What next? Use your results to decide whether to strengthen or extend your learning.

Challenge

12 Draw three different right-angled triangles with an angle of 45°.
   a Are they all similar? Explain your reasoning.
   b Repeat for right-angled triangles with an angle of 30°.

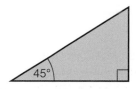

Master
P201

Check
P213

STRENGTHEN

Extend
P219

Test
P223

9 Strengthen

You will:

- Strengthen your understanding with practice.

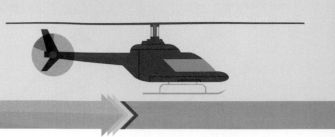

Maps and scales

1 Naomi designed this logo. Make an accurate scale drawing of the logo, using 1 cm to represent 3 cm.

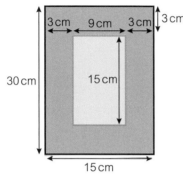

2 A map has scale 1 cm to 50 m.
What distance on the map represents a real-life distance of
a 100 m
b 300 m
c 1000 m
d 2000 m
e 1 km?

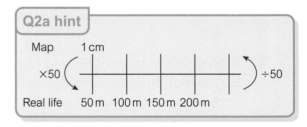

Q2a hint

Map   1 cm

×50   ÷50

Real life   50 m   100 m   150 m   200 m

3 This plan shows Adrian's garden. The scale is 1 cm to 4 m.

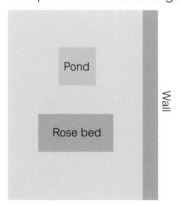

In real-life
a how long is the wall
b how long is one side of the square pond
c what is the length and width of the rose bed?

4 A diagram has scale 1 cm to 20 cm.
Calculate the real-life length of:
a 5 cm   **b** 10 cm   **c** 23 cm   **d** 42 cm.

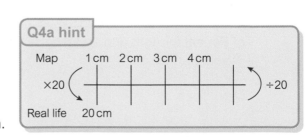

Q4a hint

Map   1 cm   2 cm   3 cm   4 cm

×20   ÷20

Real life   20 cm

5 Real / Problem-solving

This map uses a scale of 1 cm to 500 m.
Find the distance in metres between

a the Lincoln Memorial and the
Jefferson Memorial

b the Watergate Complex and the
White House

c the Lincoln Memorial and Federal
Bureau of Investigation.

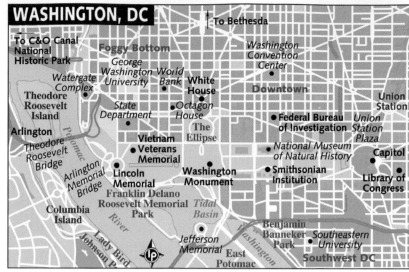

> **Q5 Strategy hint**
>
> Measure the distance on the map.
> Use the scale to work out the
> real-life distance.

6 Write each scale as a ratio.

a 1 cm to 100 cm

b 1 cm to 20 cm

c 1 cm to 1 m

d 1 cm to 3 m

e 1 cm to 1 km

> **Q6 hint**
>
> In a ratio, both numbers must be in
> the same units. Convert m and km
> to cm.

Bearings

1 Write the bearing of B from A in each of these diagrams.

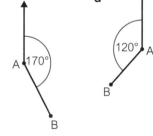

> **Q1 hint**
>
> A bearing is measured clockwise
> from north. It is always written as
> 3 digits. A 48° bearing is 048°.

2 a Mark a point, P, on a piece of paper.

b Draw an accurate bearing of 075° from P.

> **Q2b hint**
>
> Draw a north line at P first.

3 a Mark a point, Q, on a piece of paper.

b Draw a bearing of 330° from Q.

**4 Trace these points.
Measure and write
down the bearing
of**

a Y from X

b X from X

c Z from Y

d X from Y.

> **Q4a hint**
>
> Draw the north line at X. Join XY.

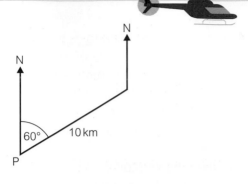

5 A ship sails 10 km from port, P, on a bearing of 060°.
It then turns and sails for 8 km on a bearing of 140°.
  a Copy and complete this sketch of the ship's journey.
  b Draw an accurate scale drawing using 1 cm to 2 km.
  c Use your diagram to work out
    i how far the ship is from port
    ii the bearing the ship needs to sail on to get back to port.

Congruence and similarity

1 Reasoning Which of these triangles is not congruent to A?

   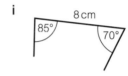

Q1 hint

If you rotated triangles B, C and D
which one would not fit exactly on A?

2 a Copy each pair of diagrams accurately. Then draw, or continue, the lines to make two triangles.

  i

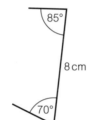 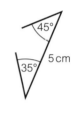

  ii

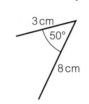 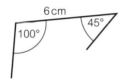

  iii

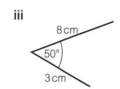

  b Use the diagrams to help you decide whether two triangles are congruent if:
    i two corresponding angles and the length of the side between them are equal (ASA)
    ii three angles are equal (AAA)
    iii the lengths of two corresponding sides and the angle between them are equal (SAS).

3 Triangles P and Q are similar.

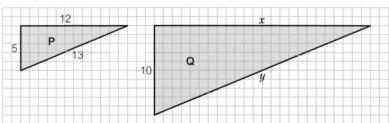

  a Copy and complete the table showing the pairs of corresponding sides.
  b Use a pair of corresponding sides to work out the scale factor from P to Q.
  c Use the scale factor to work out x and y.

P	Q
5	10
	x
13	

Q3c hint

P × scale factor = Q
□ × □ = □

Topic links: Ratio and proportion, Angles in triangles

Subject links: Geography (Maps and scales Q5, Enrichment Q9)

4 Reasoning Find the missing length x in these similar shapes.

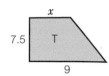

Q4 Strategy hint
Draw a table for S and T like the one in Q3.

5 Reasoning / Problem-solving All these shapes are similar. Work out the lengths marked with letters.

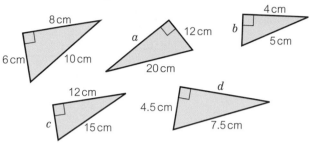
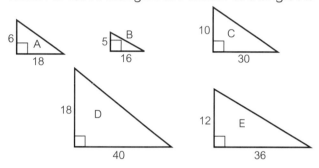

Q5 Strategy hint
Sketch the triangles the same way up.

6 Which of these triangles are similar to triangle A?

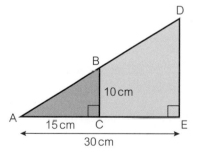

7 Reasoning The diagram shows two triangles.
  a Explain why
   i $a = b$ **ii** $c = d$ **iii** $e = f$.
  b When three pairs of angles are equal, what does this tell you about the two triangles?
  c Trace each triangle and then sketch them the same way up. Label the measurements you know. Find the missing lengths.

8 Reasoning
  a What can you say about BC and DE? Explain how you know.
  b Why does angle ABC = angle ADE?
  c What is the scale factor of enlargement from triangle ABC to ADE?
  d Work out the length DE.

Enrichment

9 a Find a map of your local area.
  b Use the map to find the distance from your school to your home.
  c Make a list of the landmarks that are within 5 km of your school.

10 Reflect Look back at the strategy hints in these strengthen lessons. Did they help you to answer the questions?
Think about a question you found difficult. Describe a strategy you used to help solve the problem.

Reflect

9 Extend

You will:
- Extend your understanding through problem-solving.

1 Use a scale of 1 cm : 1 km to draw each bearing accurately.
   a Caltown is 8 km from Mayville on a bearing of 050°
   b Georgetown is 4 km from Caltown on a bearing of 210°
   c What is the real-life distance between Georgetown and Mayville?

Q1 hint

Start with Mayville.

N ↑

Mayville •

2 Write each map scale as a ratio.
   a 2 cm to 1 km   b 4 cm to 20 km   c 6 cm to 4 km

Q2 hint

1 : ☐

3 **Real / Modelling** This map of Wales has a scale of 1 : 2 500 000.

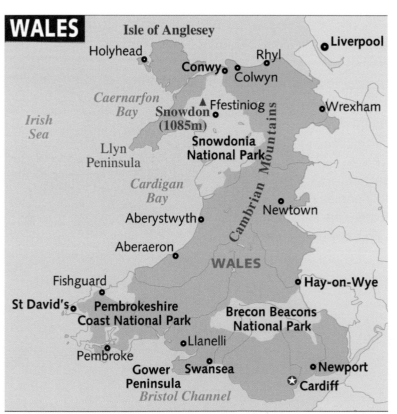

   a Calculate the real-life distance between
      i Newport and Pembroke
      ii Swansea and Aberaeron
      iii Hay-on-Wye and Conwy.
   b Estimate how long it takes to travel by car at 60 km/h between Liverpool and Swansea.
   c Why is your answer to part **b** an estimate?

Q3a hint

Give your answers in km.

4 **Real / STEM** In a Sankey diagram the widths of the arrows are drawn to scale to show how much each part represents.

Q4 hint

Measure the arrows.

a This Sankey diagram shows how the energy is used in an old-fashioned light bulb.
   i How many joules does 1 cm represent?
   ii How much energy is transferred by heat?
   iii How much energy is transferred by light?

D2 U6.4

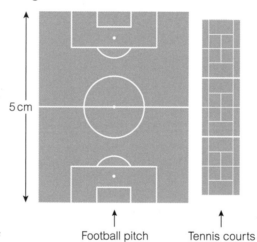

Heat energy

0.75 cm

40 J 1 cm

0.25 cm

Light energy

b Using squared paper, and a suitable scale, draw a Sankey diagram for these bulbs:
   i an energy-saving lamp with an input of 100 J, 75 J light energy and 25 J heat energy
   ii a filament lamp with input of 60 J, 20 J light energy and 40 J heat energy.

5 **Real / Problem-solving / Reasoning**
The real-life length of the football pitch is 100 m.
Use this plan of a sports field to answer these questions.

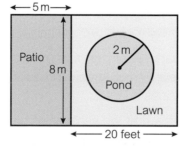

a Work out the scale used in the plan.
b Calculate the area of the football pitch.
c Calculate the area of one tennis court.
d It costs £22.50 per square metre to lay artificial turf. How much will it cost to turf the tennis courts?

5 cm

Football pitch   Tennis courts

Q5b hint

Calculate the width of the football pitch first.

6 **Problem-solving** This sketch shows the plan for Mr Jones's garden.
a Choose an appropriate scale and make an accurate scale drawing.
b Calculate the area of the patio in m^2.
c Mr Jones wants to lay paving stones on his patio. Each paving stone measures 50 cm by 50 cm. How many paving stones does Mr Jones need?
d Each paving stone costs £5. Calculate the cost of the paving stones.

←—5 m—→

Patio

8 m

2 m

Pond

Lawn

←—— 20 feet ——→

7 **Reasoning** In this arrowhead, angle BAD = 35°, angle ABD = 40°.
Calculate
a angle BDA
b angle BDC
c angle DCB.
d Explain why triangles ABD and BCD are congruent.

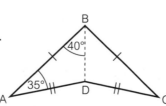

B

40°

35°

A   D   C

8 Reasoning These triangles are all congruent.
Work out the missing sides and angles.

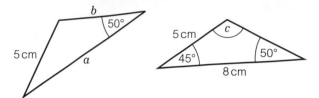

Q8 hint

Sketch them all facing the same way.
For example, like this:

9 Reasoning

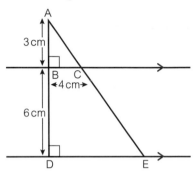

Q9 hint

You can use Pythagoras' Theorem
to find the lengths of sides in a
right-angled triangle.

a Find the length AC. **b** Find the length AE.

10 Real / Problem-solving This map shows some airports in Germany.

A plane leaves Hanover airport and travels for 200 km on a bearing of
120°. It then travels for 400 km on a bearing of 200°.
At which airport does it land?

11 Three radio masts are at the vertices of an equilateral triangle with side
30 km. Each has a range of 10 km.
a Draw a scale diagram to show the areas the radio signal can reach.
b Would you get radio if you stood in the middle of the triangle?

12 Sketch each of these situations. Use angle facts to answer the questions.
a A ship sails from port on a bearing of 050° for 10 km.
What bearing must it travel to return to port?
b A plane flies from the airport on a bearing of 230° for 100 km.
What bearing must it travel to return to the airport?

Topic links: Ratio and proportion, Angles in triangles

Subject links: Geography (Q3, Q10)

13 Reasoning Find the lengths marked x and y on these diagrams.

Q13 hint

First show that the two triangles ABD and ACE are similar.

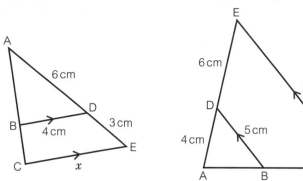

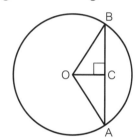

14 Reasoning AC is a diagonal of the rectangle ABCD.
Explain why triangle ABC is congruent to triangle ADC.

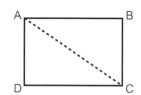

15 Reasoning The centre of this circle is O.
Prove that triangle OBC and triangle OAC are congruent.

Investigation   Reasoning

1 Are these rectangles similar?

3 cm   A   9 cm   B

4 cm   12 cm

D2 46.4

2 Write the ratio of their lengths and their areas.
3 What is the scale factor?
4 What is the area factor?

Lengths   A   ×☐   B   Areas   A   ×☐   B

3   :   9   12   :   ☐

5 Draw five pairs of other similar rectangles. Copy and complete this table.

Length	Width	Ratio of lengths	Scale factor	Ratio of areas	Area factor

6 Can you see a pattern between the area factor and the scale factor?
7 Repeat the investigation for right-angled triangles.

---

16 Reflect Copy and complete this paragraph with at least three
sentences:
When I am given a mathematics problem to solve, this is what I do...
Compare your paragraph with others in your class.
What did you learn from your classmates?

9 Unit test

Log how you did on your Student Progression Chart.

1 This is a map of some Greek islands.

   a Measure the bearing of Lipsi from Patmos.

   b Measure the bearing of Kalimnos from Lipsi.

   c Which island is on a bearing of 143° from Ag. Marina?

2 The scale on a diagram is 1 cm to 25 m.
   Calculate the real-life length of

   a 4 cm

   b 10 cm

   c 0.5 cm.

3 A map uses a scale of 1 cm to 25 m.
   What length on the map represents
   a real-life length of

   a 75 m

   b 200 m

   c 500 m

   d 5 m?

4 The scale of this map is 1 : 25 000.

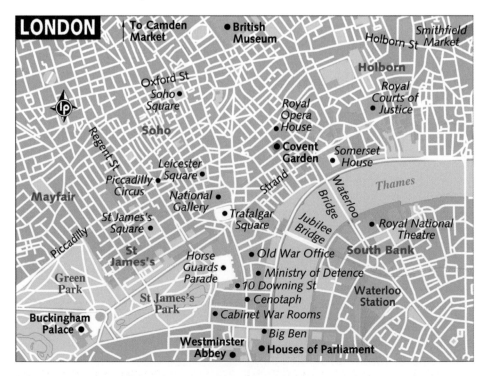

Use the map to find the distances, in metres, from

a Trafalgar Square to Westminster Abbey

b Piccadilly Circus to St James's Square.

5 A ship sails 30 km from port on a bearing of 040°.
It then turns and sails for 20 km on a bearing of 150°.
  a Use a scale of 1 cm to 5 km to draw an accurate scale
  drawing of the journey of the ship.
  b How far away is the ship from its starting point?
  c What bearing should the ship sail to return to port?

6 Triangles A, B and C are all congruent.

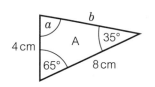
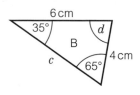
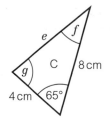

  a Work out the missing sides and angles.
  b Explain why triangle D is not congruent to the others.

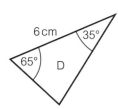

7 These triangles are similar. Find the missing lengths.

  a 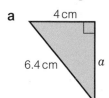   **b** 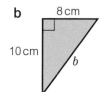   **c**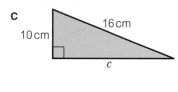

8 These trapeziums are similar. Find the missing sides.

  a 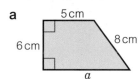   **b** 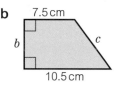   **c**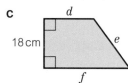

9 a Show why triangles ACE and BCD are similar triangles.
  b Calculate the length BD.
  c Calculate the length AB.

10 In this parallelogram the diagonals are drawn.
Prove that there are two pairs of congruent triangles.

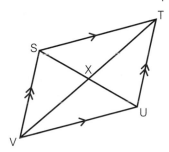

Challenge

11 Are all right-angled triangles similar? Explain.

12 Reflect Make a list of all the topics you have worked on in this
Unit where you have used multiplicative reasoning.
List some other mathematics topics that use multiplicative reasoning.
Compare your list with your classmates.

> **Q12 hint**
>
> Remember 'multiplicative' means
> 'involving multiplication or division'.
> Reasoning is being able to explain
> why.

Reflect

10.1 Plotting linear graphs

You will learn to:
- Plot straight-line graphs
- Find the y-intercept of a straight-line graph.

Why learn this?
Straight-line graphs can be used to convert between different currencies.

Fluency
What are the coordinates of these points?

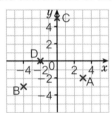

Explore
Can you predict where a line will cross the axis?

Exercise 10.1

1 Work out $y = 2x - 3$ when

  a $x = 4$ **b** $x = 0$ **c** $x = -3$

2 Write the equations of the lines.
   Discussion How many points do you need to plot to draw a straight-line graph?

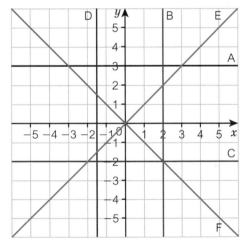

3 a Copy and complete the table of values for the equation $y = 3x - 4$.

x	−2	−1	0	1	2
y					

  b Draw a pair of axes and plot the graph of $y = 3x - 4$.

4 Plot and label these graphs. Use axes from −10 to +10.

  a $y = 5 + x$ **b** $y = 4 - 2x$ **c** $y = \frac{1}{2}x$

> **Q4 hint**
>
> Draw a table of values like the one in Q3. Choose at least three x-values. Make sure the coordinates will be on your grid.

Topic links: Using formulae, Conversions

CONFIDENCE

Warm up

Worked example

Plot the graph of $2y + 3x = 8$.

When $x = 0$:

$2y + 3 \times 0 = 8$

$2y = 8$

$y = 4$

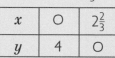

> To find the **y-intercept**, substitute $x = 0$ into the equation. Solve to find the value of y.

When $y = 0$:

$2 \times 0 + 3x = 8$

$3x = 8$

$x = \frac{8}{3}$

$x = 2\frac{2}{3}$

> To find the **x-intercept**, substitute $y = 0$ into the equation. Solve to find the value of x.

x	0	$2\frac{2}{3}$
y	4	0

> Draw a table of values with $x = 0$ and $y = 0$.

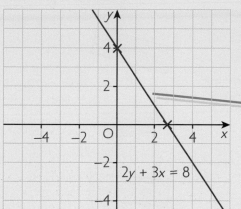

> Plot the points and join them with a straight line. Label the line with its equation.

Key point

The **y-intercept** is where a line crosses the y-axis.

To find the y-intercept of a graph, find the y-coordinate where $x = 0$.

To find the x-intercept of a graph, find the x-coordinate where $y = 0$.

5 The equation of a line is $3y - 8x = 12$.

   a Work out y when $x = 0$.

   b Work out x when $y = 0$.

   c Write down the coordinate pairs and then plot the graph.

6 On separate axes plot the graphs of:

   a $x + y = 4$

   b $x - y = 5$

   c $2x + 5y + 9 = 0$

   d $7y - 11x = 18$

Discussion Look at the equation in part **a**.

Where do you think the graph of $x + y = -3$ will cross the axes?

> **Q6 hint**
>
> You could use a graph plotting package to plot the graphs.

Investigation   **Problem-solving**

Draw a pair of axes from −5 to 5.

1 On the axes plot and label the graphs:

   a $y = x$ **b** $y = x + 1$ **c** $y = x + 3$

   d $y = x - 1$ **e** $y = x - 2$

2 Write the coordinates of the points where each line crosses the y-axis.

3 Compare your answer to Q2 to the equation of the line. What do you notice?

4 Where do you think the graph of $y = x + 2$ will cross the y-axis? Plot it to check.

7 Work out the y-intercept for each line.

a $y = 3x - 4$ b $y = 2x + 1$ c $y = x - 3$

d $y = -2x + 1$ e $y = -3x - 4$ f $y = -x - 5$

g $y = x$ h $y = -x$ i $y = \frac{1}{3}x + 1$

j $y = \frac{2}{3}x - 4$

Discussion How did you work out your answers?

8 **Reasoning** Match the equations to their graphs.

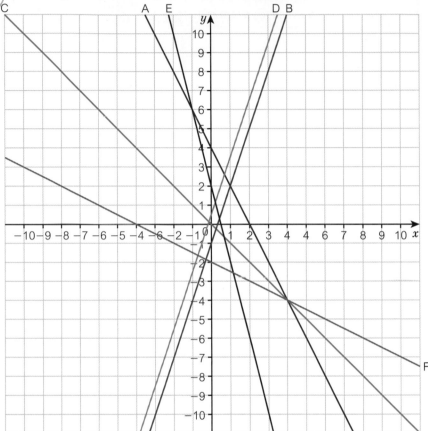

$y = 3x + 1$

$y = -4x + 2$

$y = 3x - 1$

$y = -x$

$y = -\frac{1}{2}x - 2$

$y = -2x + 4$

9 **Problem-solving** Write the equations of three lines that go through the point (0, 5).

Q9 hint

The equations all need to start $y =$

10 **Real / Modelling** A law firm uses a graph of this equation to work out the monthly pay for staff:

$y = 20x + 1750$

where x is the number of new clients and y is the total monthly pay (£).

a Draw the graph of this equation.

The pay includes a basic payment (£), and then an amount (£) for every new client.

b What is the basic payment?

Q10b hint

What is the pay when there are no new clients?

11 **Explore** Can you predict where a line will cross the axis? What have you learned in this lesson to help you answer this question? What other information do you need?

12 **Reflect** Write down what you think 'linear' means.

$y = mx + c$ is a linear equation.

Write, in your own words, what m and c stand for.

Write a hint to yourself so you can remember what they stand for.

Q12 Literacy hint

Some say the m comes from the French word 'monter', meaning 'to climb'.

Explore

Reflect

10.2 The gradient

You will learn to:
- Find the gradient of a straight-line graph
- Plot graphs using the gradient and y-intercept.

CONFIDENCE

Why learn this?
Economists use graphs to help predict profit.

Fluency
What is:
- 3×0
- $3 \times 0 + 4$
- $3 \times 0 - 7$?

Explore
What does a 'Gradient 12%' road sign mean?

Exercise 10.2

1 Find the y-intercept of each line.

a $y = 2x + 4$ **b** $y = -3x + 1$ **c** $y = 2x - 5$ **d** $y = -3x - 2$

2 Which is the steepest graph?

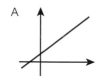 A   B   C

Key point
The steepness of the graph is called the **gradient**.

Worked example

Find the **gradient** of the line.

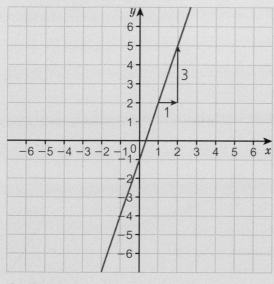

Gradient = 3

Choose a point on the line.
Draw a horizontal line 1 unit in the x-direction.
Draw a vertical line to the graph line.
When the x-value increases by 1, the y-value increases by 3.

Warm up

3 Work out the gradient of each line.

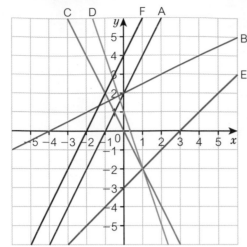

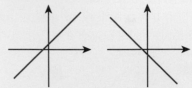

Key point

To find the gradient, work out how many units the graph goes up for every 1 unit across.

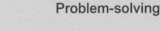

Gradients are positive (/, uphill) or negative (\, downhill).
The larger the value, the steeper the gradient.

Investigation   **Problem-solving**

Draw a coordinate grid from −10 to 10 on both axes.

1 Plot and label these graphs.

  a $y = x$

  b $y = 2x$

  c $y = 4x$

  d $y = -x$

  e $y = -2x$

2 Where do the lines intercept the y-axis?

3 Work out the gradient of each line.

4 Compare your answer to Q3 to the equation of the line. What do you notice?

5 Where do you think the graph of $y = 3x$ will be on your grid? Plot it to check.

> **Hint**
>
> You could use a graph plotting package to plot the graphs.

---

4 Alfie is calculating the gradient of a line.

He works out that for an increase of 2 in the x-direction, the y-value increases by 6.

What is the gradient of the line?

5 Draw lines on squared paper with these gradients.

  a 5   **b** −3

  c $\frac{1}{2}$ **d** −0.25

Key point

To find the gradient of a line

calculate $\dfrac{\text{change in } y}{\text{change in } x}$

6 Work out the gradient of each of these graphs.

  a

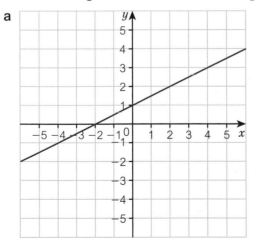

  b

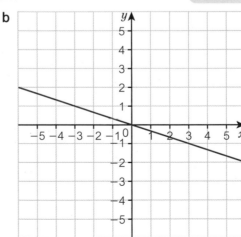

Topic links: Coordinates, Negative numbers

7 Plot these graphs. Fill in the gradient and y-intercept in the table.

Equation of line	Gradient	y-intercept
$y = 2x - 5$		
$y = x + 1$		
$y = 3x + 4$		
$y = -x + 2$		
$y = -2x - 7$		
$y = \frac{1}{3}x + 1$		

Discussion How can you find the gradient and y-intercept of a line without plotting the graph?

8 Real / Modelling An advertising company uses a graph of this equation to work out the cost of making an advert:
$y = 10 + 0.5x$
where x is the number of words and y is the total cost of the bill in pounds.
  a Where does the line intercept the y-axis?
  b How much is the bill when there are no words in the advert?
  c What is the gradient of the line?
  d How much does each word cost?

9 Real / Modelling Naomi rents a room to teach yoga to x people. She uses this equation to work out her profit, y, in pounds:
$y = 10x - 50$
  a Draw the graph of the line $y = 10x - 50$.
  b i What is her profit when 0 people attend the class?
    ii What does the y-intercept represent?
  c How much does each person pay for the class?

> **Q9 hint**
> Think about the axes you need to use.

10 Explore What does a 'Gradient 12%' road sign mean?
Look back at the maths you have learned in this lesson.
How can you use it to answer this question?

11 Reflect Write, in your own words, as many facts as you can about gradients of straight lines. Compare your facts with your classmates' facts.

10.3 $y = mx + c$

You will learn to:
- Use $y = mx + c$
- Find the equation of a straight-line graph.

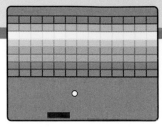

CONFIDENCE

Why learn this?
Computer games designers specify how a character moves across the screen by giving the equations of the lines they follow.

Fluency
What is the inverse of
- +3
- −2
- ×5
- ÷4
- +2x
- −3y?

Explore
Can graphs help you solve algebraic problems?

Warm up

Exercise 10.3

1 On squared paper, draw a line with gradient −2.

2 $y = 3x - 6$
  a Work out the value of y when:
    i $x = 3$ **ii** $x = -2$ **iii** $x = 0$
  b Work out the value of x when:
    i $y = 6$ **ii** $y = -3$ **iii** $y = 0$

> **Key point**
> The equation of a straight-line graph can always be written in the form $y = mx + c$. m is the gradient and c is the y-intercept.

3 Write the gradient and y-intercept of each line.
  a $y = 2x - 5$ **b** $y = 3x$ **c** $y = -\frac{1}{2}x + 4$ **d** $y = -x$

4 a Work out the gradient of the line on the right.
  b Where does the line intercept the y-axis?
  c Write the equation of the line in the form $y = mx + c$.

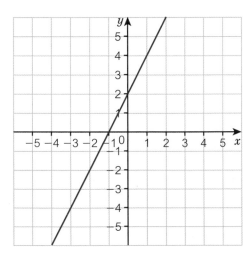

5 Match the equations to the graphs.

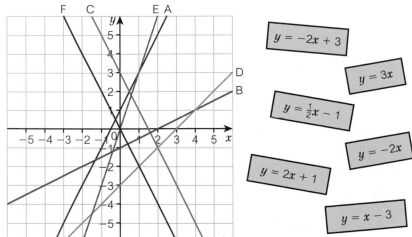

$y = -2x + 3$

$y = 3x$

$y = \frac{1}{2}x - 1$

$y = -2x$

$y = 2x + 1$

$y = x - 3$

Topic links: Coordinates, Negative numbers, Solving linear equations

6 Write the equations of these graphs in order of steepness.

A $y = x + 5$ **B** $y = 3x + 1$ **C** $y = 0.7x + 12$

7 Draw a pair of axes from –10 to +10. A line has equation $y = 3x - 1$.

   a What is its y-intercept? Plot it on your axes.

   b What is its gradient?

   c Start at the y-intercept. Draw a straight line with this gradient. Extend your line to both edges of the grid.

8 Use the method in Q7 to plot these graphs.

   a $y = 2x + 1$

   b $y = x - 5$

   c $y = -2x - 3$

   d $y = \frac{1}{3}x$

9 **Problem-solving** Which of these are equations of straight lines?

   a $y = 2x + 5$

   b $y = x^2$

   c $y = \frac{2}{x}$

   d $y = -\frac{1}{2}x + 4$

   e $y = 3x^2 + 7$

10 **Real** The graph shows the relationship between the number of cars sold and the monthly salary of a car salesman.

   a How much does he earn if he doesn't sell any cars?

   b How much does the salesman earn for each car he sells?

   c Write the equation of the line that links salary (y) to number of sales (x).

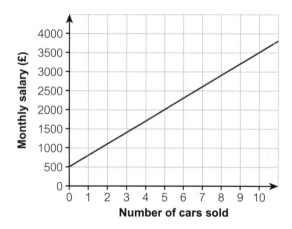

11 $y = 2x + 5$

   a Work out the value of y when $x = 3$.
   Write the coordinates (3, ☐).

   b Does the point (1, 9) lie on the line $y = 2x + 5$?

12 **Problem-solving** Which of these points lie on each line?

   A (3, −7)   B (0, 5)   C (−5, −15)   D (1, −1)
   E (3, 12)   F (−1, 5)   G (10, 0)   H (3, 4)

   a $y = 2x - 5$

   b $y = x - 10$

   c $2y = 4x - 8$

   d $2y + 6x = 4$

Q11b hint

Substitute $x = 1$ into the equation of the line.

13 **Explore** Can graphs help you solve algebraic problems?
Is it easier to explore this question now you have completed the lesson?
What further information do you need to be able to answer this?

14 **Reflect** Samina says, 'I can work out any point on a straight line just from knowing the gradient and one point on the line.'
Max says, 'I can work out any point on a straight line from the equation of the line.'
Whose method do you prefer?
How are the methods different? How are they the same?

Explore

Reflect

10.4 Parallel and perpendicular lines

You will learn to:
- Identify parallel and perpendicular lines.

Why learn this?
Architects use parallel and perpendicular lines in their drawings.

CONFIDENCE

Fluency
What do m and c represent in $y = mx + c$?
What is the product of 2 and $-\frac{1}{2}$?

Explore
How can you tell if two lines are at right angles?

Exercise 10.4

Warm up

1 Which pairs of lines are parallel and which are perpendicular?

 A   B   C   D

Key point

Lines that are **parallel** have the same gradient.

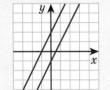

2 Write the gradient and y-intercept of the line $y = 4x - 7$.

3 What can you say about the gradients of **parallel** lines?

4 Which of the lines is parallel to $y = -x + 1$?

A $y = -x + 2$ **B** $y = x + 3$ **C** $y = 3x + 1$ **D** $y = -2x + 6$ **E** $y = 4 - x$

Discussion What other lines are parallel to $y = -x + 1$?

5 Write the equation of a line parallel to
  a $y = 3x - 5$
  b $y = -2x + 7$
  c $y = 3x$, with y-intercept (0, 4)
  d $y = -2x$, that crosses the y-axis at –5.

Q5a, b hint
c can be any number.

6 A line is parallel to the line $y = 2x + 5$ and passes through (4, 11).
  a Substitute the value of m for this line into $y = mx + c$.
  b Substitute the coordinates (4, 11) to work out the equation of the line.

Q6b hint
At the point (4, 11) $x = 4$ and $y = 11$.

7 **Real / Finance** The graphs show two companies' profits. Write the equation for line B.

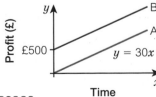

8 Work out the equation of a line parallel to $y = \frac{1}{2}x + 5$ that passes through (–2, 1).

Topic links: Coordinates, Negative numbers

Draw a coordinate grid using the same scale on both axes.

1 Plot the lines $y = 2x$ and $y = -\frac{1}{2}x$ on your grid.

2 Measure the angle between the lines.

3 Plot these pairs of lines on a coordinate grid with the same scale on both axes and measure the angle between the lines.

    a $y = 3x$ and $y = -\frac{1}{3}x$

    b $y = 4x$ and $y = -\frac{1}{4}x$

4 Which line would make the same angle with $y = 5x$? Check your answer.

9 Write the gradient of a line **perpendicular** to

    a $y = 2x - 1$ **b** $y = -3x + 12$

    c $y = \frac{1}{2}x$ **d** $y = -\frac{1}{2}x - 4$

    Discussion How did you work out the gradient of the perpendicular lines?

> **Q9a hint**
>
> $2 \times \square = -1$

10 **Problem-solving** Each line has a partner which is perpendicular except one. Which one?

A $y = \frac{1}{6}x - 3$ **B** $y = -\frac{1}{2}x + 3$ **C** $y = -3x + 1$ **D** $y = -\frac{1}{5}x + 4$

E $y = 4x - 7$ **F** $y = -6x + 1$ **G** $y = 2x - 3$ **H** $y = -x + 2$

I $y = x + 4$ **J** $y = -\frac{1}{3}x - 4$ **K** $y = 5x + 2$

> **Key point**
>
> When two lines are **perpendicular** the product of their gradients is -1.

Worked example

Find the equation of a straight line perpendicular to $y = 3x + 2$, which goes through the point $(6, 0)$.

$y = -\frac{1}{3}x + c$ — Work out the gradient of the perpendicular line. Substitute it for m in $y = mx + c$.

$0 = -\frac{1}{3} \times 6 + c$ — Substitute $x = 6$, $y = 0$ into the equation.

$0 = -2 + c$ — Solve to find c.

$2 = c$

The equation is:

$y = -\frac{1}{3}x + 2$ — Rewrite the equation with the values m and c.

11 Find the equation of the line perpendicular to

    a $y = -2x + 1$, which goes through the point $(3, 2)$

    b $y = \frac{1}{5}x + 2$, which intercepts the y-axis at -4.

12 **Explore** How can you tell if two lines are at right angles? What have you learned in this lesson to help you answer this question? What other information do you need?

13 **Reflect** Jack says, 'It's always easier to find the equation of a parallel line than a perpendicular line.' Do you agree with Jack? Write a hint, in your own words, for finding the equation of a perpendicular line.

Explore   Reflect

10.5 Inverse functions

You will learn to:

- Find the inverse of a linear function.

CONFIDENCE

Why learn this?
Functions are used to encrypt codes. Inverse functions decode them.

Fluency
Work out:
- $10 + 8 \div 2$
- $(10 + 8) \div 2$

Explore
Can you find a function whose inverse is the same as the function?

Exercise 10.5

Warm up

1 Find the missing inputs and outputs of the function machines.

a $3 \rightarrow \boxed{\times 2} \rightarrow \boxed{-7} \rightarrow \square$

b $15 \rightarrow \boxed{-6} \rightarrow \boxed{\div 3} \rightarrow \square$

c $\square \rightarrow \boxed{+4} \rightarrow \boxed{\div 10} \rightarrow 2$

d $\square \rightarrow \boxed{\times 4} \rightarrow \boxed{-30} \rightarrow -2$

Q2a hint
The function $x \rightarrow 3x - 2$ means every value of x maps to $3x - 2$.

2 Draw function machines for each function.

a $x \rightarrow 3x - 2$

b $x \rightarrow \dfrac{x - 2}{3}$

c $x \rightarrow 3(x + 1)$

Q2c hint

$x \rightarrow \boxed{+1} \rightarrow \square$

Worked example

Find the **inverse function** of $x \rightarrow 2x + 1$.

$x \rightarrow \boxed{\times 2} \rightarrow \boxed{+1} \rightarrow 2x + 1$

Write the **function** as a function machine.

$\dfrac{x + 1}{2} \leftarrow \boxed{\div 2} \leftarrow \boxed{-1} \leftarrow x$

Reverse the function machine to find the inverse function. Start with x as the input.

Inverse function of $x \rightarrow 2x + 1$ is $x \rightarrow \dfrac{x - 1}{2}$

Key point
An **inverse function** reverses the effect of the original **function**.

3 Find the inverse of each function.

a $x \rightarrow 3x + 5$ **b** $x \rightarrow \dfrac{x}{2} - 1$ **c** $x \rightarrow 2(x - 3)$ **d** $x \rightarrow x + \dfrac{2}{7}$

Q3 hint
Check each of your answers by substituting a value into the original function and then the inverse.

4 a Copy and complete the function machine for the equation of the line $y = 2x - 1$.

$x \rightarrow \boxed{\times 2} \rightarrow \boxed{\square} \rightarrow y$

b Copy and complete the inverse function machine.

$y \leftarrow \boxed{\div 2} \leftarrow \boxed{\square} \leftarrow x$

c Write the inverse function: $y = $ _____

Topic links: Coordinates, Negative numbers

5 Find the inverse function of

a $y = 3x$ **b** $y = x - 4$ **c** $y = \frac{x}{2}$

d $y = x + 5$ **e** $y = -2x$ **f** $y = -x$

6 Find the inverse function of

a $y = 3x + 7$ **b** $y = 2(x - 1)$ **c** $y = \frac{x}{3} + 4$

d $y = \frac{x - 2}{3}$ **e** $y = -4x + 7$ **f** $y = -2(x + 5)$

Investigation Problem-solving

1 Plot the graphs of $y = 3x$ and its inverse function on a set of axes.

2 These graphs are a reflection of each other. Draw in the mirror line.

3 What is the equation of the mirror line?

4 Repeat parts **1** to **3** for these graphs and their inverses.

> **Hint**
> You could use a graph plotting package to plot the graph.

  a $y = 3x + 4$ **b** $y = 2x - 5$ **c** $y = \frac{x + 1}{3}$

5 What do you notice about the mirror lines?

---

7 Work out the inverse function of the line.

Discussion Is there more than one way to answer this question?

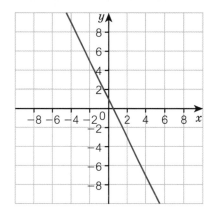

> **Key point**
> The graph of an inverse function is a reflection of the original function in the line $y = x$.

8 **Real / Problem-solving**
A teacher making a worksheet about symmetry draws two sides of a shape using a graph plotting package. Work out the equations of the two lines she needs to draw to make a shape symmetrical about the line $y = x$.

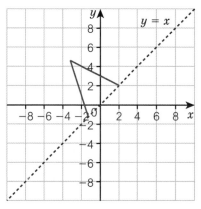

9 **Explore** Can you find a function whose inverse is the same as the function?
Look back at the maths you have learned in this lesson.
How can you use it to answer this question?

10 **Reflect** Look back at the function machines you used in this lesson.
Did they help you to work out the inverse functions?
What method did you use to work out the inverse when you didn't use a function machine? Compare your method with your classmates.

10.6 STEM: Non-linear graphs

You will learn to:
• Plot and use non-linear graphs.

Why learn this?
The population of a country usually increases each year. Politicians need to predict the future population.

Fluency
Using $T = 2Y$, work out the value of
• T when $Y = 12$
• Y when $T = 12$

Explore
How many megapixels will a phone camera have in 2030?

Exercise 10.6: Non-linear graphs

1 **STEM** The graph shows the distance Allan is from home during a bicycle ride.
  a Between which two times is he cycling fastest? How can you tell from the shape of the graph?
  b At what times does he stop for his breaks?
  c Work out his average speed for the total journey.

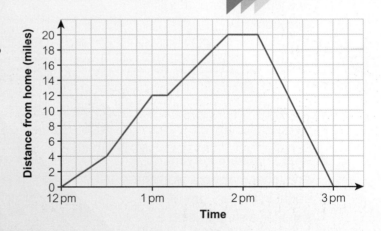

2 **STEM / Modelling** A marine jumps from an aeroplane flying at 4000 metres.
At what height does he open his parachute?
Explain how you know.

> **Q2 hint**
>
> When does he start descending at a constant rate?

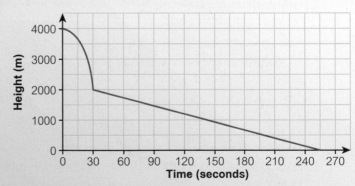

3 **STEM / Modelling** The graph shows the height of a ball thrown straight up in the air.
  a Is the ball moving faster between 0 and 1 second or between 1 and 2 seconds? Explain how you know.
  b At what time is the ball stationary?
  c How far does the ball travel in total?

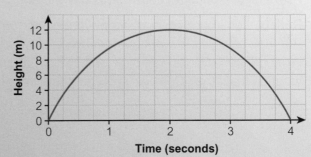

Topic links: Coordinates, Speed/distance/time, Sequences

Subject links: Science (Q1–6)

4 STEM / Modelling A scientist recorded the number of bacteria in a sample.

Time (hours)	0	1	2	3	4	5
Number of bacteria	1	2	4	8	16	32

a How many bacteria would you expect there to be after 6 hours?

b Draw a pair of axes with Time (x) from 0 to 10 and Number of bacteria (y) from 0 to 1100.

c Plot the points on the axes and join them with a smooth curve.

d Continue the curve up to 10 hours.

e Use your graph to estimate how many bacteria there will be after

   i $6\frac{1}{2}$ hours

   ii $8\frac{1}{2}$ hours.

Q4d hint

Extend the table of values up to 10 hours.

5 STEM / Modelling The graph shows the **count rate** against time for chromium-51, which is a radioactive material.

Literacy hint

The **count rate** is the number of radioactive emissions per second.

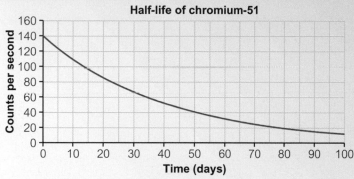

Half-life of chromium-51

(y-axis: Counts per second, 0 to 160; x-axis: Time (days), 0 to 100)

a What is the count rate after 25 days?

b After how many days does the count rate reach 50?

The half-life of a radioactive material is the time it takes for the count rate to halve.

c What is the half-life of chromium-51?

Discussion Does the count rate ever reach zero?

6 Sketch a graph to show the electricity use in a school over a 24-hour period. Explain your sketch.

7 Explore How many megapixels will a phone camera have in 2030? Is it easier to explore this question now you have completed the lesson?
What further information do you need to be able to answer this?

8 Reflect In this lesson you have looked at many different types of non-linear graphs.

a Look back at the different contexts used in this lesson.
Would you have expected them to produce non-linear graphs?

b Think about whether you would expect these contexts to produce linear or non-linear graphs.
   • The population of the Earth over time.
   • The temperature of a pot of just-boiled water over time.
   • The number of unemployed people in Britain over time.
   • The height of a burning candle over time.

Q5a, b hint

c can be any number.

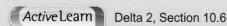

10 Check up

Log how you did on your Student Progression Chart.

Linear graphs

1 Draw a coordinate grid from −10 to 10 on both axes.
Draw the graph of $2x + y = 8$.

2 Find the gradient of this line segment.

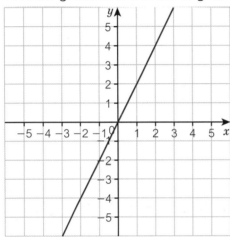

3 For each line write the y-intercept and the gradient.

a $y = 2x - 4$　　　　　　　　**b** $y = \frac{1}{2}x$

4 Which of the points lie on the line $y = \frac{1}{2}x + 3$?
A $(0, -3.5)$　　B $(9, 8.5)$

5 Find the equation of this line.

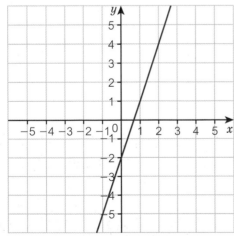

6 From the list choose

a a pair of parallel lines　　　　**b** a pair of perpendicular lines.

A $y = 2x - 5$　　**B** $y = -2x + 1$　　**C** $y = x - 5$　　**D** $y = -\frac{1}{2}x + 2$　　**E** $y = 2x + 3$

7 Write the equation of a line parallel to $y = -3x$, which goes through the point $(2, -2)$.

8 Write the equation of a line perpendicular to $y = -2x + 3$, which goes through the point $(4, 1)$.

Inverse functions

9 Find the inverse of each function.

a $x \to 5x$ **b** $x \to 2x - 7$

c $y = \frac{x}{3} + 12$ **d** $y = 3(x - 5)$

10 Use the graph lines to make 3 pairs of functions and their inverses.

A $y = 2x$

B $y = \frac{x}{2} + 3$

C $y = \frac{x + 1}{2}$

D $y = 2x - 1$

E $y = \frac{1}{2}x$

F $y = 2x - 6$

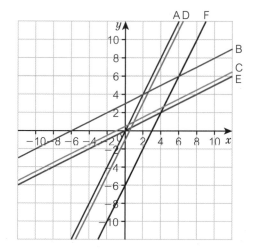

Non-linear graphs

11 The graph shows the amount of fuel in a car during an 8-hour period.
  a When is the car consuming the most petrol? How can you tell?
  b How long is the car travelling for?

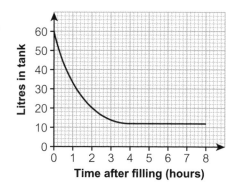

12 How sure are you of your answers? Were you mostly

😞 **Just guessing**   😐 **Feeling doubtful**   🙂 **Confident**

What next? Use your results to decide whether to strengthen or extend your learning.

Challenge

13 Write the equations of four different lines which pass through the point $(2, 4)$ and have a positive gradient.

14 a Find the equation of the line perpendicular to $y = 3x + 2$ which intercepts the y-axis at the same point.

  b Plot the two lines.

  c Work out the area of the triangle enclosed by the lines and the x-axis.

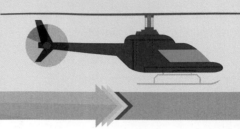

10 Strengthen

You will:
• Strengthen your understanding with practice.

Linear graphs

1 a Copy and complete the table of values for $y = \frac{1}{2}x + 3$.

x	−3	−2	−1	0	1	2	3
$\frac{1}{2}x$							
+ 3							
y							

b Draw the graph of $y = \frac{1}{2}x + 3$.

2 a Copy and complete the table of values for $x + 2y = 7$.

x	−3	−2	−1	0	1	2	3
$-x + 7$	10						
$2y$	10						
y	5						

b Draw the graph of $x + 2y = 7$.

3 Write the coordinates where each line intercepts the y-axis.

a $y = 10x - 7$ **b** $y = 2x - 5$ **c** $y = -x + 1$

d $y = \frac{1}{2}x + 7$ **e** $y = 3x - 2$ **f** $y = 4x$

4 a Which of these lines has the steepest gradient?

A $y = x$
B $y = 2x$
C $y = 3x$

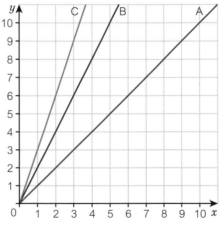

b Nico finds the gradient of the line of $y = x$ by moving 1 horizontally and counting how many squares he must move vertically to get to the line.
Copy and complete:
The gradient of $y = x$ is _____

c Find the gradients of lines A, B and C in part **a** using Nico's method.

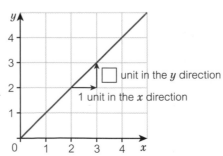

Q1b hint

What are the smallest and largest values of x and y in your table? Use these to help you decide on your axes.

Q3a hint

c is the y-intercept.
$y = mx + c$
$y = 10x - 7$

Q4a hint

Imagine you are walking up the hill from left to right – which is the steepest hill?

Q4b hint

The gradient is the number of units moved in the y-direction when you have moved 1 unit in the x-direction.

5 The diagram shows the graph of $y = 3x + 1$.

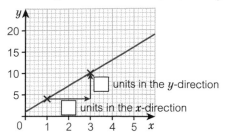
□ units in the y-direction
□ units in the x-direction

The points (1, 4) and (3, 10) have been marked.
Copy and complete the calculation to find the gradient:

Gradient $= \dfrac{\text{units in } y\text{-direction}}{\text{units in } x\text{-direction}} = \dfrac{\square}{\square}$

Q6 hint

Look carefully at the scales on the x- and y-axes.

6 a Copy the graph.

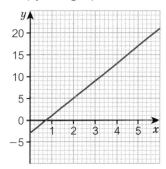

b Mark two points on the graph line with whole number coordinates.
c Draw horizontal and vertical lines similar to the red lines in Q5.
d Find the gradient of the line.

7 The equation of a line is $y = 2x - 1$.
a When x is 1, what is y?
b Fill in the missing coordinate: (2, □).
c When y is 7, what is x?
d Fill in the missing coordinate: (□, 9).

Q7b hint

When x is 2, what is y?

8 The equation of a straight line is $y = x + 5$.
a Does the point (2, 5) lie on the line $y = x + 5$?
b Which of these points lie on the line $y = x + 5$?
A (0, 5)   B (1, 7)   C (2, 8)   D (3, 9)   E (4, 9)

Q8a hint

When x is 2, does $y = 5$?

9 Copy and complete this table.

Equation	Gradient	y-intercept
a $y = 3x + 1$	3	(0, □)
b $y = 2x$		(0, 0)
c $y = x + 5$		(0, □)
d $y = 2x - 3$		(□, −3)
e $y = 5x - 7$		
f $y = -2x + 4$	−2	
g $y = -5x - 2$		
h $y = -x + 7$		

Q9 hint

For the y-intercept look back at Q3.
m is the gradient.
$y = mx + c$
$y = 3x + 1$

10 a Are these lines perpendicular or parallel?

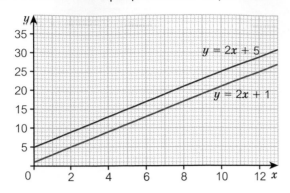

b What can you say about the gradient of both lines?

c How can you tell if a pair of lines are parallel by looking at their equations?

d Which two graphs in Q9 are parallel?

11 a Work out the gradient of this line.

Q11a hint

Use the method in Q5.

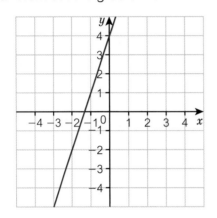

b When $x = 0$, what is the value of y?

c Write the equation of the line in the form $y = mx + c$

12 Use the method in Q11 to work out the equation of this line.

Q12 hint

The line goes downhill \, so its gradient is negative.

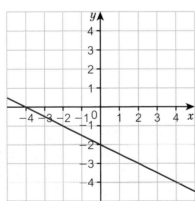

Inverse functions

1 Copy and complete the inverse function machines for each function.
Find the inverse function.

a $y = x + 7$

$x \rightarrow \boxed{+7} \rightarrow y$

$y \leftarrow \boxed{\square} \leftarrow x$

Inverse: $y = x$.................

Q1a hint

What is the inverse of +7?

b $y = 3x$

$x \rightarrow \boxed{\times 3} \rightarrow y$

$y \leftarrow \boxed{\square} \leftarrow x$

Inverse: $y = $ ....

c $y = \dfrac{x}{2}$

$x \rightarrow \boxed{\div 2} \rightarrow y$

$y \leftarrow \boxed{\square} \leftarrow x$

Inverse: $y = $ ....

d $y = x - 4$

$x \rightarrow \boxed{-4} \rightarrow y$

$y \leftarrow \boxed{\square} \leftarrow x$

Inverse: $y = $ ....

2 Charlie draws a function machine to illustrate $y = 2x + 1$.

$x \rightarrow \boxed{\times 2} \rightarrow \boxed{+1} \rightarrow y$

To find the inverse function he reverses the machine and replaces the functions with their inverse.

$y \leftarrow \boxed{\div 2} \leftarrow \boxed{-1} \leftarrow x$

Copy and complete the inverse function: $y = \dfrac{x - \text{.........}}{\text{.........}}$

3 Find the inverse of
   a $y = 3x - 20$
   b $y = 5x + 12$
   c $y = \dfrac{x + 2}{3}$
   d $y = \dfrac{x - 7}{10}$

4 Is line A or line B the inverse of the line $y = 2x$?

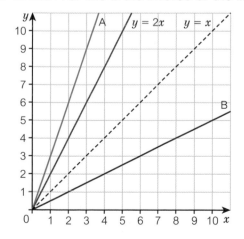

Q4 hint

The graph of an inverse function is a reflection in the line $y = x$.

Non-linear graphs

1 The graph shows how much an electrician charges her customers

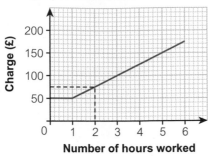

a How much does the electrician charge for 2 hours?

b How much does the electrician charge for 3 hours?

c How much does the electrician charge for each hour?

d What is the minimum amount the electrician charges?

Q1a hint

Draw a dotted line from 2 hours on the x-axis up to the graph and read across to the y-axis.

2 The height of a bean seedling is recorded over 30 days.

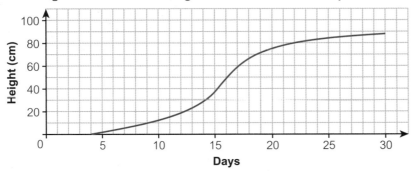

a What is the height of the plant after 10 days?

b When is the plant growing at its fastest rate?

c How many days is it before the seedling shows above the ground?

Q2b hint

Look for the part of the graph where the gradient is steepest.

Enrichment

1 $y = x$ goes through the point (0, 0).

Write the equations of five other lines that go through the **origin**.

2 Which is the odd one out and why?

A $y = 2x$ **B** $y = 2x - 3$ **C** $y = 3x + 1$

D $y = 2x + 7$ **E** $y - 2x = 4$

Q1 Literacy hint

The **origin** is the point (0, 0).

Q2 hint

There is more than one answer to the question – you must explain your answer!

3 Reflect Look back at the questions you got wrong in the check up.

Were they mostly questions about

- linear graphs
- inverse functions
- non-linear graphs?

Now look back at the strengthen questions you answered.

Write down one thing you now understand better.

Is there anything you still need help with?

Ask a friend or your teacher to help you with it.

10 Extend

You will:
- Extend your understanding with problem-solving.

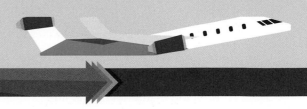

1 a Find the inverse of the function $y = -x$.
  b Is this function **self-inverse**?
  c What other function is self-inverse?

2 a Find the inverse of each function.
  i $y = 10 - x$
  ii $y = 20 - x$
  iii $y = 8 - x$
  iv $y = 1 - x$
  b What do you notice about all these functions?

3 a Work out the gradient of this line.
  b Write the equation of the line in the form $y = mx + c$.

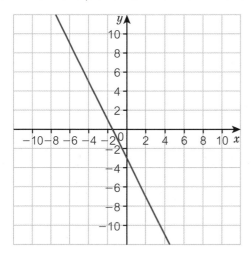

4 A line has gradient 3. It goes through the point $(-2, 4)$.
  a Write the equation of the line in the form $y = mx + c$.
    Substitute the value for m.
  b Substitute the values of x and y for the point $(-2, 4)$.
  c Solve the equation you got in part **b** to find the value of c.
  d Write the equation of the line.

5 A line has gradient -2. It goes through the point $(1, 3)$.
    What is the equation of the line?

6 Find the gradient of the line joining each pair of points.
  a $(1, 3)$ and $(4, 9)$
  b $(3, 5)$ and $(5, 11)$
  c $(4, 8)$ and $(3, 10)$
  d $(-3, 5)$ and $(1, 9)$.

Key point

A function is called **self-inverse** if the function and its inverse are the same.

Q2a i hint

Write the function as $y = -x + 10$ and then find the inverse.

Q6a hint

Sketch the points and line.
Work out the gradient.

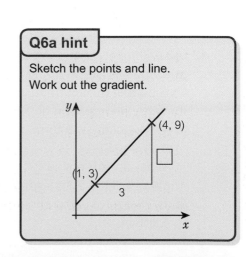

7 A straight line goes through the points (0, 6) and (1, 9).
Write the equation of the line.

Q7 hint

Work out the gradient.
Use the y-intercept.

8 **Problem-solving** A line has gradient 2.
It goes through the point (1, 4) and the point (2, a).
What is the value of a?

Q8 hint

Sketch the line with gradient 2 from
the point (1, 4).

9 Here are the coordinates of a graph
entered into a spreadsheet package.
What is the equation of the line?

	A	B
1	x	y
2	2	15
3	5	24

10 **Problem-solving** The coordinates of the endpoints of a line
segment are (1, b) and (3, 5).
Work out the value of b when the gradient is

Q10 hint

Sketch the lines.
Label the coordinates.

  a 2   **b** 3   **c** 1

  d −1   **e** −2   **f** $\frac{1}{2}$

11 **Problem-solving a** Draw a coordinate grid and plot the points (3, 5)
and (1, −1).
  b Join them with a straight line. Extend it to the edge of the grid.
  c Write the equation of the line in the form $y = mx + c$.

12 **Real** To convert from pounds (P) to rupees (R), a bank uses the
equation $R = 100P - 2000$.
  a How many rupees would you get for £50?
This graph shows the exchange rate:

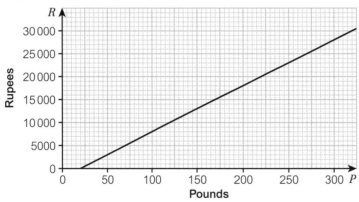

  b Use the graph to work out the cost of 10 000 rupees.
  c What is the gradient of the line?
  d Explain in words what the gradient represents.
  e Why can the graph only be used for amounts over £20?

Q13d hint

Substitute $n = 20$ into the equation of
the line.

13 An arithmetic sequence starts: 1, 4, 7, 10, …
  a Copy this graph of the sequence.
     Extend it to include as many terms as you can.
  b Write the equation of the line.
  c Work out the nth term of the sequence
     1, 4, 7, 10, …
     What do you notice?
  d What will the 20th term of the sequence be?
  e Is 23 a term in the sequence?
     Explain.

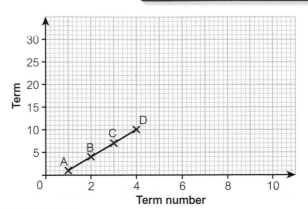

Topic links: Compound interest, Midpoint of a line segment, Sequences

14 Real / STEM The scatter graph below shows the average height and age of 20 plants over 15 weeks.

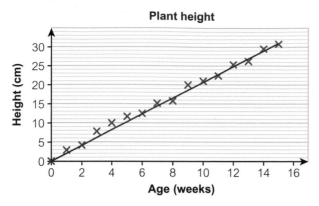

Plant height

a Work out the equation of the line of best fit.

b Use the equation to work out the height of a 10-week-old plant.

15 STEM The height of the tide in a harbour is recorded:

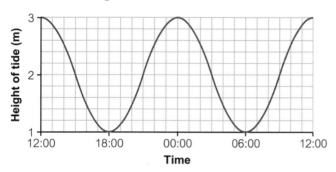

a Estimate the times when the tide is rising the fastest.

b How long is it between high and low tides?

c What is the maximum number of high tides that could occur in one 24-hour period?

A boat can sail out of the harbour when the tide is higher than 1.5 m.

d At what times of the day couldn't the boat have sailed?

16 Problem-solving The rectangle is made using four straight lines.

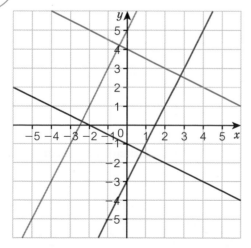

The equation of the blue line is $y = 2x - 3$.
Write the equations of the other three lines.

17 A bank pays compound interest on a savings account at a rate of 5% per year. Charlie puts £1000 into an account.

   a How much money will he have in the account after 5 years (assuming he does not withdraw any money)?

   b The bank draws a graph to show how much money will be in the account over 20 years. Which graph is correct?

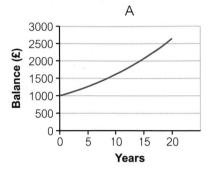
A

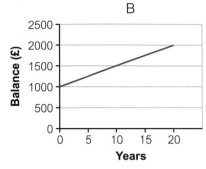
B

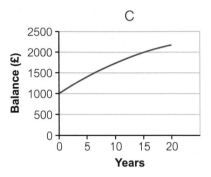
C

18 Decide if each statement about the line $y = \frac{1}{2}x - 7$ is true or false.

   a ~~It goes through the point (−1, −7.5).~~

   b It is parallel to $2y = x + 12$.

   c It is perpendicular to $y = -2x$.

   d It crosses the y-axis at (0, 7).

19 Problem-solving For the line $y = 3x + 2$, write four TRUE statements like those in Q18.

20 a What are the coordinates of the midpoint of line segment AB?

   b Work out the gradient of line segment AB.

   c A line is drawn perpendicular to the line segment and passes through the midpoint of the line. What is the gradient of the line?

   d What is the equation of the line?

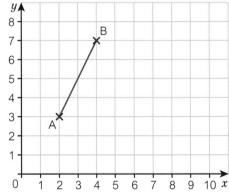

21 In which of these equations are x and y in direct proportion?

   a $y = 2x - 5$ **b** $y = -4x$ **c** $y = 3x$

   d $y = \frac{1}{3}x$ **e** $y = -\frac{1}{2}x + 2$

22 a What is the angle between the two lines?

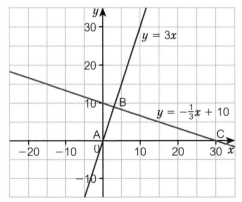

   b Work out the coordinates of the points A, B and C.

   c Work out the length of the line AB.

   d Work out the length of the line BC.

> **Q21 hint**
>
> When two quantities are in direct proportion, what does their graph look like?

> **Q22b hint**
>
> To find B work out where the two lines intercept by equating $3x$ and $-\frac{1}{3}x + 10$.

> **Q22c hint**
>
> Use Pythagoras' theorem.

23 Reflect Look back at Q18. How did you decide if each statement was true or false?

Did you find a counter example for the false statements?

10 Unit test

Log how you did on your Student Progression Chart.

1 Draw a coordinate grid with x- and y-coordinates from -10 to 10.
Draw the graph $3x + 2y = 1$.

2 Find the inverse of each function.

   a $x \rightarrow 3x$ **b** $x \rightarrow 2x - 5$

   c $x \rightarrow 3(x + 1)$ **d** $y = x + 7$

   e $y = 3x - 2$

3 Write the equation of this line.

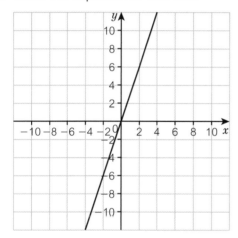

4 **a** Where does the line $y = 3x - 5$ cross the y-axis?

   b What is the gradient of the line $y = -2x + 7$?

5 Is line A, B or C the inverse function of $y = 2x + 5$?

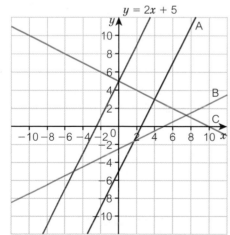

6 A line has gradient 4 and intercepts the y-axis at $(0, -3)$.
Write the equation of the line.

7 Does the point $(6, 2)$ lie on the line $y = 2x - 14$?
Show working to explain.

8 Work out the gradient of the line joining the points $(1, 5)$ and $(3, -3)$.

9 The graph shows the relationship between the length of the edges of a cube and the surface area of the cube.
Use the graph to estimate the surface area of a cube with edges of length 2.5 cm.

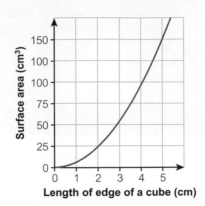
Length of edge of a cube (cm)

10 The graph shows the total amount in an investment fund over 12 years.

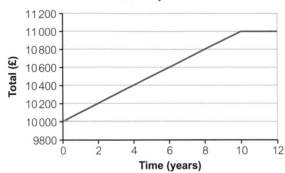
Time (years)

a What was the initial investment?
b How much did the investment increase by each year for the first 10 years?
c What happened to the investment after 10 years?

11 Which of these statements are true?
A The lines $y = 2x$ and $y = -2x$ are parallel.
B The lines $y = 2x$ and $y = -\frac{1}{2}x$ are perpendicular.
C The lines $y = 2x$ and $y = \frac{1}{2}x$ are parallel.
D The lines $y = 2x$ and $y = \frac{1}{2}x$ are perpendicular.
E The lines $y = 2x$ and $y = 2x + 1$ are parallel.
F The lines $y = 2x$ and $y = 2x + 1$ are perpendicular.

12 The graph of $y = -2x + 5$ is shown. What is the equation of line A?

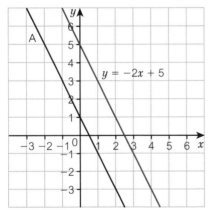

Challenge

1 A graph has equation $y = mx + c$
Given that it goes through the point (1, 3) what is the relationship between the possible values of m and c?

Q1 hint

Work out a couple of possible equations of the line.
Then look at the relationship between m and c.

2 **Reflect** Look back at the questions you answered in this unit test.
• Which took the shortest time to answer? Why?
• Which took the longest time to answer? Why?
• Which took the most thought to answer? Why?